The Citizenship of Christian Parenthood

You Are One of the **2.9 billion** *Citizens of* **God's Kingdom**,
By **wisdom** *a house is built, and through* **understanding** *it is established*

I am He; I am he who will sustain you. I have made you, and I will carry you; I will sustain you, and I will rescue you, Isaiah 46:4

Gabriel Marcelin

Copyright © 2025 by **Gabriel Marcelin**
The Citizenship of Christian Parenthood.
All rights reserved.
U.S. Copyright Registration Number: 114937455871

This book is protected under the copyright laws of **the United States of America**, and **Canada**. All applicable international treaties. No part of this publication may be copied, stored, or transmitted in any form: electronic or mechanical, without prior written permission from the author, except for brief quotations used in reviews or articles.

Permission will be granted upon request. Unless otherwise identified, Scripture quotations are taken from the King James Version. **Copyright ©1982, 1984, by Thomas Nelson, Inc. Used by permission. All rights reserved, Scripture quotations marked NIV are taken from the HOLY BIBLE, NEW INTERNATIONAL VERSION, © 1973, 1978, 1984**

International Bible Society and used by permission of Zondervan.

This book is a work of nonfiction. Any references to historical events, real people, or the Bible are accurate to the best of the author's knowledge.

The Citizenship of Christian Parenthood: written and edited by **Gabriel Marcelin**.

U.S. Copyright Registration Number: 114937455871

Scripture References:

Unless otherwise noted, Scripture quotations are taken from the Holy Bible, New International Version® (NIV®). Copyright © 1973, 1978, 1984, 2011 by Biblica Inc. Used by permission. All rights reserved worldwide

All ideas, stories, and teachings in this book are original and authored by **Gabriel**. A big thank you to the editors who supported the refinement process, ensuring clarity and quality without altering the heart of God's Kingdom.

Published by: Heavenly Citizen.
shop www.heavenlycitizen.shop
Contact: heavenlycitizenshop@gmail.com

ISBN (Paperback): 978-1-0696240-1-7
ISBN (Hardcover): 978-1-0696240-2-4
ISBN ……..(eBook): 978-1-0696240-0-0

Dedications

This book is dedicated to my wife, **Angelique Umutoniwase Marcelin**. In the quiet moments of true love, my heart is forever drawn to you. With every smile, your warmth flows, a gentle grace that helps me grow. You are the design God made for my heart. I am forever grateful that you are mine. In the name of our Lord Jesus, our children will bear witness to my love for you as a divine art. I love you.

To my three sons, **Gabriel Marcelin Jr., Isaiah Marcelin and Gershom Marcelin**

I want you to know how much you are loved. You are my greatest blessings, and every moment spent with you fills my heart with joy. Gabriel Jr., your strength and kindness shine brightly, and Isaiah, your wisdom and compassion inspire me every day. The Lord blesses Gershom, your curiosity to acquire knowledge.

Watching you grow into the incredible young men you are. May you grow to be a man after God's own heart, clothed in wisdom, intelligence, and covered in grace. With all my heart and love, I love you.

To my dear mom, **Anna Pochette**,

I am forever thankful to you. Heaven rejoiced when you embraced the Christian faith and were baptized in 2024. Today, I want to take a moment to convey how much you mean to me. Your love, wisdom, and strength have molded me into the person I am today. Thank you for being the heart of our family, for your countless sacrifices, and for embodying the true meaning of love.

As a **Christian family**, we continually turn to the Scriptures for knowledge and wisdom to strengthen our home. We pray for guidance from the Holy Spirit to fulfil the parenting role God has entrusted to us entirely. Our commitment to God and one another remains unwavering.

May this book inspire you to adopt the same leadership principles and apply them within your own family. Joshua 24:15: "**My family and I will serve the Lord forever**".

Introduction

I want to thank all readers of this book sincerely. As you turn each page, may you discover the blueprint of Christian family faith, and may it inspire a renewed commitment to walk in God's grace and fulfil His purpose within your family. You will explore God's master plan for your family, which will help align every decision and step with His knowledge and understanding.

You will come to understand that faith isn't just a belief in things we can't see, but a way of life, an appreciation for how the Lord guides your life and the lives of your loved ones through many challenges and blessings. Christian parenthood is a sacred partnership with the Lord, built on knowledge, wisdom, and spiritual insights. The family is designed to reflect God's nature, grounded in faith, love, and spiritual instruction, illustrating His creative power and passion for the faithful family.

Parenthood is a lifelong spiritual partnership with God, calling fathers and mothers to fulfil a sacred objective of faith that dignifies the foundation of raising a Godly family. Within this divine and holy framework, this book is designed to equip parents with the wisdom to guide their children's hearts and minds toward the Lord, nurturing them for a higher purpose.

The Bible presents parentship as a privilege, a gift from God, and a responsibility for mothers and fathers. *These words, which I command thee this day, shall be in thine heart: and thou shalt teach them diligently unto thy children, and shalt talk of them when thou sittest in thine house, and when thou walkest by the way, and when thou liest down, and when thou risest up.*

(Deuteronomy 6:6-7).

That's how crucial the role of parents is in shaping the next generation. Parents are summoned to embody God's love, knowledge, and wisdom in their children. They are their children's primary caregivers, healers, protectors, teachers, and mentors.

Through this divine partnership with the Lord, parents will be empowered to build a legacy of faith that will impact not only their children but also them, so that they stand out from the crowd and culture around them.

TABLE OF CONTENTS

Chapter One 1
Chapter Two 11
Chapter Three 22
Chapter Four 32
Chapter Five 42
Chapter Six 53
Chapter Seven 64
Chapter Eight 74
Chapter Nine 84
Chapter Ten 94
Chapter Eleven 102
Chapter Twelve 113
Chapter Thirteen 123
Chapter Fourteen 133
Chapter Fifteen 143
Chapter Sixteen 152
Chapter Seventeen 161
Chapter Thirteen 172
Chapter Nineteen 181
Chapter Twenty 190
Chapter Twenty-One 200
Chapter Twenty-Two 210
Chapter Twenty-Three 219
Chapter Twenty-Four 230
Chapter Twenty-Five 250

HEAVENLY CITIZEN

CHAPTER ONE

Unless the Lord builds the house, the builders labor in vain. Unless the Lord watches over the city, the guards stand watch in vain. Psalm 127:1

The Foundation of a Christian Family

God's Design for Parenthood and the Divine Blueprint for Fathers. God laid the foundations of fatherhood and motherhood by creating the first man and woman, Adam and Eve, thus establishing the very first Christian family in His image. The sixth day marked the completion of God's creation of all living beings and culminated in the creation of humanity. Our parents are the first doctors and healers we meet after birth.

From the moment of conception, your child instinctively seeks love, comfort, and care. Even in the womb, your baby begins to recognize and respond to your voices. Mom and Dad prepare to welcome their tiny one home, as the baby enters the world by uttering God's name, Yahweh, or YHWH, which means "**Breath**".

This sacred name is said to be the very first word spoken with every breath at birth, and the last word spoken by each of us leaving this earth as we take our last breath when we leave this world. Every time you place your hand on your mother's womb, your child feels your presence, and a sacred connection begins to form, linking your hearts long before you ever meet face-to-face.

The bond between a baby and its parents is exactly what our Creator said: *"Before I formed you in your mother's womb, I knew you, and before you came out of her womb, I had anointed you". (Jeremiah 1:5)* Soon after birth, the baby begins to recognize your voice, faces, and smells, quickly identifying those who will provide love and care.

Let me share a personal experience with you. When my wife was pregnant with my first child (a son), I started talking to the baby in the womb from the time she was a few weeks pregnant until the baby was born. I know that I'm not the only father to do this; to be honest, as a first-time parent, I was preparing myself to welcome and care for a little person. So, I was one of the fathers who began reading and singing to my baby while he was still in the womb.

When I got home from work, I'd tell the baby about my day, and in the evening, I'd hold my wife's belly to pray for my son.

There was no happier moment than when he moved every time I touched him, and a name was chosen for my boy, Isaiah, which means "the Lord is salvation".

Standing on the Threshold of Fatherhood

All our family and friends were eager to see Isaiah arrive, filled with excitement and anticipation. Advice poured in from all sides on how things would change for us and how to care for the boy. Every suggestion came from well-meaning loved ones who wanted to share their wisdom. Every piece of advice we received was valuable, reminding us that every baby is unique and that, ultimately, we would learn as we went along. During all the preparations, one thing was sure: **Isaiah** was already deeply loved; we couldn't wait to welcome him home.

I wanted to give his room a special touch, so I made all the decorations myself. I'm not a handyman and had never decorated anything before, but as his father, I was determined. It took me a long time, but I created a welcome banner with his name on it, stretching from wall to wall behind his crib in his room. By this stage, Daddy and Isaiah had already formed a bond.

Every time I spoke to him or touched his mother's belly before he was born, he always responded with a kick.

One morning, as I was getting ready for work, she calmly said, "**You're not going to work today, Mr**. It's time, and I think Isaiah wants to meet you in person today".

You're not going to work today; that was me repeating out loud what she had said.

My heart started beating fast, and a wave of nervousness washed over me. I packed everything we needed for the hospital, even though everything was already packed, and double-checked that we hadn't forgotten anything.

I started praying out loud, as if I were talking to someone next to me, hoping for the best.

I drove her to the hospital; we lived about seven miles from the hospital, from Hyde Park, Massachusetts, to Boston Medical Center (BMC) in **Massachusetts**, USA.

Her water broke in the car while we were driving about a mile away from the emergency room, which took charge of her as soon as we arrived. The doctors confirmed it! **Yes**, "your wife is in labor and her water has already broken".

Full stop. Have you ever been in a position where you expected something extraordinary in your life for the first time, and you knew, with God's truth, that you were ready to receive it?

When the doctors told me that my son would be joining me in a few hours, I was very disappointed in myself, because I had prepared myself for nine months very well to know how to behave in the hospital, how to react when I saw him, and what to say to him for the first time, our first photo together, right? I had a complete list of things ready, **but no.... Now the moment had arrived, and it was real**.

When my wife started screaming across the room, I couldn't remember anything. I felt a mixture of joy, fear, and wonder that left me with a sense of uncertainty about how to begin navigating this new chapter in my life.

Very soon, another name would be added to my life, another little creature would call me! "**Daddy**" would soon be here, yes, right here. I would soon be holding my boy in my hands for the first time. But first, the more she screamed, the more I forgot and panicked that he was about to arrive.

My wife went into labor *at 2 PM on Friday, March 3rd, 2006*, enduring **13 hours** of intense contractions before finally giving **birth at 3 AM on March 4th**. It was a long and exhausting journey, filled with anticipation and wonder, pain, and fear, yet marked by her unwavering strength as she brought our child into the world in the quiet, early hours of the morning.

At that moment, the room was filled with a wide range of emotions; three people were crying, while others were smiling with joy. **My wife, my son, and I were crying with happiness as we held our newborn baby in our arms**. His tiny body, so fragile yet full of life, rested in my arms as he looked up at me with a random little smile; when his big eyes met mine, a deep bond was formed.

Then there was silence; it was as if the world stopped for a few seconds, and I felt a bond of unspoken words, a love so deep it transcended words. I whispered to him, my eyes filling with tears! **Welcome to Papa Fiston**. Your name is Gabriel Marcelin Jr., and your nickname is also Gabe, just like your **daddy**.

These names had perfect meaning, spiritual weight, purpose, and legacy. I knew he would inherit his father's strength, faith, and love. I knew without a doubt that this boy would grow up to embody all the qualities that defined his father: his unwavering strength, resilience, and boundless love.

As I stood in the hospital room, surrounded by joy and smiles, my heart burned with gratitude. I couldn't help but silently thank God for the gift of a beautiful, healthy boy. In that sacred moment, I realized how often we forget to give sufficient thanks for many of the blessings we take for granted.

Have you ever had one of those moments, when looking back, you realized you forgot to thank God for something in your life?

As a faithful servant, the weight of memories hits you when you step back and reflect on a deeper, quieter level. That's when your mind begins to recall the countless miracles, big or small, that have shaped your life. You start to remember moments from the past, the number of times the Lord manifested Himself for you, and yet how easily you took Him for granted, forgetting everything he has done in the hustle of your busy life!

If you're expecting something from the Lord again,

now's the time to stop and spend some time alone with him, talk to him, and tell him you remembered.

Don't let Jesus ask you the following question!

In Luke 17:17, Jesus asks, "**Were not all ten cleansed? Where are the other nine?**"

This question follows the miraculous healing of ten lepers, only one of whom, the Samaritan, had remembered his wound and had also left the scene.

Yes, he had left the place like the others. However, only one of the ten lepers returned to thank Jesus.

The question highlights this human tendency to receive blessings without gratitude. The other nine, who had waited so long to receive the Lord's healing, though now cured, failed to recognize the source of their restoration.

This moment is a **powerful reminder** that gratitude is not a mere politeness, but an act of faith, which consists in recognizing God's hand in our lives. True faith is not just about receiving from God, but also reciprocating with a grateful heart.

Have you ever forgotten to thank God for something or remembered something for which you hadn't expressed gratitude? Do you sometimes overlook the essential things the Almighty has done for you?

Healing and Health: Healing from illness, encompassing both physical and emotional recovery, as well as maintaining overall well-being. I will restore your health and heal your wounds (Jeremiah 30:17)

Wisdom and discernment: Clarity in decision-making, integrity, and sound judgment. (Proverbs 2:10-11)

"For wisdom will enter your heart, and knowledge will be pleasant to your soul. Discretion will protect you, and understanding will guard you."

Strength & Protection*: Courage to overcome challenges, safeguarding from harm and negative influences.* Psalm 46:1-2 "God is our refuge and strength, an ever-present help in trouble."

Forgiveness & Salvation*: Personal repentance, spiritual growth, and a deepened faith.* "This is my blood of the covenant, which is poured out for many for the forgiveness of sins. Matthew 26:28

Happiness Fulfilment*: Joy, contentment, and a sense of purpose in life.*

"May the God of hope fill you with all joy and peace as you trust in Him, so that you may overflow with hope by the power of the Holy Spirit." Romans 15:13

Unity & Fellowship: Strong relationships, harmony in communities, and spiritual renewal.

"But if we walk in the light, as He is in the light, we have fellowship with one another, and the blood of Jesus, His Son, purifies us from all sin." 1 John 1:7

Guidance & Leadership*: Effective and wise leadership, opportunities for service and outreach, words of Solomon.*

"Trust in the Lord with all your heart and lean not on your own understanding; in all your ways submit to Him, and He will make your paths straight. "Proverbs 3:5-6"

Compassion & Justice: Relief for those suffering, an end to injustice, and support for those in need.

"The Lord is gracious and compassionate, slow to anger and rich in love." Psalm 145:8 *Personal blessings, self-esteem, a fulfilling marriage, the blessing of children, and the well-being of the family, all with respect for privacy and human dignity.*

The Christian Vision of Family

The way a Christian views family is profoundly different from that of a non-believer. Some may disagree with this, but the truth remains: the people of God are entrusted with a sacred calling. From the very beginning, believers have been charged by the Lord to center their lives on family and community, and to multiply under His command.

Family is not a human invention or cultural tradition; ***it is a divine institution, designed and blessed by God Himself.***

By contrast, the world of the 21st century is hectic, racing ahead without God, which often leads the modern generation to minimize the value of family. In some societies, children are not considered a blessing but a burden. Some cannot imagine adopting a child, let alone bringing one into the world, because their view of life is limited to personal comfort or financial calculation.

This difference of worldview highlights the sacred privilege given to the Christian community. To raise a family in faith is not merely a choice; it is an act of obedience to the Lord's command and a way of honoring His design for humanity.

God, in His mercy, certainly understands the difficulties faced by those who suffer from a medical condition that may limit their ability to conceive. His grace is sufficient in all situations. Such a person is free to choose whether or not to adopt a child, for adoption itself is a reflection of the heart of God, who makes us His sons and daughters through Christ.

Yet the Lord's command to humanity remains clear:

The purpose of the family is rooted in fertility, the call to reproduce and pass on life. When this is not possible naturally, God's compassion and wisdom provide His people with alternative ways to honor His purposes.

In 2 Corinthians 12:

Jesus said to apostle Paul: "My grace is sufficient for you, for my power is made perfect in weakness."

We should feel deeply blessed to have the opportunity to glorify God through family life. What may seem to the world like an ordinary pattern: marriage, children, and community is, in truth, the unfolding of heaven's law on earth. God established this law from the very first generation.

When He created Adam, He gave him work to do: to tend and keep the garden.

Yet God declared that it was not good for man to be alone, so He created Eve, his companion, helper, and equal. Together, they were charged with the responsibility of multiplying, stewarding creation, and living under God's protection. This pattern remains eternal.

Every time a man and woman enter into marriage, they are not simply signing a contract or forming a household; they are stepping into a covenant. In the eyes of God, the two become one.

Scripture declares: *"It is not good that the man should be alone"* (Genesis 2:18) and again, *"Two are better than one; because they have a good reward for their labor"* (Ecclesiastes 4:9). Marriage is a divine mystery where unity creates strength, and partnership produces fruitfulness.

Consider the example of two different lives. A single person may live alone, working hard and accumulating wealth. At first glance, it would appear that such a person would save more than a father working to provide for his wife and children.

Yet reality, as well as Scripture, teaches otherwise. The one who labors alone often finds emptiness in his gain, while the one who works within God's design, in unity with spouse and family, finds purpose, joy, and long-term fruit. The Bible's wisdom proves true: two are indeed better than one.

Ecclesiastes 4:9:

Two are better than one, because they have a good return for their labor.

The power of two united under God's law is greater than the sum of their parts. When a husband and wife walk together in faith, guided by the Spirit, they combine their strengths, ideas, and prayers to form a powerful unity. Their joined lives are not only more resilient, but more fruitful. They can arrive at their destination faster and with greater blessing than the solitary traveler, because their journey is not built on human effort alone, but on divine partnership.

This truth extends beyond marriage into the broader Christian community. The family is the seedbed of the Church, and the Church is the larger family of God. Just as the Lord commanded Adam and Eve to multiply and fill the earth. Christians are called to build communities rooted in faith, love, and discipleship.

A Christian family does not exist only for itself, but for the advancement of God's Kingdom. At home, children are taught to love the Lord, honor their parents, and serve others. From that foundation, they step into the world as beacons of light in the darkness, carrying with them the values of heaven.

The family is therefore both personal and missionary in nature. It is the place where God's commandments are put into practice daily, in love, discipline, and sacrifice. It is also the place where God's mission develops, one generation teaching the next, one home strengthening another, until communities and nations are transformed.

That is why the Christian vision of the family cannot be reduced to a simple matter of biology or social convenience. It is a spiritual calling, a mission for the Kingdom.

Non-believers may see family as optional, negotiable, or even disposable. But for those who belong to Christ, family is sacred, with an eternal purpose, and foundational to God's design. Marriage and parenthood are not temporary arrangements; they are covenants.

That reflects the love of Christ for His Church. In

laying down His life for His bride, Jesus provided the ultimate model for every Christian.

Husband. In the Church's devotion to Christ, we find the picture of a faithful wife. In the Father's love for His children, we see the standard of Christian parenthood.

This is why Christian families are distinct. They do not exist to survive or to prosper materially. They exist to honor God, to embody His truth, and to multiply His Kingdom on earth. A godly family testifies to the world that God's design is good, that His Word is accurate, and that His ways bring life.

To embrace this calling is to embrace both privilege and responsibility. It is a privilege because family life is a gift from heaven, a daily opportunity to walk in God's blessings. It is a responsibility because every Christian family is a living witness of the Kingdom of God. Our marriages, our parenting, and our households must shine with the light of Christ, showing the world that God's way is higher and better.

Ultimately, the Christian view of the family is not about personal fulfillment, but about obedience to God. It is about aligning our lives with the heavenly plan, the original design of the Master Architect. It is about recognizing that in marriage, in raising children, and in community, we are not just building homes, we are building the Kingdom of God.

Psalm 1:1

Blessed is the person who does not walk in the counsel of the ungodly, nor stand in the way of sinners, nor sit in the seat of the scornful.

HEAVENLY CITIZEN

CHAPTER TWO

*T*he Spirit himself testifies with our spirit that we are God's children. Now if we are children, then we are heirs, heirs of God and co-heirs with Christ, if indeed we share in his sufferings so that we may also share in his glory. Romans 8:16

The greatest gift of all is to realize that it's never too late to take just thirty seconds out of your busy day to express gratitude and thank the Lord. If you were to hear me praying or thanking God for something, you'd find it hard to focus on anything else, because when I pray, it's like having a deeply personal conversation with someone right next to me.

I've grown so close to my Lord during these conversations that I've developed the habit of praying even for the most minor things he's done for me. So, I never forget to say thank you or ask for forgiveness. At the same time, I can ask him lots of questions and explore all the possibilities he has in store for my life and my family.

When my son was born, he became more than a son to me; he became the bearer of a legacy, the continuation of a story I had started.

His name, Gabriel Marcelin Jr., was carefully chosen by the Lord, and he was a bridge between generations, a testament to the strength, perseverance, and love that had defined my own life. As I held him in my arms for the first time, I saw the limitless potential of his future in his little face. He would carve his destiny while carrying the essence of his father before him.

With every cry, every breath, and every slight movement, he revealed to me that God had granted me the privilege of molding and guiding another soul. I envisioned the challenges he would face, the triumphs he would accomplish, and the lessons he would learn along the way. All of this was bound together by the name he inherited from his father; Gabriel Marcelin Jr. was more than a name or an angel who sat in the presence of God. He was a promise, a symbol of hope, a beacon for generations to come, just as the Lord intended.

As you read this book, I encourage you to learn to pray as if the Lord is standing or sitting next to you, wherever you are right now. Consider making this a priority, and you'll see how God will show up for you. The Lord told the prophet in Isaiah 43:19, **"Behold, I will do a new thing; now it shall spring forth; shall you not know it?" I will even make a way in the wilderness, and rivers in the desert.** He said, **"You are mine."**

He will make a way in the darkness, and rivers flow in the desert of our lives." These powerful words remind us that God specializes in the impossible. When you feel like there's no way forward, no path through the pain or confusion, remember that the Lord has never slept. *"The eyes of the Lord are upon the righteous, and his ears are open unto their cry."* (Psalm 34:15).

Because of your value in His eyes, your story isn't over yet. What looks like the end to you is where He begins to work miracles, pouring life into the driest places of your soul and creating paths where none exist.

If certain areas of your life lack purpose, it's as if they have no water. Hold on to this word from God: "You are mine". I made you and formed you." This means that no one can deceive you about who you are. When you pray, you have an intimate conversation with the Lord. It's a private moment with the only person you can fully trust, the master of the universe.

This is why we often close our eyes during prayer, to reduce distractions and focus entirely on God in the spiritual realm. Find your own way to draw nearer to Him, and you will uncover your true purpose and peace.

From now on, you have a new beginning and renewed hope through the Spirit. If you're reading these words, I encourage you to pray as if the Lord were right beside you. Wherever you are, make it a priority to set aside a special time, you and the Lord, to be alone with Him from this moment forward.

How to start a private conversation channel to spend special time alone with the Lord, away from the distractions of the world?

Prayer is a way for guidance to be received by those seeking it, whether they are husbands, wives, or young people who feel lost or uncertain about their purpose. **Those who pray in this way will receive an answer from Abba.**

You can trust Jesus with whatever you can't share with your family or friends, knowing He understands and cares deeply for you.

The prophet Jeremiah said: "**Do not trust a neighbor; put no confidence in a friend. Even with the woman who lies in your embrace, guard the words of your lips**.". God is the only one who can keep all your secrets. Jesus said that when you pray, go into your room, close the door, and pray to your Father, who is in heaven. Then your father, who sees what is done in secret, will reward you. (Micah 7:5)

In Isaiah 41:18, **"I will make rivers flow on barren heights, and springs within the valleys for you. I will turn the desert into pools of water, and the parched ground into springs."**

Brethren, if parts of your life seem barren and dry, as if you lack spiritual water, you may begin to wonder in those moments of hardship, if life has no purpose or hope. However, God is always at work, cutting a path through your desert and causing water to flow through your wastelands. What may seem lifeless and empty today can be transformed by his divine power.

How many of us, after making the mistake of walking away from a dream, our church, or someone we love, find ourselves filled with regret? We convince ourselves that we have time, that opportunities will always present themselves again, only to realize later that time waits for no one, and you may never get another chance.

We delay important decisions, thinking we have control over the future, whether it's pursuing our vocation, committing to a relationship, or returning to God. Yet life moves on and opens doors that are completely shut forever. If God stirs your heart, don't let fear, doubt, or procrastination hold you back; take a step-in faith while there's still time. Just as water brings renewal and growth to dry soil, God can restore your purpose, bringing joy and fulfilment to areas of your life that seem stagnant.

There are seasons when you may feel lost, drained, or uncertain about your future. Looking back, and at your age now, you alone made these decisions that did not serve you well, but God's promises remain steadfast.

He specializes in turning wastelands into gardens and making a way where there seems to be no way. Even when you cannot see the changes happening, trust that He is working behind the scenes, preparing something new for you. His timing is perfect, and His plans are far greater than anything you could imagine.

Jeremiah 29:11-12 *"For I know the plans I have for you,"* declares the Lord, "plans to prosper you and not to harm you, plans to give you hope and a future. Then you will call on me and come and pray to me, and I will listen to you."

Trust in him alone, my brothers and sisters, for he is the source of all life and restoration. Don't trust your own understanding or strength; you once thought you were smarter, didn't you?

How did that work out for you?

Now is the time to surrender all the dry, broken parts of your life to Him. If you have faith, He will renew your spirit and guide you towards some abundant blessings. Rivers of His grace will flow into every lifeless area, bringing transformation, healing, and purpose. Keep your faith anchored in Him, and in time, you will see the beauty of His work unfold in your life.

In Isaiah 43, the prophet reminds us that God is with us when we find ourselves at life's crossroads and when we make poor choices. He has asked you to adapt to a new mindset and be open to learning new things. Man's plans are many, but the purposes of the Lord will prevail in our lives as Christians (Proverbs 19:21).

How many times have you presented your plans to God, only to realize that He had a very different path planned for you?

We often make our own plans, thinking we know what's best! But God's wisdom and purpose are beyond anything we can imagine. While it's natural to dream and set goals, we must learn to trust the Lord with our plans. We must believe that His ways are higher and His timing is perfect. Sometimes we desire certain things without realizing that they don't meet our needs.

God's plan is carefully designed to lead us to deeper fulfilment and lasting alignment with his will.

All the fantasies of love and wealth you see online today are ephemeral; they're not meant to last. They won't bring you or your family eternal happiness or enrichment. True joy and contentment come from deeper values of faith, meaningful relationships, and a life aligned with God's purpose; they don't come from superficial desires or material success.

Do you recall the name we chose for my firstborn, Isaiah? A prophet of God.

But instead of bringing a prophet into our home, God made a change and gave us a messenger, Gabriel, a name we hadn't chosen. I glanced at my wife to see if I was in trouble for giving our son a name we hadn't discussed or even known about. But she smiled, happily confirming the choice God had just made.

When Christians have to choose a name for their child

Many Christian parents are inspired by their faith to choose a name for their child with biblical significance, a name that will serve as a blessing for the child. Some parents select a name based on the circumstances of the child's conception or a pivotal moment, a blessing they have received, to remember.

God's promises and blessings. For example, names like Grace, Samuel, or Elijah not only honor notable biblical figures but also symbolize divine favor, prayer, or strength.

Christian parents are encouraged to choose names that express the core values of their faith, such as Faith, Hope, Joy, Job, Esther, or Elijah. These names are found in Scripture and Christian tradition, and they carry meanings that align with love, perseverance, and divine purpose. Such choices serve as a powerful reminder to both parent and child of the profound calling God has placed on their lives. More than simple words, they become daily affirmations of truth, character, and legacy.

Choosing a meaningful name is essential.

It's a good idea to avoid giving children names that are entirely invented or so unusual that their meaning is unclear. Names whose origin or definition isn't recognized, and names that don't appear in any dictionary or historical context, may create confusion rather than identity.

Ecclesiastes 1:9 reminds us that:

There is nothing new under the sun," suggesting that originality should not overshadow the meaning.

Unlike the tendency of some celebrities to give their children abstract or ambiguous names, such as "**X**" or "AI", Christian parents are being advised to prioritize clarity, with grace and purpose in mind, when naming their children.

A meaningful name can be a blessing in a child's life. It can hold prophetic significance for their future, shaping how they perceive themselves and their role in God's plan of salvation. When parents intentionally choose a name for their child, selecting one rich in biblical or spiritual meaning, they are planting seeds of identity and destiny for their child. The name becomes a compass that guides them through life's challenges while reminding the child of God's promises and presence.

Ultimately, for Christian parents, the goal is to honor God through the choice of their child's name. Whether inspired by Scripture, Christian heroes, or virtues such as love, courage, and wisdom, the child's name should embody values that nourish their soul. A name is more than just a label; it's a legacy. When chosen prayerfully and with discernment, a name can serve as a powerful expression of faith, shaping a child's character and guiding them toward the calling God has placed on their life.

In the Bible, a woman named Hannah prayed for many years at the temple in Shiloh, asking God to give her a son. (Shiloh was Israel's first capital for nearly four centuries and is about nine kilometers from Bethlehem, the birthplace of Jesus, is not far from Jerusalem.) Hannah's husband, Elkanah, was a Levite from Ramah, a town in the mountainous region of Ephraim.

He had two wives: Hannah, who had been barren for many years, and Peninnah, who had several children.
Elkanah was a servant of God, wealthy and well-regarded in the region. Although Hannah had no children, Elkana loved her more than Peninnah; she was beautiful and wise.

Hannah prayed with all her heart to have a son and promised to dedicate him to God once her prayer was answered. However, she remained barren for many years, and God stayed silent about her situation. Despite this silence, Hannah's faith never faltered. She continued to go alone to the temple, praying passionately and asking God to give her a son, again promising to dedicate him to the Lord.

Her unwavering trust in God's plan pushed her to keep praying, even when it seemed her prayers weren't being heard. She believed that if only God listened to her cry, her life would be forever changed. **Have you ever presented your case before the Lord, fully aware that only He can resolve your problem, yet felt as though He was silent for what seemed like an eternity?**

In those moments, faith alone must sustain you. Like Hannah, you may find yourself clinging to hope, praying earnestly, and trusting that answers will come, even when it seems you're waiting in silence. Your prayers may feel unanswered, but remember that God sees you, hears you, and your name is on His calendar; He will act according to His will.

Finally, the Lord answered Hannah's prayers. He opened her womb and granted her the desire of her heart. Hannah conceived and bore a son, Samuel, whom she dedicated to the Lord, as promised. The Lord continued to bless her, and she received grace with three more sons and two daughters. Through her patience and faith, God not only gave her a child but also blessed her abundantly, showing that His plans for us are often much greater than we can imagine

(1 Samuel 2:21).

She must have felt desperate, yet God had a plan for her. The Bible shows that God waited until Hannah was spiritually mature enough to welcome her son before answering her prayer. **God desires believers to gain the knowledge and wisdom to handle**

His blessings and mature in understanding before receiving His grace.

He doesn't withhold answers to our prayers out of unwillingness, but out of wisdom. He wants to make sure we are ready to handle His blessings. Until that time comes, we must remain patient, continue to grow in knowledge, and prepare our hearts to receive His grace.

The Lord said, 'Instead of your shame.' *You will receive a double portion, and instead of disgrace, you will rejoice in your inheritance. And you will inherit a double portion of your land, and everlasting joy will be yours. For I, the Lord, love justice. In my faithfulness, I will reward my people and establish an everlasting covenant with them. (Isaiah 61:7-8)*

After many years of prayer, Hannah became pregnant and gave birth to a son, whom she named Samuel, saying, "**It was for this child that I prayed**:' I prayed for this child, and the Lord granted me what

I asked of Him. 1 Samuel 1:27-28 The name Samuel means *"God has heard."*

Hannah kept the promise she made to God, saying, *"I prayed for this child, and the Lord has granted me what I asked of him. So now I give him to the Lord. For his whole life, he will be given over to the Lord." And he worshiped the Lord there."* She chose a name connected to her prayers and gratitude to thank God for His involvement in the process.

Now you, yes you...! How many times have you broken your promises to God?

You signed a contract with God. He granted your requests long ago, whether last year or recently, but you've continued to live your life as if you did it all alone! Let me share a little advice I received from one of my pastors: God didn't bless you so you could boast to others. **God resists the proud but gives grace to the humble**.

(James 4:6).

Your blessings should be your testimony, yours alone, with kindness and thanksgiving. You must not use them to boast to others; you must receive them with humility and preferably in secret, so that it is God who is honored, not you.

After waiting and praying for a long time, you've received favor and grace from heaven, but you've already forgotten God. You keep posting and calling other people who don't even like you to share! Now, one day, you'll be "pregnant" again, facing more demands and waiting for another miracle from the Lord, won't you?

Yes! Hannah just told you her story and what she did! Your temple can be anywhere where you can be alone with God in a safe and private setting. Your Shiloh is not in Israel; it's right here, where you are, in the city where you live. Find your Shiloh as soon as possible to present your gratitude, before you complain to the Lord. So, be very careful how you live, not as the unwise, but as the wise.

My brethren, remember that when you are pregnant with your Samuel, it is based on the promises you have made to God in your own words. You may not yet know whether your Samuel will become a king, but one thing is sure: if you have enough faith to understand the spiritual realm, God will answer you.

One reason you might experience delays or silence in your life is that the Lord loves you deeply. He sometimes separates you, drawing you into solitude so He can speak to you. But to hear His voice, you need to be willing to pause, stop talking, stop venting, and truly listen to His voice.

Only you can hear His voice as He prepares you to receive the abundance of the treasure He is about to deliver into your life. When God answers your prayers, don't forget to show your gratitude, regardless of the situation you're in at the moment. Be careful not to display your holiness in front of others just to be seen when the Lord gives you what your heart desires, or your heavenly Father will not reward you.

Truth and Obedience to God

At King Herod's birthday celebration, Salome, the daughter of Herodias, who was both Herod's wife and his niece, performed a dance that greatly pleased the king. At her mother's urging, Salome demanded the head of John the Baptist on a platter. Herodias and her daughter were deeply offended by John, for he had boldly denounced their immoral life. Thus, John was beheaded for speaking the truth.

When the Lord sends His Holy Spirit to deliver a message, He often chooses people close to us or individuals who can profoundly capture our attention. These moments are not mere coincidences; they are divine interventions, intentionally placed to redirect, correct, or encourage us along our path.

God's messages may take the form of a whisper in a conversation, a thought during a moment of silence, or an action carried out by a loved one. Whatever the form, each message bears the mark of His wisdom. Designed to lead us into the fulfillment of His will, they testify to the Lord's inexhaustible compassion, as He bends toward us, speaks intimately to our hearts, and longs for us to listen.

Yet, when we choose to ignore or reject the presence of the Holy Spirit, we cut off the very flow of life. It is as though every door to progress closes and the path ahead grows dark. Until we humble ourselves, acknowledging and respecting God's power and authority, every area of our existence risks becoming Stagnant.

Projects, relationships, careers, and personal growth all come to a halt when we refuse to submit to our inner voice.

Obedience to God paves the way for His blessings to flow into our lives, while resistance brings only delay and hindrance. Until we align ourselves with His will, we remain inactive, waiting for that divine movement which only prayerful obedience can unlock.

When Zechariah doubted the message of the angel Gabriel, he thought it impossible that his elderly family could bear a child. Many Christians today would respond the same way, since science and medicine affirm that a woman in her forties, fifties, or sixties can't conceive. But God, the sovereign Creator, transcends every human limitation, demonstrating that His power surpasses all earthly understanding.

Psalm 3:3

But thou, O LORD, art a shield for me; my glory, and the lifter up of my head.

HEAVENLY CITIZEN

CHAPTER THREE

For no matter how many promises God has made, they are "**Yes**" in Christ. And so, through him, the "**Amen**" is spoken by us to the glory of God. 2 Corinthians 1:20

When God Says Yes

His Ways Are Higher, His Blessings Made for You. God alone possesses the unlimited power to see every person on Earth simultaneously and to guide every soul according to His perfect will. His sovereignty is unique, and no force can limit His jurisdiction. This kind of divine power is attributed only to Him, beyond all human understanding or knowledge. If He chooses to bless you and answer your prayers, He does so of His own free will, without anyone else's permission.

His plans are unstoppable, and His grace is freely bestowed, according to His perfect wisdom.

When God chooses to transform His servant's life, nothing and no one can stand in His way. He requires no permission, neither yours nor anyone else's. Whether you are ready or not, faithful or not, His work in your life is a testament to your worth in His eyes and a story for you to tell others that you belong to Him alone. He sees beyond the present, knowing your future and shaping it according to His divine will.

This idea probably doesn't make sense to many of you. Furthermore, for those who have more questions, we are glad you are here reading this truth, regardless of the names you choose to call God in your own language.

Your curiosity about this knowledge is of great importance. God does not hide the truth from anyone willing to seek understanding of where everything comes from.

As Prophet Isaiah said:

*"For this is what Jesus said, the one who created the heavens, He is God, the one who fashioned and made the earth. He founded it; He did not create it to be empty, but formed it to be inhabited. "I am the LORD, and there is no other". (*Isaiah 45:18)

Absolute trust in God: One of Jesus' twelve apostles, James 1:17, says, "***Every good and perfect gift is from above, from the Father of heavenly lights, who does not change like shifting shadows***."

This reminds us that no one can change what God has planned for us. His grace has been more than sufficient in the past, and it will continue to be more than satisfactory in the present and future.

In 2006, the Lord took control of my life and my family, turning the whole situation around just when we needed it most. This experience taught me an important lesson: even if we don't always have an accurate view of the situation, our heavenly Father, in His infinite wisdom, knows exactly when and how things should unfold.

His ways may be beyond our imagination, but they always lead us in the right direction.

Even when things take longer than expected, we must remember that we are His children, keep the faith, and follow His example. The story of my second son, Isaiah, testifies to this truth.

The time had not yet come for us to take the prophet home. God, in his omniscience, knew we had to wait a little longer. He first gave us Gabriel Marcelin junior, who bears the same nickname as his father, "**Gabe**". This name is that of an angel who lives in the presence of God and who came to interpret the prophet's vision in (Daniel 9:20-27), and who delivers the prophecy of the seventy weeks, foretelling essential events in Israel's history, including the coming of the Messiah and the destruction of the temple.

Gabriel appeared to Zacharias, who was a priest, to announce that his wife, Elisabeth, would give birth to a son, despite their advanced age. The angel announced that this child would play a crucial role in preparing the way for the Messiah by preaching and baptizing people in the Messiah's name. That child was John the Baptist, who later became a distinguished preacher and baptized Jesus in the River Jordan. However, he was eventually executed by King Herod.

The Sovereignty of God and the Impossible Made Possible

During King Herod's birthday celebration, Salome, the daughter of Herodias, who was both Herod's wife and niece, performed a dance that greatly pleased the king.

At her mother's request, Salome demands the head of John the Baptist on a platter. Herodias and Salome were very angry with John because he had condemned their immoral lifestyle. As a result, John was beheaded for speaking the truth.

When the Lord sends his Holy Spirit to deliver a message, he often uses the people closest to us, or individuals who can deeply captivate our attention.

These moments are not mere coincidences, but divine interventions, purposely placed to redirect, correct, or encourage us on our path. God's messages can take the form of a whisper in a conversation, a thought in a quiet moment, or an action by a beloved being.

Whatever the form, each message is a reflection of His wisdom. Designed to direct us toward the fulfillment of His will, the Lord, in His inexhaustible compassion, reaches out to us, speaking intimately to our hearts and wanting us to listen.

However, when we choose to ignore or reject the presence of the Holy Spirit, we disrupt the flow of life itself. It's as if all the doors to progress are locked, and the path ahead is unclear.

Until we humble ourselves, acknowledging and respecting God's power and authority, every aspect of our lives risks becoming stagnant and unfulfilling. Projects, relationships, careers, and personal growth all come to a halt when we refuse to submit to our inner voice. Obedience to God paves the way for His blessings to pour into our lives, while resistance only brings delays and hindrances. Until we align ourselves with His will, we remain in a place of inactivity, waiting for the divine movement that only prayerful obedience can unlock.

When Zechariah doubted the angel Gabriel's message, he tried to believe that his aging family could not have children. Many Christians today have the same mindset if they were in his situation, as science and medicine today suggest that it would be impossible for women between the ages of 40 and 60 to give birth to a child. However, God, the ultimate Creator, transcends human limits, demonstrating that His power surpasses any earthly understanding.

King David demonstrated his reverence for God's sovereignty over creation, his daily care for the earth, and his provision for all living creatures. He said:

"How many are your works, O Lord! You have done them all wisely, and the earth is full of your creatures. (Psalm 104:24.)

This is not the same as a scientist who, based on his understanding, studies the complexities of the world and declares certain things to be impossible. Such limitations do not bind those who have witnessed your greatness firsthand. Thanks to their profound experiences, they have come to the conclusion that nothing is impossible for the Lord.

These servants, willing to give their lives for their faith, have left us messages to understand that God's power far surpasses all human reasoning. Their testimonies teach us that the Lord works beyond what we can comprehend, calling us to trust in His unlimited ability to accomplish the impossible.

When everything seems dark and impossible, when healing seems out of the question, when a couple has been waiting in vain for a child for a long time and is faced with infertility, or when a loved one is ill in the hospital. When a surgical operation goes wrong, or when a spouse has given up on staying married. God's power remains greater than all circumstances. No illness, not even cancer or any other fatal disease, escapes his power of deliverance.

When the doctors say there's no hope, God can still make a new way. He is the great healer, the one who gives life where there is none, and the God who turns impossibilities into miracles. What seems to be the end for man is only the beginning of God's divine intervention.

Sometimes life can seem impossible, complicated, and overwhelming, and you can find yourself in the dark, surrounded by uncertainty, with no one around to offer you an answer.

This servant of the Lord lived his life in deep darkness. Job was a man of great faith and righteousness, but he faced unimaginable suffering. In a single day, he lost all his wealth, his servants, who had nothing to do with his faith or his relationship with God but were part of his household, and his ten children, who were all tragically killed. Yet he never wavered in his devotion to God. On the contrary, he humbly declared:

"The Lord has given and the Lord has taken away; blessed be the name of the Lord" (Job 1:21).

God is the ultimate mathematician, perfectly calculating every soul's solution to the challenges we face. There is no greater physician than He, for He heals not only the body but also the soul, restoring what is broken and making whole what seems impossible. His philosophy surpasses all understanding, and His ways surpass all human knowledge. No one has ever surpassed the depth of His love for those who place their faith in Him alone.

Jesus looked at them and said: "**To men it is impossible, but not to God; all things are possible to God**" (Mark 10:27).

Jesus wanted to teach Christians that while human restrictions may make some things impossible, nothing escapes God's power. He knows the intimacy of our hearts, the desires we carry, and all the prayers we have addressed to Him. Trust that God will send you everything you need from your list of blessings, and when His angels bring you the answers, don't be afraid. Welcome this guidance, knowing that it is a sign of His presence and a reminder that now is the time to be blessed, bringing you closer to Him.

The appearance of the angel Gabriel: fear and faith.

However, the appearance of the angel Gabriel often seems strange, even intimidating. In Scripture, every time Gabriel appeared to someone, his presence inspired awe, underscoring the awe-inspiring and extraordinary nature of encountering the divinity of the Almighty.

Daniel describes what he saw when he met with the archangel Gabriel in vivid detail: "I lifted my eyes and looked, and behold, a man clothed in linen, with a belt of fine gold from Uphaz around his waist.

His body was like beryl, his face like lightning, his eyes like flaming torches, his arms and legs like the gleam of burnished bronze, and the sound of his words like the roar of a multitude. Daniel alone saw the vision, and the men who were with him did not see it, but they were terrified of the presence. (Daniel 10:5-7)

Though Daniel recognizes this as a messenger from God, as a prophet of God, he still struggles with doubt. How often have we done the same, hesitating to trust the message God has placed before us? We may have been called to remain silent, yet we rushed to confide in a friend.

Gabriel then said to Zechariah, the father of John the Baptist:

"Even a fool who keeps silent is considered wise; when he closes his lips, he is deemed intelligent." (Proverbs 17:28)

"I am Gabriel. I stand in the presence of God, and I have been sent to speak to you and to share this good news with you. And now you will

be silent and not able to speak until the day this happens, because you did not believe my words, which will come true at their appointed time."
Luke 1:18-20.

Later, the angel Gabriel announced Mary's pregnancy to her cousin Elisabeth, as a sign for Mary to understand that God was in the story. In a dream, the angel Gabriel also tells Joseph not to be afraid to take Mary as his wife, for her pregnancy is a result of the Holy Spirit. He also tells him to name the child Jesus, for he will save his people from their sins. Gabriel helps and protects the holy child from King Herod to ensure Jesus' safety.

Can you imagine yourself in this story? What would you do?

Imagine you're in a situation where you're about to marry someone who's already pregnant, and when you dated her, she wasn't, now, not by you or someone in your town.

You and your fiancée are both foolish enough to listen to the explanation given by the angel of God. You are both deeply committed servants of the Lord, and yet you find yourselves facing these immense challenges and a very difficult one. It all boils down to one word: "***FAITH***".

The law of your country could condemn you both to death, and the gossip around town could tarnish your family's names and reputations.

How many followers would you have on social media?

The weight of your family name, their lineage reputation, cultural values, and the social norms pressing down on both of you could lead to shame and even risk your lives.

How would you handle such an unimaginable trial?

This is far more challenging than receiving bad news from a doctor, being diagnosed with cancer, or facing any other disease for which humans have studied the process of a plan. The physical burden of navigating such a responsibility, as a man or a woman, is overwhelming. The question of how to emerge on the other side of this for your family is daunting.

When Christian families face trials, it's common to doubt God's timing, wonder if He's still at work, and question whether the messages we've received are truly from Him. The waiting time of these challenges can make us impatient, as we long for immediate answers. At such times, we often turn to our friends for comfort, but many of them are not believers, which can make the situation even more complicated.

In difficult times, it can feel as though God is silent, especially when change seems slow and our problems persist. We often struggle with patience, desiring God's intervention on our timeline, quickly and decisively. However, we must remember that the knowledge of God is vast and encompasses everything:

With Jesus are the keys of the unseen, except Him. And He knows what is on the land, and in the sea. Not a single leaf falls without His knowledge. Nothing escapes His sight, and everything unfolds according to His perfect wisdom; even when we cannot yet see it.

Nothing in all creation is hidden from God's sight. Everything is uncovered and laid bare before the eyes of him to whom we must give account. **(Hebrews 4:13)**

When he met Moses, the Lord said, "*I will have mercy on whom I will have mercy: I will have mercy on whom I will have mercy, and I will have mercy on whom I will have mercy.*" **(Exodus 33:19).**

This does not depend on human desire or effort, but solely on God's mercy. In these moments, our faith is tested, and we learn to trust God more and more.

The Lord said, "When the time comes, I, the Lord, will make it happen." The Lord will carry out His plans at the right time, according to His will and wisdom." (Isaiah 60:22)

The Lord will fulfill His purposes in His time, according to His will and wisdom.

You remember my first child, originally to be named Isaiah, but who came home as Gabriel, don't you? On March 24, 2008, we welcomed our second boy, Isaiah, precisely two years later, keeping his name on the same banner in Gabriel's room as a reminder that the Lord had more blessings to bring us. During those two years, even when we didn't understand God's plan, we trusted Him with total control of our family, allowing Him to guide us while we submitted fully to His will.

Isaiah 55:8-9

"For my thoughts are not your thoughts, neither are your ways my ways," declares the Lord. As the heavens are higher than the earth, so are my ways higher than your ways and my thoughts than your thoughts."

Does this sound familiar to you?

Having the patience to wait for something from God is a virtue. Waiting for a vital answer often requires faith, especially when you feel that your prayers and efforts are met with silence or delay. Waiting is not something Christians do well. Praying and then having to wait for answers from God can be one of the most complex parts of faith.

Our human nature craves immediate solutions, but we must resolutely trust in His ordained timing and perfect design. We often don't have the complete picture of what he's orchestrating behind the scenes for us, and in those moments of uncertainty, our faith needs to be stronger than ever, as it is tested and refined.

The waiting period is an opportunity for growth, as God uses this time to prepare our hearts, to strengthen our character, and align us with His plan.

Remember, God's delay is not a rejection of your case.

His plans for you are good, and his timing is perfect.

The Certainty of God's Promises. Has anyone ever seen a promise of God fail to come to pass?

The answer is a resounding "**NO**". Every word the Lord has spoken is accurate, and His promises are sure. Scripture affirms, *"God is not a man, that He should lie, nor a son of man, that He should repent. Has He said, and will He not do it? Or has He spoken, and will He not make it good?"* (Numbers 23:19).

Our Father cannot be mocked, nor does He deceive anyone. His Word is steadfast, His faithfulness unshaken.

In a world where men and women break their word daily, where contracts are violated and trust is often misplaced, the promises of God stand as an eternal anchor. If we think ourselves wiser than others, boasting in our intellect, talents, or status, we deceive ourselves. **The Lord resists the proud but gives grace to the humble** (James 4:6). Pride closes the heart to God's wisdom, while

Humility opens the soul to learn, to grow, and to be transformed by His Spirit.

For this reason, regardless of what happens in life, Christians are called to keep their faith firmly rooted in God. Trials will come, challenges will test us, and disappointments may wound us, but none of these things can cancel the promises of the Lord. The faithful believer continues to pray, to seek the face of God, and to act in alignment with His Word. Faith is not passive; it is active. It listens to God's law, responds with obedience, and shapes every part of the family and community life according to His design.

We must never forget: you and your household belong to Him. From the moment you surrendered your life to Christ, you were no longer your own. Paul reminds us, *"Do you not know that your body is the temple of the Holy Spirit who is in you, whom you have from God,*

and you are not your own? For you were bought at a price; therefore, glorify God in your body and in your spirit, which are God's." **(1 Corinthians 6:19–20).**

To belong to Him means we cannot think, speak, or act as unbelievers do. We are called to be holy, set apart, and distinct as citizens of a Kingdom, not of this world.

The Kingdom of God is our true homeland. While we walk on this earth, we live as ambassadors of

Christ, representing His values, His truth, and His love. Our families are not merely social units but sacred spaces where His promises are lived out. When we raise our children in His ways, when we honor our spouses, when we practice humility and walk in obedience, we are testifying to the world that God's Word is true.

So let us hold fast to His promises without wavering. Not one of them has ever failed, and not one ever will. We are temples of His presence, citizens of His Kingdom, and heirs of His eternal covenant. Our faith rests not in human strength, but in the God who cannot lie and whose Word endures forever.

Psalm 4:8

I will both lie down in peace and sleep, for thou, LORD, only makest me dwell in safety.

HEAVENLY CITIZEN

CHAPTER FOUR

*W*hen God Says Yes, God is like no other.

As a father, God is like no other; his love, wisdom, and guidance surpass all men's understanding. Unlike earthly fathers, who can falter or fail us, God's fatherhood is perfectly reliable, unwavering, and eternal. His love for us is unconditional.

Faith is a fundamental necessity, especially when you feel that despite all your prayers and efforts, God remains silent. David said:

Psalm 18:6:

"In my distress, I called upon the Lord, I cried to my God for help. From his temple, he heard my voice, and my cry reached his ears."

But nothing helped; he was confused, uncertain, and discouraged.

Sometimes, we approach God as if we are frustrated with the approach and technique, He uses to manifest Himself to us. We want to see some manifestation. I've seen people pray aloud as if God is far away, weep emotionally as if their emotion would get God's attention, or touch His heart.

He will answer our prayers in times of trial, but it's essential to know and understand who God is and seek to know how He hears and answers the prayers of all the other servants who have gone before us.

"***Whatever you ask in prayer, you will receive, if you have faith***" **Matthew 21:22**.

The key is not to prove yourself as a good servant or to pray more than others, but to be still, seek wisdom through the Scriptures, and take time to listen to God's voice.

The Lord said, "**Be still, and know that I am God**."(Psalm 46:10)

The Lord pays attention to our prayers: "**Before they call, I will answer; while they are still speaking, I will hear.**" **(Isaiah 65:24)**

His love and counsel are beyond human understanding. In the whirlwind of life, we often find ourselves asking Him for specific blessings, whether large or small. Even if we don't always understand His ways, we can rest in the truth that He's always working behind the scenes, orchestrating things for our good.

Even in moments of uncertainty, when circumstances seem insurmountable, we can take comfort in knowing that what is beyond our control is entirely in his hands.

God's promise to all believers is that we are never alone, even in our weakest moments. He strengthens and sustains us, offering his steadfast grace when we feel weary. Isaiah 41:10 He said to the prophet, "Do not fear, for I am with you; do not be afraid, for I am your God. I will strengthen you; I will help you; I will uphold you with my righteous right hand."

When fear and doubt invade us, confusing us, we must remain faithful and stand firm in our faith, knowing that God's plan is greater than anything we could imagine. Trusting him means giving up all our worries and embracing his peace, knowing that he is always faithful to his promises.

***Those who live in the shelter of the Most-High will find rest in the shadow of the Almighty.* (Psalm 91:1)**

In times of adversity, we all need someone to turn to. Take a moment to reflect on your life experiences and consider who that trusted person is. It's not just anyone; you need someone who genuinely desires the best for you and your family, someone whose care and guidance are unwavering.

While parents, friends, spouses, and colleagues may offer support, the only one truly worthy of your complete trust is the Lord. When you surrender your life and your family to

You will witness the profound transformation that comes from His fatherhood, love, and care.

The waiting seasons. Every faithful person will experience a season of waiting. Along the way, we will encounter friends and good people who are not part of our lives, but who stay with us for only a season or two. So, don't be surprised when they suddenly leave. When their presence fades away, like waters that run dry in a valley, it simply means their season in our lives has come to an end, and we must let them go.

Rather than seeing this trial as a loss, hurt, or anger, we should welcome it as an opportunity for growth. In these moments, God prepares our minds, strengthens our character, and aligns us with His purpose. His blessings are immense, but to receive them fully, we often need greater discipline to manage His grace well.

Remember that God's delays are not a rejection. He hasn't forgotten you or your family. His plans are always good, and you need to stand firm in faith. Be patient, hang on a little longer, and trust that he's doing everything for your good. When the time is right, he will show up for you.

Take the example of Elijah in the desert, exhausted and overwhelmed, he cried out to God, saying, "Take my life." Yet as he slept under a juniper tree, an angel of the Lord came to give him food and strength for the journey ahead, sustaining him for forty days and forty nights (1 Kings 19). Likewise, as you wait, God provides exactly what you need to walk in His purpose.

In **Deuteronomy 9:9**, Moses fasted on Mount Sinai for 40 days and 40 nights, without eating or drinking. Likewise, Jesus was led by the Holy Spirit for 40 days and 40 nights. As Christians, you're familiar with these powerful lessons that teach us the value of patience and the need to entrust our burdens to our Lord, knowing that He will show up for you.

Before any critical endeavor: fasting and consecration

Before engaging in any important task, Christians are often invited to fast, submitting their concerns to the Lord, renouncing their flesh, and seeking His divine intervention, so that no one on earth can hinder what God has ordained.

God sees you even in the shadows, hears your praises, and knows when you feel hidden from the world. His light surrounds you, and every whisper of faith, every silent prayer rises to Him like a fragrant offering. He understands your secrets, your joys, your silent sorrows, your deepest aspirations, your most intimate doubts, and struggles. Nothing escapes him, and his love watches over you with infinite tenderness. May your heart always sing in adoration, for he hears your cries, and his faithfulness is there to protect you and your family.

«The spiritual treasures of the Kingdom are revealed to all Christians who walk in faith. The mysteries of the Kingdom of God have been revealed to all believers.»

I rejoice in the way God reveals himself, in ways both unexpected and profoundly meaningful. He did it in the burning bush with Moses, as he did for Elijah in the cave, as he appeared to John the Baptist in the Jordan, or to Saul on the road to Damascus. He always manifested himself in such a way that even the people around him couldn't claim anything other than to say, 'Only God did it.'

"I know that thou can do all things, and that there is nothing against thy thoughts." (Job 42:2)

I also love that when people around me become aware of my miracles, including my wife, they have to say, "**Yes, only God can do it**".

Most of the time, we feel like we've had enough, that more than 40 days and 40 nights is too long, but His clock is in perfect tune with our needs. After enduring the sufferings of the cross and conquering death, Jesus revealed Himself to His disciples, showing and teaching them the undeniable proof of His resurrection.

"**Whoever has seen me has seen the father**" before Abraham was born, I am. I am in the father, and the father is in me. (John 14:9)

"All things have been delivered to me by my father. No one knows the son except the father, and no one knows the father except the son. (Matthew 11:27)

Forty days of revelation and faith

For 40 days and nights, he taught them, revealing even more of the mysteries of God's kingdom. By his presence and teaching, he strengthened their faith, dispelled their doubts, and prepared them for the evangelical mission ahead. This precious time spent with the Lord after His resurrection was a vivid confirmation of God's victory over death, sickness, and infirmity, and a call to proclaim our complete trust in Abba.

"*Because you are his sons, God sent the Spirit of his Son into our hearts, the Spirit who calls out, 'Abba, Father.'*"

Galatians 4:6:
The Mighty King's Name is « I AM ».

When you and your family claim citizenship in the kingdom of heaven, you no longer have to face adversity as others do. You don't have to be shaken or moved like the world around you. You don't have to complain like non-believers. Instead, you hold onto your faith, trusting that the name « *I AM* ». Will always be there for you and your family.

The God whose name is « *I AM* ». It is not a vague or distant force for Christians; it's a personal, ever-present, all-powerful being who promises to reveal himself to you. His presence is divine and infallible, never wavering, always ready to meet you in your hour of need to give you wisdom, healing, strength, and boundless love. Whether you're going through trials or rejoicing in blessings, she is constant, independent of time and circumstance.

As the eternal God, without beginning or end, He is your invincible provider, of unsurpassed greatness and unlimited power. His presence knows no boundaries, simplifying exactly what you need at the perfect moment. In Him, there is no lack, no uncertainty, only unwavering faithfulness.

*Moses asked God, "**If I go to the Israelites and say to them**, 'The God of your fathers has sent me to you,' and they ask me, '**What is his name?**' what will I say to them?" God said to Moses, "**I AM THAT I AM**". This is what you will speak to the Israelites: "**I AM**" has sent me to you.* **Exodus 3:13-14**

When faced with trials and uncertainty, remember that you are a child of the great *I AM*. As a citizen of God's kingdom, you are not alone; you are not defined by fear, illness, weakness, or the struggles of this world. The same God who sent Moses, parted the Red Sea, and reigns sovereign over all creation, is the same God who walks with you today. Stand firm in your identity, knowing that the great *I AM* has called you, sustains you, and will never abandon you.

wisdom and power of silence

The wisdom of silence is a theme that resonates deeply in Scripture, particularly in the teachings of King Solomon. Proverbs 21:23 draws attention to the importance of keeping our mouths shut as Christians, reminding us that.

Guarding our tongues can protect our souls from unnecessary trouble.

Words can often lead to misunderstandings, conflicts, and sin; not everything needs to be shared. Solomon's counsel is a reminder to exercise restraint in using our tongues as Christians. Silence is not merely the absence of speech but a choice to avoid causing harm through reckless words.

When we control our speech, we not only safeguard our relationships but also maintain our inner peace.

King Solomon teaches profound wisdom about the power of words and the importance of controlling our mouths. Proverbs 21:23 warns Christians that those who keep their mouths and tongues shut will preserve their souls from trouble, redirecting the link between our words and the state of our hearts.

James 1:19 adds to this advice, exhorting believers to be quick to listen, slow to speak, and slow to anger, warning Christians that their reactions and responses will determine their relationships and inner peace.

In addition, Solomon said in Proverbs 13:3 that guarding our words preserves our lives, while careless words lead to ruin. Taken together, these verses teach us that wisdom and peace come not from speaking freely, but from choosing carefully when and how to say, and learning to listen with patience and understanding.

By following this divine advice, we can protect ourselves from unnecessary conflict and maintain the harmony God desires for our lives. King Solomon further expands on the idea of being silent, when necessary, in Proverbs 17:28, stating that even a fool, when quiet, can be perceived as wise.

This passage is a powerful reminder that wisdom isn't always about having the correct answers or knowing more than others, but instead that it's often better to know when to speak up and when to remain silent. In a world where people usually feel pressured to express their opinions and dominate conversations, to like other people's posts and comment on everything, silence can serve as a shield against unnecessary pride, arrogance, and rash decisions.

Choosing silence in certain situations can help prevent us from getting entangled in conflicts that distract us from God's will and from each other.

The book of James also echoes the dangers of the tongue. James 3:6 warns Christians that the tongue is like fire, capable of great destruction. A single word can set off a chain of events that spins out of control, causing hurt and division, shattering families, friendships, marriages, governments, and much more.

By adopting the wisdom of silence, we can avoid contributing to the conflagration James warns us about. In moments of tension, the choice of silence can be a reflection of strength, tempering our reactions and allowing God to guide our responses.

The Bible teaches Christians to place their trust in God rather than relying solely on human relationships. King David, in Psalm 118:8, states that it is better to take refuge in the Lord than to rely on human beings. Even if they seem trustworthy, men are imperfect and can disappoint us. God, on the other hand, remains steadfast and faithful, always bringing us stability and wisdom.

Trusting God's guidance, rather than depending solely on our friends or peers, allows us to find true peace and direction in life. It is through this trust that we are better equipped to discern when to speak and when to remain silent.

Heavenly Father,
Almighty Lord,
Set a guard over my mouth and watch over my lips.
So that my words can bring peace rather than division.
Teach me to listen more than I speak.
Be patient, slow to anger, and quick to understand.
Please help me choose silence when it guards my soul. And to speak only when my words build up, comfort, or glorify Your Name.
Fill my heart with your peace.
And grant me the wisdom to depend on you alone, rather than relying on others for security. Lord, I place my trust in you, for you are my refuge, my guide, and my strength.
May my tongue and my heart always serve your Kingdom.
In the name of Jesus Christ, **Amen.**

The Wisdom of Waiting and Consecration

God is like no other. From the beginning of creation to the end of time, His majesty, holiness, and sovereignty set Him apart from everything and everyone else. To know Him is to discover a reality greater than human reason, a love deeper than human affection, and a power beyond human strength. Every believer who bows before the Mighty King encounters the living God whose Name is *«I AM »*, the One who was, who is, and who is to come.

The Waiting Season of a Christian's Life and Family. One of the greatest tests of faith is the waiting season. Christians are often called to be patient, trusting that the Lord's timing is perfect, even when our hearts long for immediate answers. Waiting is not passive resignation; it is an act of worship, a declaration that God's plan is wiser than ours.

In the silence of waiting, our faith is stretched, our character is refined, and our hearts are trained to recognize the gentle movements of the Spirit. The waiting season is therefore not wasted time, but sacred preparation.

Fasting and Consecration Before Every Big Endeavor

Before any critical endeavor, the people of God are invited to fasting and consecration. These disciplines are not empty rituals but expressions of total dependence on the Lord. To fast is to say, "**Man does not live by bread alone**," and to consecrate oneself is to declare, "**My life belongs to God's purposes**."

Before engaging in any important task, Christians are often invited to pray, lifting their hearts to heaven in surrender. Through fasting, consecration, and prayer, the believer aligns his will with the divine will, ensuring that the Spirit leads every step forward.

The spiritual treasures of the Kingdom are revealed to all Christians who walk in faith. These treasures are not material riches, but eternal gifts: peace that surpasses all understanding, joy that remains unshaken in the face of trials, and hope that anchors the soul. The mysteries of the Kingdom of God have been revealed to all believers who open their hearts to the Word and allow the Spirit to teach them. Through Scripture, prayer, and fellowship with the Body of Christ, believers discover that the Kingdom is already among them, present within them, transforming their daily lives.

The Wisdom and Power of Silence, among the treasures of the Kingdom, is a testament to the wisdom and power of silence. Too often, words spoken in haste wound others and dishonor the Lord. Scripture warns us that life and death are in the power of the tongue.

Therefore, let not your tongue and your heart get you in trouble with the Lord. Silence, when guided by wisdom, becomes an instrument of peace. In silence, we hear the voice of God more clearly. In silence, we guard the unity of the Body. And in silence, we cultivate humility, remembering that our words must always build up, never tear down.

The believer's body is a temple of the Holy.

Spirit. As such, it must remain holy, consecrated, and devoted to divine service. Let your temple always serve your Kingdom. What you think, what you speak, and what you do either honor or dishonor the King. To serve faithfully, the Christian must cultivate purity of heart, obedience to God's Word, and a life marked by prayer and worship. The temple is not merely an individual's body but also the collective Church, the dwelling place of God's Spirit. Together, Christians form a living sanctuary where the glory of the King is displayed to the world.

Conclusion

To live as a Christian is to walk in the assurance that God is like no other. The waiting season, though difficult times, prepares the heart for greater blessings. Fasting and consecration before any endeavor remind us of our dependence on Him.

The spiritual treasures and mysteries of the Kingdom are open to all who believe. The wisdom and power of silence keep us from stumbling, and the temple of our lives must continually serve the purposes of the Kingdom. In all things, may we bow before the Mighty King, whose Name is « *I AM* », and live as faithful citizens of His eternal Kingdom.

Psalm 5:12: *For thou, LORD, wilt bless the righteous; with favor wilt thou compass him as with a shield.*

HEAVENLY CITIZEN

CHAPTER FIVE

*F*or we are co-workers in God's service; you are God's field, God's building. 1 Corinthians 3:9

Grounded in Grace: Building Kingdom Families in a Troubled Century.

A father's leadership to protect, educate, and train the next generation in partnership with God.

A Christian family is more than just a home; it's a divine partnership with God, built on the foundation of His love and understanding. Parenthood is a journey full of grace, joy, growth, goals, and challenges. In today's world, the definition of parenthood is often shattered by cultural norms, media influence, and societal demands.

However, as believers, we are summoned to a higher standard, one that aligns with the heart of God and the purpose of His kingdom. We live under a different authority because we are under a different government that responds to God's desire and the purpose of his kingdom.

God's divine plan for raising children is embedded in love, faith, discipline, and discipleship.

How can parents overcome the challenges of today's society to raise their children according to the Lord's plan?

By embracing this goal, even in a world where Christians often stray from God's truth. Today, the temptation is great to overlook the biblical principles, faith stories, and timeless wisdom that Scripture provides when it comes to raising children.

Many faithful families struggle to raise their children in accordance with the values of the Kingdom of God. Amid a culture that is moving further and further away from them and changing at a rapid pace, it is becoming increasingly challenging to realign our children.

However, God's partnership gives all Christian parents the authority and responsibility to make conscious decisions about how and where our children are raised and educated. This is an essential responsibility for all parents, especially fathers, in a rapidly changing world.

The spiritual legacy of parents

The values and teachings we pass on to our children must be firmly grounded in God's Word, knowing that outside influences can easily lead them astray. Our task as parents is to actively and prayerfully reorient their lives, ensuring they are rooted in the truth of God's kingdom, even as the world around them constantly changes.

Paul says:

"Do not conform to the pattern of this world, but be transformed by the renewing of your mind. Then you will be able to test and approve what God's will is, his good, pleasing, and perfect will." (Romans 12:2)

Understanding God's mission for the family

Only then will you be able to test and discern God's mission, His good, pleasing, and perfect will for your home. Our fundamental responsibility is to provide for and protect our family.

Just as the outer shell of a coconut protects the nourishing water and flesh inside, the protective fibrous envelope also preserves what is precious. Likewise, our families are safer when we relinquish total control to God.

This highlights the role of fathers as teachers and mentors who impart wisdom and stewardship in accordance with God's truth. These faithful leaders direct their families with wisdom, love, and understanding of His purposes. When we align ourselves with God's plan, we provide our families with the protection and guidance they need, and the Holy Spirit dwells in our homes, just as the coconut shell preserves what's alive inside.

The spiritual mission of the fathers

The Bible teaches that the father's mission is to be the spiritual leader of the home. As Scripture indicates:

"A father is to bring up all children, training and nurturing them according to the Lord." **(Ephesians 6:4)**

As spiritual leaders, protectors, and providers, fathers are called to exemplify God's fatherly love. They must lead their families with kindness, wisdom, and leadership.

God's wisdom is beyond all human understanding. He directs the Christian family through His Word, proposing orderly principles that lead to a life of justice, peace, and fulfillment. Christian fathers have the responsibility to apply this wisdom, disciplining and counselling their children with grace. They teach values rooted in faith, emphasizing integrity, compassion, and a commitment to God's truth.

An example of patience and humility

Fathers must govern with patience and humility, setting an example for their children. Through their actions, they develop self-respect and strengthen family ties in a way that honors God. This cultivates a home where love, respect, and faith shine brightly.

Fathers must actively foster a loving environment where children can grow in their relationship with family members and with God, laying the foundations for strong morals.

By consistently practicing prayer, worship, and fostering family cohesiveness, the Christian father helps build a home that embodies God's grace and purpose.

This provides the family with a sense of security, direction, and closeness, which has a positive impact on children's personal development and the quality of their relationships.

A spiritual foundation to equip the next generation

This spiritual foundation helps children face life's challenges with faith and confidence, knowing they are supported by both their earthly parents and their heavenly Father.

A strong father provides a constant presence in the lives of his children, giving a model of responsibility, resilience, integrity, emotional support, spiritual grounding, and intellectual growth. By setting a strong example, fathers teach their children essential life skills that shape their character and influence their development.

When fathers entrust their children with tasks, such as paying bills and managing family finances, it teaches them the discipline of financial responsibility and the value of saving. Tasks like grocery shopping and stocking supplies not only teach children how to manage practical matters but also instill good manners and teamwork; furthermore, they learn to avoid waste. Similarly, maintaining a clean house encourages self-reliance, discipline, and cleanliness.

These daily responsibilities help children develop independence and a sense of accomplishment, which in turn contributes to their overall development.

A culture of responsibility and leadership

As a father, I encourage my sons to take responsibility for household chores and to maintain high standards of education and personal development.

I always remind my sons that, even when I'm not physically present, they are the men of the house, and that their role is to keep the family safe, clean, and well-nourished.

This responsibility goes beyond household chores; it's about creating a culture of accountability, leadership, and dedication to the family. I'm convinced that by entrusting them with these responsibilities, I'm preparing them to succeed in life by teaching them to balance work and solidarity, while developing their potential to lead with determination, guided by the knowledge and integrity of a father.

The irreplaceable presence of a father

Thank you to all the fathers who teach their children the balance between love and discipline. The presence of a father creates a profound sense of belonging and trust, providing a solid foundation that enables children to face challenges with confidence and build healthy, lasting relationships.

The stability and support of a Christian father play a significant role in a child's overall well-being, promoting emotional, spiritual, and mental development. With this guidance, children are equipped with the strength and wisdom they need to navigate the outside world, knowing they have a stable, loving figure to turn to for support and guidance.

Heavenly Father, I praise you for all Christian children.

For Your hands wonderfully create them. Your works are extraordinary, and I thank You for the unique and precious personalities they are. I pray that they will never forget their value in You and remain strong in the truth of Your Word.

As Paul wrote in 1 Timothy 4:12, I ask:

«***Don't let anyone look down on you because you are young, but set an example for the believers in speech, in conduct, in love, in faith and purity***." May they live with integrity and honor, behave with confidence and respect, knowing that they are your beloved children.

Lord, help them guard their hearts above all else, as King Solomon teaches in **Proverbs 4:23**, "***Guard your heart more than anything else, for from it come the springs of life***."

I pray they hold to your wisdom, protecting their hearts from the influence of this world and staying faithful to your will. I declare that they are intelligent and anointed by the Holy Spirit, equipped to navigate life with strength and grace.

May your presence guide them as they walk in self-respect and the purpose you have planned for them. In Jesus' name, ***Amen***

The mission of fathers in a turbulent world

In today's world, non-believers often promote numerous theories and ideas that are usually in direct opposition to God's purpose for Christian families. We are being bombarded by multiple experts delivering contradictory advice on television and all social networking platforms, not to mention false prophets and new apostles who offer people a series of keys on how to successfully raise a family, each embracing philosophies and methods that differ from those in God's word.

However, in many cases, human wisdom is imperfect and subject to change, leading to confusion and uncertainty. Many of these so-called experts are ironically divorced or living far from their own families, while their failed experiences make them first-rate advisors and influencers.

That's why God established Christian fathers in homes, not to adapt to changing cultural trends or societal norms, but to anchor their families and align them with God's eternal truth. A father's job is to instill God's teachings in the hearts and minds of his children, to guide them in righteousness, and equip them to navigate the world with faith, wisdom, understanding, and integrity.

In addition, the Lord has partnered with Abraham in making a covenant that no one can ever break on earth. "*I will establish my covenant as an everlasting covenant between me and you and your descendants after you for the generations to come, to be your God and the God of your descendants after you. The whole land of Canaan, where you now reside as a foreigner, I will give as an everlasting possession to you and your descendants after you; and I will be their God."*

Then God said to Abraham, "As for you, you must keep my covenant, you and your descendants after you, for the generations to come. **(Genesis 17:7-9)**

Protecting and strengthening children's identity in Christ.

By leaning on God's Word rather than worldly opinions, fathers fulfil their divine calling to lead their families in the way of God's principles. This means shielding them from harmful influences, including bullying, by instilling in them a strong sense of identity in Christ, helping them understand their own identity.

The Word of God teaches kindness, respect, self-esteem, and the value of each person. Empower children to stand firm against abuse while responding with grace and wisdom. By defending biblical truths, parents give their children the strength to reject and speak out against fear and insecurity, knowing that they are deeply loved and protected by God.

We should remind them that they are intelligent, kind, loving, and beautifully made just as they are. In a faith-based home, intimidation has no place, for God's love lifts each spirit, giving it unshakable confidence and protection.

Protecting families from cultural and digital influences, Christian parents face the challenge of protecting their children from harmful cultural influences, including the pressures of social exploitation. This requires the wisdom and discernment of a spiritual leader, especially at a time when privacy is increasingly diminished.

Safeguarding the family from potential risks involves open and thorough communication about online behavior, educating children about privacy, and being vigilant when sharing personal information on the internet. God has placed a responsibility on fathers to lead and guide their families, including setting clear boundaries on what can and cannot be shared, especially when it comes to personal details, privacy, geolocation, and photos of underage children.

To preserve the privacy of our family, it is essential to guide children on the right path. As **Proverbs 22:6** says, «Train up a child in the way he should go, and when he is old, he will not depart from it. »

Fathers as Spiritual Leaders and Providers

The Bible taught that fathers have a vital role as educators, molding children's hearts and minds through Godly instruction.

Moses said to fathers, "And these commandments, which I give you this day, shall be in your heart: and you shall teach them to your children, and shall speak of them when you are in your house, and when you go on your journey, and when you lie down, and when you rise. **(Deuteronomy 6:6-7)**

The enduring nature of a father's teaching extends beyond formal education and encompasses the everyday moments of daily life. Fathers are the primary spiritual leaders and educators, instilling biblical values through both their words and deeds. By teaching the Scriptures, modelling the character of Christ, and leading a prayerful home, they create an environment where faith thrives.

Fathers: educators, protectors, and providers. Fathers are not only spiritual educators but also protectors of their children's minds and providers of various forms of wealth, including wisdom, knowledge, and material provision. They should teach their children a strong work ethic and the understanding that wealth is earned through diligence, integrity, and enterprise.

Teaching children the value of saving and planning for the future helps them avoid impulsive spending and unnecessary debt.

As **Proverbs 22:7** says: **"The rich rule over the poor, and the borrower is the lender's slave."**

Through financial management and innovative strategies, fathers empower their children to meet economic challenges wisely.

In addition, children should be encouraged to develop a generous heart, recognizing that giving is an act of worship and a mirror of God's provision. Through these biblical principles, they will learn to honor God and their parents with their finances, manage money responsibly, and cultivate a spirit of generosity and faithfulness.

A father's role extends beyond worldly education; he must protect his children from ungodly influences and ensure they are grounded in the truth about finances. Money is not inherently evil, but excessive love can lead to many sins. On the contrary, money should be used and managed wisely.

The truth about money and familial prosperity.

Children should learn that wealth acquired through honest work, business, and diligence is a blessing, while laziness and dishonesty lead to poverty and trouble.

As King Solomon, a very wealthy man, said, "***Wealth acquired Dishonestly dwindles, but he who gathers money little by little will increase it.***"

(Proverbs 13:11)

A father's instruction is deeply personal, shaping character, instilling values, and promoting spiritual growth toward wealth and prosperity.

Just as God provides for His children, fathers are ordained with the responsibility of providing for their families' material and emotional needs, alongside mothers, forming a strong system of support. A father's presence in the home should reflect God's unwavering love, giving both discipline and encouragement to nurture strong, faithful individuals who will be embraced and respected by the world.

Fathers are the best educators in the home, best placed to guide their children in traditional faith and wisdom. As the prophet Daniel wrote:

Daniel 1:17:
"To these four young men God gave knowledge and understanding of all kinds of literature and learning. And Daniel could understand visions and dreams of all kinds."

By assuming the role of educator that God has entrusted to them, the fathers prepare their children to become wise, competent, and God-fearing individuals who will be able to pass on His truth to future generations.

The **Bible** has stressed the importance of passing on the faith through intentional teaching. "When your children ask you, **'What does this ministry mean?' you will answer, 'It is the sacrifice of the Lord's Passover**" **(Exodus 12:26-27).**

In this way, God reinforced their identity as the chosen people. Likewise, Christian families are set apart for His kingdom, called to defend His truth and justice in every generation.

God's Fellow Workers: Parents Building a Spiritual Foundation

The apostle Paul reminds us, *"We are God's fellow workers"* **(1 Corinthians 3:9).**

This profound truth reshapes the way Christian parents see their calling. We are not left to navigate the complexities of raising children in a world filled with distractions and dangers alone. Instead, God's partnership gives all Christian parents the authority and responsibility to make conscious decisions about how and where our children are raised and educated. To parent is not only a sacred duty but also an act of stewardship, where we work hand in hand with our Creator to prepare the next generation.

Parents today face challenges that previous generations could scarcely imagine. From digital influences that capture young minds to cultural ideologies that distort truth, the task of guiding children has never been more demanding. Yet, by the strength of the Spirit, parents overcome the challenges of today's society to raise their children according to the Lord's plan. The same God who entrusted us with this responsibility also equips us to fulfill it. His Word is a lamp to our feet and a light to our path, showing us how to protect and nurture our families in a hostile world.

A Culture of Responsibility under the Leadership of Men

As a father, I encourage my sons to take responsibility for household chores and to maintain high standards of education and personal development. These seemingly small acts, washing dishes, studying diligently, and serving with kindness, are the building blocks of a strong life. Responsibility is not a burden but a gift, for it prepares them to carry weight, to serve others, and to one day lead their own households. Leadership is not about dominance but about serving with wisdom, protecting with strength, and guiding with love.

Every decision made in the family home contributes to a spiritual foundation to equip the next generation. Education is more than academics; it is a form of discipleship. Training a child is more than preparing them for a career; it is shaping their heart for eternity. Parents who ground their children in Scripture and prayer prepare them to stand firm against life's storms.
The lies of culture will not easily sway a child who knows the truth of God's Word.

A Prayer for Christian Families

Heavenly Father, I praise You for all Christian children. Thank you for entrusting them to our care. Protect families from cultural and digital influences that seek to distort their minds and hearts. Strengthen parents with wisdom and endurance. May every Christian household reflect the light of Christ, raising children who will one day shine as leaders in the world and faithful citizens of Your Kingdom. In the name of Jesus. Amen.

Psalm 9:10:

And they who know your name will put their trust in you: for you, Lord, have not forsaken those who seek you.

HEAVENLY CITIZEN

CHAPTER SIX

*Y*our family belongs to God, set apart to honor

and glorify Him in all things.

P**aul asks**, *"Do you not know that you are God's temple and that God's Spirit dwells in you? If anyone destroys God's temple, God will destroy him. For God's temple is holy, and you are that temple".* **(1 Corinthians 3:16-17)**

This means that your home is more than just a place of residence; it's a sacred space where God's presence is intended to dwell. Every word spoken, every action performed, and every value upheld must manifest his love and justice.

When you dedicate your family to God, you are establishing a firm foundation that acknowledges that everything within your household belongs to Him. This act of surrender opens doors for the Holy Spirit to work within your family, providing strength, guidance, healing, protection, and peace through every season of life. It's a commitment to not only trust God in times of joy but also to rely on His wisdom and grace in times of struggle or uncertainty.

By dedicating your family to God, you open the door for Him to lead you, creating an environment where His presence can transform your home into a sanctuary of faith and love.

In this journey of faith, it's important to remember that no one is perfect. Jesus calls all who are weary, burdened, and broken, giving them rest and healing. God does not demand perfection; on the contrary, he invites us to approach him with a humble heart.

As God told Samuel, *"The Lord does not look at the things people look at. People look at the outward appearance, but the Lord looks at the heart".*

What God desires is a heart ready to seek him, even if it's imperfect or failing. By opening our hearts to His love and guidance, we can draw closer to Him and find peace in His grace.

Sometimes we take a small step back, thinking others are watching and judging our every move, asking questions. We often do so without really understanding the blessings God has bestowed upon us. People may focus on our actions, scrutinize our words or lifestyle, and form opinions based on limited knowledge, assuming they have the right to know.

However, the Lord sees ***our hearts***, and His vision for us is always filled with love, grace, and blessings. God understands the deeper reasons for our actions, the intentions behind our words, and he knows our struggles. While others may misinterpret or criticize, the Lord remains steadfast in his love, continuing to bless us abundantly and guiding our every step with his wisdom.

A clear example is when someone asks you a question, expecting a specific answer, but chooses to respond differently or deflect the conversation. If the person interprets our answer as a lie or a deflection, the question arises:

Have we deceived them, or have they misinterpreted our intentions?

At times like these, it's important to remember that God knows our hearts and understands our true intentions.

While others may form judgments based on their perspectives, the Lord sees the whole picture, and His vision is always one of grace, forgiveness, and understanding. It is in this divine perspective that we find peace, knowing that God is the ultimate judge and protector of our hearts.

"God is a righteous judge". **(Psalm 7:11)**
Don't waste your energy explaining your life to anyone except God, because, in the end, no one else truly understands or cares the way He does.

The believer's body: a sacred temple

The body of every believer is a temple, a sacred place where God dwells to communicate with His people. God will fight to protect His temple, which is you, yes, you. It doesn't matter what you've done or how you've lived your life.

Paul wanted **all Christians to understand the importance of becoming a servant of the Lord**. He wanted Christians to take this faithful journey very seriously. The fact that God himself will destroy those who wish to destroy his people, that he will stand up for you, and that our battle belongs to Jesus.

"**Do not be afraid or discouraged because of this vast army of Angels to fight your battles, for the battle is not yours, but Jesus**" (2 Chronicles 20:15).

This verse calls believers to live a life of holiness and unity; as believers, we must be mindful of how we conduct ourselves, knowing that we bear the presence of God in every aspect of our lives.

Whether it's in relationships, the work we do, or our daily interactions. Holiness is self-control, living a life set apart for God's purposes, striving to distinguish one faithful person from another. Our attitudes and behaviors are imbued with awe, peace, and love. Believers are always called to promote love, peace, and harmony among themselves and with others, recognizing that all believers are part of one body in Christ.

Together, a community of believers must be united to bear a powerful witness to God's transforming grace for the world. A selfless, transformative love that represents the very nature of heaven. This love, often referred to as agape love in Scripture, transcends all human understanding and conditional love. 1 John 4:8 says: "**He who does not love does not know God, for God is love**".

Heavenly Father

Thank you, a million times, over for your grace and many answers to our prayers. When we feel misunderstood or judged by others, we turn to You for comfort and strength. Lord, you alone are the righteous judge. You know our hearts, the intentions behind our actions, and the true story of our lives. While others may misinterpret or criticize, we find peace in knowing that You see the whole picture and that Your perspective is always filled with love and understanding.

Help us, Lord, to avoid wasting effort trying to explain ourselves to others, and instead focus on seeking Your approval and wisdom. You are our ultimate protector and guide, and we trust that Your love and grace will carry us through every trial. May we always rely on Your leadership, knowing that You are the one who truly understands us and will never fail.

We find peace in the assurance that You are with us every step of the way. When you are in control and we feel safe, we always find security. In Jesus' name, Amen.

Unconditional love

God's love doesn't depend on merit or worth; no one has to be perfect; it's freely given to everyone, regardless of their faults or failures. This love seeks out the broken, lost, and unworthy, offering them redemption and acceptance. As a bonus, it allows everyone to repent, even in the last moments before death.

Let's examine how straightforward this is in Romans 10:9. Paul teaches a simple truth about salvation: by confessing with our mouth that Jesus is Lord and believing in our heart that God raised Him from the dead, we receive eternal life. This verse captures the heart of the Gospel, showing that salvation isn't earned by works, worth, merit, titles, or religious rituals but is a gift of grace through faith. Remarkably, God has made the way to His heavenly kingdom so simple!

Yet, despite its simplicity, which might seem too easy, many people overlook or reject this truth, either out of unbelief, distraction, or a lack of understanding of God's love and justice.

Matthew 22:37: "*And he said unto him, thou shalt love the Lord thy God with all thy heart, and with all thy soul, and with all thy mind*". A wise person once said, "*If more than 2.9 billion people believe in something, and are willing to lay down their lives to share it, it's worth taking the time to explore one curiosity.*"

It's heartbreaking to realize that millions of people don't recognize the meaning of these words. Many think that, since God is loving, everyone will automatically have a place in heaven, regardless of their beliefs. However, the Scriptures make it clear that salvation is a personal decision; everyone, one way or another, will have the opportunity to confess it on their own free will or reject Jesus.

Each person must choose to accept Jesus as their Savior. God's love is immense, but he won't force anyone to enter his kingdom.

That's why, as believers, we continue to share the good news with those who haven't yet understood it, praying that they will open their hearts to the truth or become curious enough to seek the kingdom for themselves.

Jesus is asking you, "Do you want my kingdom?"
Paul said **Acts 16:31:**
"Believe in the Lord Jesus, and you will be saved, you and your household."

Our mission is to spread the Word of God to all nations, free of charge, as Jesus commanded. We share the Gospel out of love, not self-interest, and are willing to give freely so that others may know the joy of salvation.

Romans 10:13 reinforces this by saying, "***For everyone who calls on the name of the Lord will be saved.***

Christian communities are everywhere, in every city of every country, ensuring that anyone who wants to know more about God has access to His truth, whether in print or online. We are convinced that God will work through His Word to transform lives, bringing more Christians to the saving knowledge of Jesus Christ. Salvation is a gift, and we look forward to sharing it with you.

For faithful communities, whether Christian or Muslim, all believe in the words of our Lord Jesus: no one will be saved unless they heed the answer, he gave to the apostle Thomas in John 14:6: Jesus answered, "***I am the way, the truth, and the life. No one comes to the father except through me***".

These words do not come from pastors, imams, prophets, apostles, preachers, or any other man or woman of God, but from Jesus Himself. The only way to the kingdom of heaven is through Jesus.

Isaiah 45:5 Jesus said, "***I am the Lord, and there is no other; besides me there is no God***." There is no God but me. Similarly, the prophet Isaiah said in chapter 44:6 states, "*Thus says the Lord, the King of Israel, and his Redeemer, the Lord of hosts: 'I am the first and I am the last; besides me there is no god.'*"

In essence, this verse declares the absolute sovereignty of the God of Israel, affirming His eternal existence as the one true God, without equal or rival, from eternity past to future eternity.

Regardless of your beliefs or religious affiliations

Do you believe in Jesus?

Did Jesus tell the truth, or was he a liar?

If you believe he was telling the truth, Jesus asks you this question in **Matthew 16:15:** "He said to them, **'But who do you say that I am?**

If you believe Jesus is credible in His words, let's explore a couple of the things Jesus said. He told Philip, "Whoever has seen me has seen the Father" **(John 14:9).** Jesus forgave a man's sins; the intellectual scribes and all religious leaders asked, "Who can forgive sins but God alone?" **(Mark 2:7).**

When Jesus calmed the storm, His disciples questioned, "Who then is this, that even the wind and the sea obey him?" **(Mark 4:41).** These accounts reveal His divine nature and authority.

Do you have some darkness in your life?

Huge, massive storms with many wins around your
life? Matthew 28:6 says: "He is not here, for he has risen, as he said he would. "Everyone else who has died remains in their tombs, but not Jesus. Hallelujah! He is risen, he is alive, and he reigns forever!

Only God is worthy of worship, as stated in Deuteronomy 6:13; yet, Jesus accepted worship multiple times. Thomas called Him "My Lord and my God" after His resurrection (John 20:28), and Jesus did not rebuke him. In Isaiah 9:6, the Messiah is referred to as "**Mighty God" and "Everlasting Father**." Romans 1:4 affirms that Jesus " who through the Spirit of holiness was appointed the Son of God in power by his resurrection from the dead: Jesus Christ our Lord."

The evidence of Christ's divinity is undeniable.

The world is filled with many denominations, and beliefs are diverse across various religious sects. However, each person must choose whether they want it or not. A choice will be made on your behalf. Will you believe the words of Jesus, or will you reject them? Will you accept His gift of salvation, or will you turn away?

These questions are not about religion but about truth. The truth is that Jesus is the only way to eternal life. And Jesus is standing right now at your door, and Jesus is asking you, **"Do you want my Salvation"?**

The world is home to numerous denominations and diverse beliefs in various religious doctrines. However, every person has to make a choice, whether good or bad; a selection will be made for you. Will you believe Jesus' words or reject them?

Will you accept his gift of salvation or turn away from it? These questions are not about religion, but about truth. The reality is that Jesus is the only way to eternal life. And Jesus is standing at your door right now, asking: **"Do you want my salvation**? "Do you want my salvation?

As believers, we are called to share this truth with determination and conviction. It's not a question of imposing faith on anyone, but of freely offering the message of salvation. Christ's love drives every Christian to speak, to give, and to serve. Every soul is important to God, and he desires that all should repent and receive His salvation through Jesus.

The invitation is open. But the question still stands:
What will you answer Jesus?

The love of the Kingdom of God enables us to love others in the same way. It gives believers the heart to forgive, to show kindness and grace, even to our enemies. With the Holy Spirit, this divine love becomes a guiding force for **millions of faithful Christians worldwide.**

I know you agree with this statement: ***Christians, Buddhists, and Muslims are by far the kindest, gentlest, most devout, and most trustworthy of people, simply because of God's love.***

As spiritual heads of their households, fathers have a sacred responsibility to protect, provide for, and guide their families, following the example of God's fatherly care. Despite cultural or linguistic differences, to maintain the rules and discipline of our home, the fundamental commitment remains the same: to raise children who surpass us in faith, wisdom, and character. God has charged men with the duty of guiding their children in His ways, ensuring that their words and actions represent His love.

A father's role goes far beyond meeting material needs; it's about nurturing his children's hearts and souls, training them to walk in faith and integrity. No friend, teacher, or colleague should shake their confidence because they stand firm in the trustworthiness their father has instilled in them.

A father must teach his children to honor and respect their earthly and heavenly Father. His presence in the home is a living testimony to God's unconditional love and compassion.

The father's authority is a source of strength for the whole family. He is called to lead as a servant, guiding with humility and grace. He never dominates, but always offers direction rooted in God's Word. His leadership embodies divine patience, understanding, and justice, fostering a home where love, respect, self-esteem, and grace prevail. Through these examples, children will learn the balance between discipline and mercy in their relationships with God and others.

A father's unwavering presence is a solid environment conducive to spiritual and emotional growth, providing stability and security. By modelling

God's fatherly love, we must teach our children to trust God's guidance and embrace life with unshakeable faith.

Fathers are not perfect, but God is. While earthly fathers may strive to lead and guide their children, they are limited in knowledge, presence, and power. Unlike them, God is omniscient, omnipresent, and omnipotent, making Him the ultimate source of power, wisdom, and authority for our family.

Recognizing this distinction helps us understand the importance of honoring both our earthly fathers and our Heavenly Father.

God's Fellow Workers: Parents Building a Spiritual Foundation

The apostle Paul reminds us: ***"For we are God's fellow workers"*** **(1 Corinthians 3:9).**

This profound truth reshapes how Christian.

Parents understand their calling. We are not left alone to face the complexities of raising children in a world filled with distractions and dangers. Instead, God's partnership gives every Christian parent the authority and responsibility to make intentional decisions about how and where their children are raised and educated. Parenting is not only a sacred duty; it is also an act of stewardship, where we work hand in hand with our Creator to prepare the next generation.

Today, parents face challenges that previous generations could hardly have imagined. From digital influences that capture young minds to cultural ideologies that distort truth, the task of guiding children has never been more demanding. Yet, by the strength of the Spirit, parents can overcome the pressures of today's society and raise their children according to the Lord's plan. The same God who entrusted us with this responsibility also equips us to fulfill it.

His Word is a lamp to our feet and a light to our path (**Psalm 119:105**), showing us how to protect and nurture our families in a hostile world.

A father is called to bring up his children by training and nurturing them according to God's Word. His leadership is not harsh or authoritarian but rooted in love, discipline, and faithfulness. A father's role is to plant seeds of truth, water them with prayer, and trust the Lord to bring forth growth. By modeling humility, integrity, and courage, fathers shape a culture of responsibility and leadership within their homes. Such leadership ensures that children grow not only in knowledge but also in character, learning to value faith, family, and community above fleeting pleasures.

A Culture of Responsibility under the Leadership of Men

As a father, I encourage my sons to take responsibility for household chores and to pursue high standards in education and personal growth. These seemingly small actions, washing dishes, studying diligently, and serving with kindness, are the building blocks of a strong life. Responsibility is not a burden but a gift, for it prepares them to carry weight, to serve others, and one day to lead their own households. Leadership is not about domination but about serving with wisdom, protecting with strength, and guiding with love.

Every decision made in the home contributes to a spiritual foundation that equips the next generation. Education is more than academics; it is a form of discipleship. Training a child is not only about preparing them for a career; it is about shaping their heart for eternity. Parents who root their children in Scripture and prayer prepare them to stand firm against life's storms.

The lies of culture will not easily shake a child who knows the truth of God's Word.

A Prayer for Christian Families

Heavenly Father,

I praise You for all Christian children. Thank you for entrusting them to our care. Protect families from cultural and digital influences that seek to distort their minds and hearts. Strengthen parents with wisdom and endurance. May every Christian household reflect the light of Christ, raising children who will one day shine as leaders in the world and faithful citizens of Your Kingdom. In Jesus' name. Amen.

Psalm 16:11

Thou wilt shew me the path of life: in thy presence is fullness of joy; at thy right hand there are pleasures for evermore.

HEAVENLY CITIZEN

CHAPTER SEVEN

*T*he Example of Jesus After His Resurrection:

Rabbouni, The Master of All

The powerful example of this principle is found just after Jesus' resurrection. When Mary Magdalene recognized Him, she called out, "**Rabboni!**" (Meaning Teacher), but Jesus responded:

"Do not touch me, for I have not yet ascended to my father. But go to my brothers and say to them, 'I am ascending to my Father and your Father, to my God and your God'" **(John 20:16-17)**.

In this moment, Jesus demonstrated His reverence for His Father, prioritizing His relationship with God above all else.

Before allowing anyone to touch Him, Jesus first ascended to His Father, seeking His approval. This act demonstrated His obedience and reverence for divine authority, setting a powerful example for all believers. Similarly, our daughters are to seek their father's approval before entering into marriage.

Just as Jesus honored His Father before continuing His earthly mission, daughters should honor their fathers by seeking wisdom, guidance, and blessing before taking such a significant step. A father's role is to protect, provide for, and guide his daughter, ensuring that she enters marriage with a strong foundation of love, faith, and security. By following this biblical principle, families can uphold God's design for marriage, promoting respect, accountability, and lasting commitment.

This act shows the biblical principle of honoring parental authority. Just as Jesus placed His Father's will above human interactions, children are called to respect and submit to their parents' guidance. This principle extends to family structure; until parents release their children, they remain under their care and instruction, preparing them for their future responsibilities.

Ultimately, Jesus' obedience to His Father led to His continued ministry on earth for 40 days and 40 nights, during which He strengthened His disciples and laid the foundation for the Church. ***His faithfulness bore incredible fruit, resulting in over 2.9 billion Christians worldwide today.***

His example serves as a potent reminder that honoring and submitting to godly authority leads to lasting impact and spiritual growth.

God designed the family as His sacred institution, a foundation on which society is built. From the very beginning, He established the roles and responsibilities of each family member to ensure that love, faith, prayer, worship, and unity are at the center of every home.

Christian families are created to obey God's divine command, living by His Word and seeking His guidance in every aspect of life. When families align themselves with biblical principles, they create an environment where faith flourishes, children grow up righteous, and marriages are respected and strengthened.

Christian families can actively partner with God to build a strong relationship and a foundation of faith-filled homes. By following biblical principles, listening to the testimonies of those who have witnessed Jesus Christ's actions, and taking practical steps, we can deepen our relationship with God and with one another.

The Bible is full of wisdom on how to lead our families in faith, and when we apply its teachings, we witness transformation in our homes. The stories of God's faithfulness are potent reminders that he is always at work, guiding and providing for those who trust in him.

From a young age, I decided to stay close to God and never stray from my faith, regardless of the challenges I faced. The foundation of my commitment is based on the truth of the Bible. The disciples of Jesus, who walked with Him and witnessed His miracles, remained steadfast in their faith despite facing brutal persecution.

At that time, there were no human rights in the country to protect the disciples of Jesus as they faced the choice of either hiding in fear or boldly proclaiming the gospel. Yet, despite the threats of persecution, imprisonment, and even death, they chose to stand firm in their faith.

This unwavering commitment suggests that they had encountered a truth so powerful and undeniable that they could not keep it to themselves. Rather than recant or remain silent, they willingly faced suffering and martyrdom, ensuring that the message of Jesus Christ would be spread to the world, no matter the cost.

If they were willing to endure suffering and death for what they saw and knew to be true when they were physically with the Lord, then their testimony carries undeniable weight. Their sacrifices confirm to me that the Gospel is real and that Jesus is the living God. No one will see the kingdom if you don't accept him.

James and John, the Baptist, were both killed (beheaded) by King Herod. Philip was stoned to death, while Bartholomew endured the agony of being flayed alive before being beheaded.

Thomas, the disciple who initially doubted Christ's resurrection until he saw proof, was speared to death while spreading the gospel. Matthew was stabbed and burned, Thaddeus was axed to death, and Simon the Zealot was crucified. Even Judas Iscariot, who betrayed Jesus, was consumed by guilt and took his own life. Matthias, chosen to replace Judas, was also beheaded for his faith **(Acts 1:26).**

Now, ask yourself: would you willingly die for something you knew to be a lie?

These men did not suffer and die for mere stories or legends. They endured persecution because they had seen the truth with their own eyes. They walked with Jesus, witnessed His miracles, saw His crucifixion, and later encountered Him resurrected.

Their unwavering faith, even unto death, is a powerful testament that Jesus is who He claimed to be: the Son of God, the Savior of the world. Their sacrifices reinforce my belief that the gospel is not just history but living truth.

Because of this, I will never turn away from my faith, no matter what trials come my way. I trust in God's plan, knowing that my life is part of something far greater than people can understand. Even in suffering, I find purpose in serving Jesus, who gave His life for me. The thought of abandoning my faith or taking my own life has never crossed my mind because I know that my hope and salvation rest in Christ alone. He is my strength, my comfort, and my eternal reward.

If they were willing to endure suffering and death for what they saw and knew to be true when they were physically with the Lord, then their testimony carries undeniable weight. Their sacrifices confirm to me that the Gospel is real and that Jesus is the living God.

No one will see the kingdom if you don't accept him.

Consider the immense problems endured by the twelve disciples; one after the other died, and the next one, even hearing the news of the death of the other, continued to preach, knowing that the same outcome was near for them. None of them stops preaching the gospel.

Peter was crucified upside down in Rome, feeling unworthy to die in the same manner as Jesus. **Andrew** was crucified on an X-shaped cross, refusing to renounce his faith.

James and ***John***, the Baptists, were both beheaded by King Herod. ***Philip*** was stoned to death, while ***Bartholomew*** endured the agony of being flayed alive before being beheaded. ***Thomas***, the disciple who initially doubted Christ's resurrection until he saw proof, was speared to death while spreading the gospel.

Matthew was stabbed and burned, ***Thaddeus*** was axed to death, and Simon the Zealot was crucified. Even Judas Iscariot, who betrayed Jesus, was consumed by guilt and took his own life. Matthias, chosen to replace Judas, was also beheaded for his faith **(Acts 1:26).**

Now, ask yourself: would you willingly die for something you knew to be a lie?

These men did not suffer and die for mere stories or legends. They endured persecution because they had seen the truth with their own eyes. They walked with Jesus, witnessed His miracles, saw His crucifixion, and later encountered Him resurrected. Their unwavering faith, even unto death, is a powerful testament that Jesus is who He claimed to be: the Son of God, the Savior of the world. Their sacrifices reinforce my belief that the gospel is not just history but living truth.

Because of this, I will never turn away from my faith, no matter what trials come my way. I trust in God's plan, knowing that my life is part of something far greater than people can understand. Even in suffering, I find purpose in serving Jesus, who gave His life for me. The thought of abandoning my faith or taking my own life has never crossed my mind because I know that my hope and salvation rest in Christ alone.

He is my strength, my comfort, and my eternal reward.

If you are a Christian, take a moment to think back on the depth of your faith. If you have not yet come to know the truth of God's word, consider being curious about reading it. What drives the way you live your life? What is your reason for holding the beliefs you do? My faith in Jesus is unshakable because He is the way, the truth, and the life.

Now, I ask you. What is your reason for living? My life is a testament to God's goodness and faithfulness. Through both trials and triumphs, I have witnessed His guiding hand, His protection, and

His provision. There were times when challenges felt insurmountable, yet He always made a way, strengthening our family and drawing us closer to Him.

I am certain you, too, have experienced moments when God showed up unexpectedly, proving His love and faithfulness for you and your family.

Our daily lives are often consumed by ungodly distractions that keep us busy, limiting our time and focus on spiritual matters. The demands of life, especially for husbands, usually pull them away from home, making it difficult for them to be present for their families. However, despite the responsibilities and challenges they face, godly husbands find ways to care for their families and nurture their faith. It is through intentional effort and reliance on God that families can stay strong and united, keeping Christ at the center of their home.

When my father passed away at the age of 70, it left a deep void in our family. His absence was felt in every aspect of our lives, and though I was the second son, I found myself stepping into a role of greater responsibility.

The weight of providing for both my family materially and spiritually rested on my shoulders, a burden I never anticipated having to carry. Yet, during my grief and uncertainty, I turned to Jesus, trusting Him to equip me for the challenges ahead.

Through His guidance and strength, I found the courage to lead and support my family. There were moments of doubt and exhaustion, but God remained my constant source of wisdom and provision. He taught me that authentic leadership is not about position but about serving with love and faithfulness. As I leaned on Him, I saw His hand at work, strengthening our bond as a family and reminding us that even in loss, His presence is our strength.

If you have a story of your own, I encourage you to write it down and share it as a testimony of God's grace over your life. Express your gratitude for His goodness, even in the difficult moments. If you have experienced loss, share how you coped with the pain and found strength in God's presence.

Your story may be precisely what someone else needs to hear, a reminder that God is always faithful, even in the darkest times and places.

As Christians, each of us has a unique testimony of God's love and provision. Whether through trials or triumphs, His hand is always at work in our lives. Don't hesitate to tell everyone how He has been good to you and your family. Whether you write it down or speak it to those you meet, your testimony can inspire and uplift others, pointing them to the unfailing grace of God.

God's blueprint for the Christian's family **is** embedded in His perfect design, established from the very beginning. In Genesis 2:24, God instituted marriage, saying, *"That is why a man leaves his father and mother and is united to his wife, and they become one flesh."* This union is the foundation of the Christian family, built on love, unity, and faith. He calls parents to take responsibility, guiding their children in His ways, as King Solomon says, *"Train up a child in the way he should go"*.

A godly family is not just about living together, but also about growing together in faith and preaching God's love to everyone.

Marriage is not merely a contract between two individuals, but a sacred covenant before God, a divine union designed by His love and faithfulness. A praying family is a powerful force in God's kingdom, standing firm against life's challenges through faith and unity. Trials, though difficult, can become testimonies of God's goodness, shaping our character and drawing us closer to Him.

If you have a story of your own, I encourage you to write it down and share it as a testimony of

God's grace over your life. Express your gratitude for His goodness, even in the difficult moments. If you have experienced loss, share how you coped with the pain and found strength in God's presence.

Your story may be precisely what someone else needs to hear, a reminder that God is always faithful, even in the darkest times and places.

As Christians, each of us has a unique testimony of God's love and provision. Whether through trials or triumphs, His hand is always at work in our lives. Don't hesitate to tell everyone how He has been good to you and your family. Whether you write it down or speak it to those you meet, your testimony can inspire and uplift others, pointing them to the unfailing grace of God.

God's blueprint for the Christian's family **is** embedded in His perfect design, established from the very beginning. In Genesis 2:24, God instituted marriage, saying, *"That is why a man leaves his father and mother and is united to his wife, and they become one flesh."* This union is the foundation of the Christian family, built on love, unity, and faith. He calls parents to take responsibility, guiding their children in His ways, as King Solomon says, *"Train up a child in the way he should go"*.

A godly family is not just about living together, but also about growing together in faith and preaching God's love to everyone.

Marriage is not merely a contract between two individuals, but a sacred covenant before God, a divine union designed by His love and faithfulness. A praying family is a powerful force in God's kingdom, standing firm against life's challenges through faith and unity. Trials, though difficult, can become testimonies of God's goodness, shaping our character and drawing us closer to Him.

Our families are not just called to be spiritually strong within our homes but to be lights in the world, shining Christ's love through our actions. By serving together in ministry, engaging in outreach, and performing daily acts of kindness, we show the world what it means to live in His grace and truth.

Leaving a **legacy of faith** means building a family that reflects God's love and truth for generations to come. A strong Christian family is a testament to **God's faithfulness**, a light in a dark world, and a beacon of hope for others. May our homes be places where His love shines brightly, inspiring future generations to walk in His grace and carry His truth forward.

Thanksgiving to God as the source of all blessings

Heavenly Father,

I come before You with gratitude and reverence, acknowledging that every family in heaven and on earth derives its name from You. You are the Creator and Sustainer of all life, and it is through Your glorious riches that we find strength and power. I pray that, by the Holy Spirit, you may empower each one of us in our inner being, so that Christ may dwell in our hearts through faith. Let Your love be the foundation of our lives, strengthening us to walk in faith and the fullness of Your grace.

Lord, I pray that we, being firmly rooted and established in love, may comprehend the vastness of Christ's love, how wide, long, high, and deep it truly is. May this love surpass all knowledge and understanding, filling our hearts with the fullness of God. Help us to grow in our knowledge of this divine love, so that we may reflect it in every aspect of our lives. May it empower us to love one another with the same passion that Christ has shown us, and may it be the driving force behind all that we do.

To You, O God, who can do immeasurably more than all we ask or imagine, be glory forever and ever. Your power is at work within us, and we trust that You are working in our lives in ways that go beyond our comprehension. We give You all the glory in the church and Christ Jesus, for through Him, we have received every blessing and promise. We praise You for Your eternal greatness and the limitless love that You pour out upon us.

We come before You, Lord, with hearts full of humility and reverence, recognizing that every blessing, every relationship, and every moment we experience is a gift from You. By dedicating our family to You, we are not simply making a declaration but laying down a spiritual foundation rooted in Your eternal truths.

We confess our need for You in all areas of life, our hopes, our hurts, our celebrations, and our challenges, and we invite You into every space of our hearts and home. We trust that through Your infinite love, you will strengthen us in weakness, guide us in confusion, and surround us with peace that surpasses understanding.

Father, let Your Holy Spirit be the very atmosphere of our home, shaping it into a place where Your presence is not only welcomed but central. As we walk together as a family, may our lives reflect Your character and Your truth.

In surrendering control to You, we find the most incredible freedom, knowing that You are sovereign and that nothing concerning us escapes Your care. We thank you for being our anchor in uncertainty and our source of joy in abundance. May our home always shine with the light of Christ, bringing hope and love to all who enter. We pray in the name of Jesus. **Amen**

Word of life

"*Do not be anxious about anything, but in every situation, by prayer and petition, with thanksgiving, present your requests to God. ⁷ And the peace of God, which transcends all understanding, will guard your hearts and your minds in Christ Jesus*". **(Philippians 4:6-7)**

Psalm 18:2

The LORD is my rock, and my fortress, and my deliverer; my God, my strength, in whom I will trust; my buckler, and the horn of my salvation, and my high tower.

HEAVENLY CITIZEN

CHAPTER EIGHT

J**esus** is my family's salvation (Acts 16:31).

Following Jesus will set you free.

I was born into a family without spiritual devotion that considered itself Catholic or Christian, but no one was genuinely committed to faith. Like many families today, we recognized God's existence but didn't actively seek a relationship with Him. God was viewed more as a distant, higher power, a being or creator of the world, but His role in our lives wasn't explored.

Conversations about faith were rare, and when they did happen, they were often dismissed as pointless or unimportant. Reading the Bible, praying, or trying to understand who God is was not a priority. Religion was more of a tradition for others than a meaningful part of my family's life.

My father was a farmer who employed many workers, and my mother was a small businesswoman, both consumed by the demands of their work. They focused on financial stability, providing for the family, and making sure we received a good education, were safe, and had everything we needed materially.

Their dedication to our well-being was evident, but their spiritual life remained barren and untouched. Church attendance was occasional, and faith was more a cultural identity than a personal conviction. Like many other families, they thought it was enough to be a good person, without realizing that a free book found all over the world contains the knowledge needed to know who the Almighty is and the map to his heavenly kingdom.

Despite this, we were not deprived of access to the Gospel.

The message of salvation was available to us through various means, including church services, preachers, my cousin Venor Maurice, who is a local pastor, and even Christian media channels. However, like many people, we let ignorance, self-sufficiency, and worldly distractions keep us from truly seeking God. It was easy to dismiss spiritual teachings as something irrelevant or something to worry about later in life.

I've heard many people say they'd hand the rest over to God, which means that when they're old and can no longer live as they please, they'll do a few rituals to get saved. Instead of recognizing the need for repentance and faith in Jesus Christ, many members of my family assumed that as long as they avoided major sins, they were on the right path to heaven.

Paul said in **2 Corinthians 6:2,** *"**Behold, now is the favorable time; behold, now is the day of salvation.*** « No one is promised tomorrow. Delaying repentance is dangerous.

This mindset is common to many families who consider themselves religious or who have a basic knowledge of God, but who don't understand how great and simple the Lord is. The world tends to believe that morality alone is sufficient for salvation. Heaven is not the default destination for the good and wealthy; it's the reward for those who trust Jesus as Lord and Savior.

This misconception leads many people away from the truth and makes them spiritually blind, even if they hear the Gospel everywhere. John the Baptist was the last prophet to prepare the way for the Messiah. It was he whom the prophet Isaiah had foretold: "The voice of one crying in the wilderness, 'Prepare the way of the Lord, make straight paths for him.

Matthew 3:15-16 Jesus answered, ***"Let it be so now; we should do this to fulfil all righteousness."*** *John and over 2.9 billion faithful Christians worldwide understand when the Lord says,* **"My sheep listen to my voice; I know them, and they follow me."** As soon as Jesus was baptized, he rose from the water. At that moment, the heavens opened, and he saw the Spirit of God descend like a dove and land on him. A voice from heaven said, "This is my Son, whom I love; in him I am well pleased."

Every time Jesus rises, whether from the waters of baptism or the grave in his resurrection, a divine revelation is manifested. These are not simply physical manifestations, but sacred milestones in the story of God's redemption. At his baptism, as Jesus emerges from the waters, the heavens open and the Holy Spirit descends like a dove. This moment marks more than the beginning of his ministry; it is his anointing by the father, a public affirmation of his divine identity and purpose.

Through this sacred act, Jesus is empowered by the Holy Spirit to embark on his mission to bring salvation, healing, and restoration to all who believe in Him. Just as the Holy Spirit filled him at his baptism, preparing him to face darkness and proclaim the Kingdom, the resurrection declared his ultimate victory over sin and death. These resurrection moments reveal the fullness of God's plan: a Savior sent not only to walk among us, but also to redeem and renew all who seek and receive him by faith.

As the Holy Spirit descends upon Jesus, the Father's voice echoes from heaven: "This is my beloved Son, in whom I am well pleased." This divine proclamation is not only a declaration of Jesus' identity, but also a profound moment of anointed agreement of heavenly connection. God the Father affirms that Jesus is the one appointed to fulfil the mission of redemption, and the Holy Spirit empowers him to accomplish the task ahead. The Father's voice, as he stood in the water, and the Holy Spirit descending in the form of a dove, reveal Jesus' eternal truth and divine nature.

The descent of the **Holy Spirit upon Jesus** signifies much more than an outward manifestation; it is a divine act of consecration and dedication. It marks the beginning of Jesus' earthly ministry, imbued with authority and determination. When the Spirit rests on him, it symbolizes the anointing of God's chosen one, the Messiah, who is set apart to carry out the redemptive work that will culminate in his death and resurrection. Jesus is not only empowered by the Spirit; he also confirms the eternal agreement that he came to earth for a specific purpose: to bring salvation to humanity and restore the broken relationship between God and his people.

When Jesus rises from the dead, He demonstrates His power over the ultimate consequence of sin: death itself. His resurrection is the definitive proof that He has triumphed over sin and the grave, giving eternal life to all who place their faith in Him. ***Jesus promises that anyone who believes in Him, even if they die, they will live forever. (John 11:25).***

His victory over death transforms the Christian hope, for it assures all Christians that death is no longer the end, but a passage to eternal life with Him. Jesus, in His rising, has conquered the darkness of sin and death, ushering in the hope of new life for all who believe.

King David, with his prophetic foresight, knew that Jesus would come to save his followers and everyone who would preach the gospel long before he ascended into heaven.

King David made a prophetic declaration about ten centuries before the birth of Jesus. It is he who, through his death and resurrection, will offer all the faithful the promise of redemption and restoration.

As **Ephesians 1:7** Paul said, "***in him we have redemption through his blood, the forgiveness of our trespasses, according to the riches of his grace***".

Jesus's sacrificial death brings forgiveness of sins, and his resurrection guarantees all Christians eternal life with him, even after this life on earth. To prove this, He descended into the abyss of the dead to redeem all the faithful servants from many past centuries, even those who had lived before He came to earth.

David believed this truth so deeply that, just before his death, he said in **Psalm 16:9-11,** "Therefore my heart is glad and my tongue rejoices; my body also will rest secure, because you will not abandon me to the realm of the dead, nor will you let your faithful one sees decay. You make known to me the path of life; you will fill me with joy in your presence, with eternal pleasures at your right hand".

In the light of his ultimate sacrifice, Jesus issues an invitation to everyone reading this book right now: **"Do you want my salvation?"** It's up to you to choose to accept or disapprove. If we decide to follow him, as he promised the thief on the cross, "***Today you will be with me in paradise***" (Luke 23:43). This offer of salvation is the heart of the Gospel. Through his blood, we receive redemption and forgiveness, and through his resurrection, we are assured of eternal life.

Jesus is the way, the truth, and the life (John 14:6), and no one comes to the Father except through him. The question is whether you will accept his offer of salvation and walk in faith with him.

Jesus Christ is the trustworthy source of life, both physical and spiritual. He declares: "***I am the way, the truth, and the life. No one comes to the father except through me***" **(John 14:6).** In him is eternal life, an unlimited life that no one else can offer. Jesus is also the water of life, that which quenches the soul's most profound thirst:

"***If anyone is thirsty, let him come to me and drink***" **(John 7:37).** He said to the Samaritan woman: "***Whoever drinks the water I give him will never thirst; it will become in him a wellspring of water springing up into eternal life***" **(John 4:14).** Without Jesus, no

One can inherit the kingdom of God, for it is only through him that we receive salvation, forgiveness of sins, and reconciliation with the Father.

As **Acts 4:12** affirms, *"**There is salvation in no other; for there is no other name under heaven given among men by which we must be saved**."*

No one, no matter how great, can ever say or do what Jesus did. No servant, prophet, apostle, pastor, imam, priest, or person of any human nature can promise eternal life, which is not limited to Muhammed, be able to raise the dead or forgive sins, acts that belong solely to divine power.

Jesus healed the sick, gave sight to the blind, made the mute speak, and resurrected the dead, not in the name of another, but in his name and by his authority. These miraculous works are not simply prophetic signs, but manifestations of Christ's divinity. Jesus is more than a prophet: he is the Almighty made flesh.

The Gospel of John makes this clear: "In the beginning was the Word, and the Word was with God, and the Word was God. In the beginning, the Word was with God. All things were made through it, and nothing that was made was made without it. In her was life, and the life was the light of men." **(John 1:1-3)**. Jesus was present at the creation of the world. These truths show that Jesus' promises and deeds can only come from the eternal, **all-powerful God.**

*"**He is the image of the invisible God, the firstborn of all creation. For in him were all things created that are in heaven and on earth.... All things were created through him and for him. He is before all things, and in Him all things hold together. Not only is Jesus before creation, but He made everything and is for Him* **(Colossians 1:15-17).**

A Prayer of Redemption and Salvation

Heavenly Father,

We come before You in awe and gratitude for the profound moments in which Jesus rises, whether from the waters of baptism or the grave in His resurrection. These sacred events reveal the fullness of Your redemptive plan for all who seek You and accept Your truth.

We thank you for sending Your Spirit to empower Jesus, for His anointing at His baptism, and for the divine proclamation from the Father declaring His identity as your beloved Son. Through the Holy Spirit, Jesus began His mission of redemption, and through His death and resurrection, He offers us reconciliation and eternal life.

Lord, we celebrate His victory over sin and death, and we hold fast to the promise of new life through Him. We thank You for the prophetic words of King David, which remind us of Your eternal plan, fulfilled through Jesus' sacrifice.

We accept the invitation of salvation He extends to us, choosing to follow Him and live by faith in the power of His resurrection. In the name of Jesus, the Way, the Truth, and the Life, we pray. **Amen.**

Looking back, I see how much we were missing in our home in terms of our faith. While we had material provisions, we lacked spiritual nourishment. My parents worked tirelessly to make sure we had food on the table, clothes on our backs, education, and opportunities for success. Yet, beneath all the surface stability, our hearts longed for something deeper, something eternal. Our souls remained hungry for truth, guidance, and the peace that only God can provide.

Over time, I came to understand that true life is not ultimately found in wealth, success, or even commendable deeds. However, each Christian should strive for a good portion of these. Rather, it is found in wholehearted surrender to God and a faithful walk in His ways. Faith, I've realized, is not a mere label or tradition; it's a transformative relationship with Jesus.

Christ. It demands commitment, obedience, and trust in His plan, even when it seems to contradict our understanding of it.

As Paul writes in **Romans 10:17**, "*So then faith comes from hearing, and hearing through the word of Christ.*" It is through His Word that our faith is born and strengthened.

Jesus Himself emphasized the life-giving power of His words. In **John 6:63**, He said, "*The words that I have spoken to you, they are full of the Spirit and life.*" And in **Matthew 7:24**, He painted a picture of wisdom and stability: "*Everyone who hears these words of Mine* *and does them will be like a wise man who built his house on the rock."*

His words are not temporary but perpetual; they are eternal foundations toward the Lord's kingdom. Furthermore, the Lord said, **"Heaven and earth will pass away, but My words will never pass away**."

The words of Jesus carry divine authority, eternal truth, and the power to transform our lives. To hear, believe, and obey them is to step into the life God always intended for every soul now and forever.

Everyone in my family used to laugh at my commitment to the Christian faith, teasing me as if it were just a passing phase. To them, I was the unexpected one; the least likely to follow Jesus. And honestly, I understood why. When people are familiar with your past or your business, they often feel entitled to define your present.

Family and friends will remember your struggles, your flaws, and the life you once lived. So, it will be easy for them to assume that your faith wouldn't last. But here I am, 28 years later, still walking with the Lord. They couldn't see what only God can see, the heart.

As it says in **1 Samuel 16:7**: «***The Lord does not look at the things people look at. People look at the outward appearance, but the Lord looks at the heart***. ».

Victory belongs to the Lord, and to every one of us who still keep the faith. And if you're facing something similar in your life, if others are judging your present through the lens of your past, take heart, you are not alone. Even King Solomon, in all his wisdom, recognized this truth.

Proverbs 21:2 says: *"People may be right in their own eyes, but the Lord examines their hearts."*

In truth, I carried the weight of my imperfections. I had to face the reality of being a lustful man, someone whose eyes didn't always honor God. That part of me was genuine, and I don't deny it; I assume it. But I also repented of it. I presented it to the Lord with sincerity, and I continue to fight every day to walk in the Spirit.

Yet, at the time, I felt utterly alone in my faith journey. It's a difficult thing when those who know you best can't see the change in you because they're still focused on what you used to be. Their doubts didn't just discourage you; they isolated you from others.

But a few years later, something remarkable happened.

My little sister, **Marjorie**, the one who was as doubtful as the rest, decided to get baptized. I was stunned. It was a quiet but powerful moment, as if God was reminding me, "I see your heart, and I'm not done with your story."

***Marjorie's** decision had a ripple effect. One by one, other members of our family began taking a step of faith, including my mother, who was baptized at the age of 72 in October 2024.*

Each of them publicly declared that they were following Jesus, not because I had persuaded them, but because God had touched their hearts. What looked like loneliness turned into a celebration of salvation. I saw my prayers come to life.

In 1998, I was asked to preach for the very first time without any preparation. It happened during a visit to someone's home after the passing of a loved one. At the time, I had just been baptized and knew very little about preaching or the Word of God, let alone how to bring comfort to a grieving family. So, I leaned on what I did have:

Kindness, compassion, and the values instilled in me by my family and education. From there, I began teaching little by little in Sunday school at my church, even to the elders. And as you might expect, sometimes the elders ended up teaching me more than I taught them. Many of them knew the Scriptures far better than I did, but they were always gracious and encouraging, helping me grow in both confidence and understanding.

Now, after all these years of walking with the Having been shaped through life's trials, I can confidently say that my testimony of the gospel is both deep and authentic. To anyone reading this:

Do not delay your journey of faith. Please, don't wait until it is too late.

One day, when we stand in heaven, we will not want to meet Peter, John, or Paul and realize all the blessings we missed, not because God withheld them, just because we were not spiritually prepared to receive them, or because we drifted from the presence of the Lord for a time.

Let us not lose another season of purpose by hesitating in our faith. Seeing my family take steps of obedience and say "**yes**" to Jesus is a victory won by the blood of Christ alone. It is nothing I could have orchestrated; it is all a matter of grace.

So, if you are reading this and you are the first in your family to follow Jesus, or even the only one, take heart. You may be planting seeds today that will bloom years from now. And if you must take that first step alone, take it. Jesus will meet you there. In His time, He will open the way for others to follow as well.

As the Lord Himself promises: *"I will instruct you and teach you in the way you should go; I will counsel you with my loving eye on you"* **(Psalm 32:8).** And again: *"I will make a way in the wilderness and rivers in the desert"* **(Isaiah 43:19).**

Psalm 19:14

Let the words of my mouth, and the meditation of my heart, be acceptable in thy sight, O LORD, my strength, and my redeemer.

HEAVENLY CITIZEN

CHAPTER NINE

*H*ow Generational Faith Shapes Eternal Legacies: The Power of a Parent's Prayers

One of God's greatest gifts to me was knowing her. She took me to church and nurtured my love for Him from an early age. When she got ready for church, it wasn't just a routine; it was a sacred ritual, as if she were preparing to meet the Lord in person. She often reminded me, "The Lord watches everything you do, so be wise. Don't worry about the rest, he'll take care of it.

Today, many Christians approach worship with a casual attitude, entering the house of God as if they were heading to the grocery store. The reverence we once had has faded in some places. There was a time when we dressed for church as if we were going to meet our Lord and Savior face-to-face, because in truth, we are.

We wore our cleanest clothes, carried ourselves with dignity, and prepared our hearts and bodies to stand in His presence. If we are indeed the temple of the Holy Spirit, how should that temple be presented, torn and careless, or clean and prepared?

Some say, "**God looks at the heart**," and while that's true, our outward presentation often reflects our inward reverence.
Think of how you would present yourself if you were meeting the President or a dignitary. Wouldn't you take care to dress appropriately? *Does not God, who is far above any earthly authority, deserve even greater respect?*

Too often, choir members, gospel artists, and congregants come to worship dressed in ways that are more fitting for a concert or a street corner than for the house of God. The issue is not about wealth or fashion, it's about honor. The heart matters most, yes, but we should not neglect the way we present the Lord's temple, ourselves in worship.

The Bible calls the Christian families to modesty, humility, and holiness in both spirit and appearance. *"Women should adorn themselves in respectable apparel, with modesty and self-control; with what is proper for women who profess godliness with good works"* **(1 Timothy 2:9-10)**. And again, in **1 Peter 3:34**, Paul said that our beauty should come from the inner self, a quiet and gentle spirit, but that doesn't mean we dismiss respectability in our dress. Paul reminds us in **Romans 13:14** to *"put on the Lord Jesus Christ, and make no provision for the flesh."*

Let our attire, like our attitudes, be marked by reverence, purity, and a desire to honor the One who gave His life for us.

Grandma's warmth and wisdom spread through our family, passed on to my mother, Anna, and my aunt Ninide. Grandma's love was like a tapestry woven with threads of patience, faith, and an almost ethereal warmth that transcended generations. For our family, she was more than a matriarch. She was a sanctuary, a keeper of secrets, and a guiding light on our spiritual journey; her name was **Marcine Dodin.**

She prayed unceasingly for our family. She always had something to give, whether it was her prayers, a kind word, a cup of coffee, or the simple comforts of home. I still remember that she always had coffee, bread, and fruit to share with us. Thanks to her, our house never lacked food, and our hearts were never deprived of love.

Grandma used to light a small candle in her kitchen when she had to pray. It wasn't just about the light, but the intention and the belief. The flame, she said, was a symbol of hope, a reminder that even in the darkest of times, a spark of love and faith could light the way when we trusted in God. Grandma's spiritual guidance went beyond comforting words. She taught our family to find beauty in ordinary things and to draw strength from the face of challenges.

Despite the many grandchildren who came and went, she took the time to care for every one of us. She taught us the importance of trusting God and calling on him whenever we stumbled or found ourselves in trouble.

It was in these moments of silent prayer that the family felt the depth of her love most acutely. Grandma's prayers weren't loud or dramatic. They were simple heartfelt whispers, "Bless them," *she would murmur, with her eyes closed, "with health, with peace, and with the strength to walk their path when it is difficult."*

Her faith was not a sermon, but a way of living, a soft, steady undercurrent that carried her family through life's storms. After many years since her passing, every member of our family has a favorite moment of hers. Grandma's love was not limited by time or distance while living. Even when her grandchildren grew up and moved far away to different countries and cities, they took her lessons with them.

When life feels overwhelming, we hold on to her words and teachings, her unwavering voice of faith reminding us that God will always show up. If one of your grandparents is still with you, or your parents are still here, don't wait another moment to call them or visit. Experience a little piece of true love while you still can, one more time. Seeing their smile countless times will never be enough, because once they go home to God, you will miss them for a lifetime. They will remain our most outstanding teachers forever.

I never had the chance to know my grandfather personally, but his life and legacy were passed down to us through my younger brother, Frederick, the fifth child of our family. Through him, we came to know our grandfather's wisdom, which was deeply rooted in love, care, and quiet strength. That wisdom still lives on in us today, in every lesson we remember, every story we share, and every tear we shed for those we've lost.

For over 2,000 years, the King has been proclaimed, first by His disciples and prophets, and today by billions of faithful Christians worldwide. What began with just twelve believers has evolved into a worldwide movement, now comprising over **2.9 billion members and still growing.**

Through local churches, evangelistic campaigns, and the vast reach of social media, the message of salvation has never been more accessible. The vision given to John in Revelation, the announcement of God's eternal Kingdom, is being preached freely in this book you are reading right now, and around the world, fulfilling Christ's promise to make disciples of all nations.

Jesus asks, "***Can any of you by worrying add a single hour to your life***"? (*Matthew 6:27*) **One** day, my mom got sick, and while we were at the emergency room in Boston, Massachusetts, she taught me something I've never forgotten. Looking around the hospital, she said, "*Wow... this place.*" Curious, I asked her what she meant. She explained, "***Hospitals and funerals are the two places on earth where every person's strength and pride are stripped away. They reveal just how fragile life is.***"

She continued, "*In a hospital, even the most powerful people become as vulnerable as children; completely dependent on others as they face sickness they can't control. And at a funeral, the finality of death humbles everyone who witnesses it. It's a sobering reminder that no amount of achievement or money can stop our return to dust."*

Then she looked at me and said, *"But there is another place, my son, the ultimate place."* She paused, then said I don't remember the verse in the bible, but Jesus said: he would prepare a place for us by referring to this quote from **John 14:1-3:** 'Let not your heart be troubled: you believe in God, believe also in me. In my father's house are many mansions; if it were not so, I would have told you.

I'll prepare a place for you.

With quiet strength, she reminded me that beyond hospitals and funerals, beyond all the ruptures of this life, there is a promised place, a home prepared by Christ himself, where grief ends and eternal peace begins. As the world competes to see who has the most net worth, we lose sight of our spirituality.

We have no time to pray, no time to worship, and zero time to make arrangements to reserve a place in the kingdom of heaven until it is too late. Now that you've made it this far in the book, I'd like to ask you some basic questions.

Have you ever been curious about what the Bible has to say?

What do you think Jesus was really about, beyond what you've heard second-hand? What's your view on who Jesus was? What do you think happens after we die? Would you be open to hearing one of the things Jesus said that changed my life?

However, consider this: when the apostle Matthew said, "You are far more precious to the Lord than you think," it is clear that you cannot serve God and money at the same time. The eye is the lamp of the body; if your eyes are healthy, your whole body will be full of light. However, if your eyes are unhealthy, your entire body will be shrouded in darkness. So, if the light in you is darkness, how great is that darkness!

These moments of weakness and sorrow will teach everyone that we need God's mercy and the eternal hope we find in Jesus Christ. His sacrifice and resurrection confirm to us that sickness and death do not have the last word on our lives. Do you believe this? Jesus gave you this answer and said, 'I am the resurrection and the life; he who believes in me, even though he dies, yet shall he live.' And whoever lives and believes in me will never die.

This gospel is not for sale and never will be for money; it is a gift from God, given freely with an enormous sacrifice, to each of us who seeks the truth. While the world often attaches a price to everything, the reality of the kingdom of Jesus Christ is, and always will be, freely available, offering us peace, redemption, and eternal life.

Hospitals and funerals will remind you that our time on earth is temporary.

Pancreatic and lung cancer, liver and brain cancer, stomach and ovarian cancer, colon cancer, thyroid cancer, stroke, and multiple organ failure are all future problems for us. Still, the promise of God's kingdom is eternal.

May we humble ourselves before the Lord, recognizing that true life is not found in earthly riches or status, but in surrender to Christ, who alone holds the keys to life and death.

Jesus said: "Surely, I am with you always, even to the very end of the age. Never will I forsake you. And though you walk through the darkest valley, you need not fear, for I am with you. My presence, like a comforting rod and staff, will guide and protect you, bringing peace through every trial."

My grandfather was a man of principle who always put his family first and stood firm in his convictions, qualities that his little brother, Frederick, took to heart. Everyone who knew my grandfather says the same thing: Frederick is the spitting image of him. He has inherited not only his traits but also his values, making him a living reminder of our grandfather's legacy.

As parents, you have a sacred, God-given responsibility to teach and guide your children or grandchildren from birth. These principles help parents raise their children according to God's will, nurturing them spiritually, emotionally, and physically, so they are prepared to face the world with faith and strength.

Moses asked every Christian to teach the word of God diligently to their children, and shall speak of them when you sit at the table, when you go on your journey, when you lie down, and when you rise." This passage invites Christian parents to internalize God's word and teach it faithfully to their children.

By instilling God's laws and decrees in their hearts, parents help their children stand firm in the faith, whatever challenges they face; they will know who they are and to whom they belong, that is, to the Almighty. As **Job 5:17** reminds us, "Blessed is he whom God corrects; despise not the discipline of the Almighty."

God's plan for raising a strong, faithful family. These disciplines, grounded in love and wisdom, are integral to God's plan for raising strong, loyal followers of Christ. By embracing His guidance, parents can shape their children's character and faith, equipping them to walk confidently in His ways. God's correction is not punitive but transformative, designed to align believers with His will and purpose.

Although His discipline may be complex, it is intended to lead Christians to repentance, so that we may dwell in Him alone. In other words, God's chastening is His way of bringing us back into alignment with Him for our ultimate good.

Paul often compared the Christian life to that of an athlete, emphasizing the need for discipline, self-control, and perseverance just as athletes undergo rigorous training, sacrifice, and self-denial to compete for medals and prizes.

We must cultivate spiritual discipline to deepen our relationship with God and live-in accordance with His will. This requires dedicating time to prayer, which is the foundation of spiritual growth. Through worship, believers communicate with God, seek His guidance, and deepen their understanding of His presence in their lives.

Regularly reading and meditating on Scripture also strengthens faith, providing wisdom and encouragement to navigate life's challenges. By committing to these practices, we will establish a solid spiritual foundation that enables us to remain steadfast in our walk with Christ.

In addition to prayer and faith-building, Christians must also strive for purity in their thoughts, words, and actions. The Bible calls believers to live holy lives, resisting temptations that lead them away from God's righteousness. This requires self-control and a conscious effort to reject sin, aligning one's heart and mind with God's standards.

Holiness is not just about avoiding wrongdoing but also about pursuing what is good, noble, and pleasing to God. Through spiritual discipline, believers can reflect Christ's love and holiness, becoming a light in the world and drawing others closer to Him. "*But just as he who called you is holy, so be holy in all you do; for it is written: Be holy, because I am holy.*" **(1 Peter 1:15-16)**

Unlike the fleeting rewards of this world, the ultimate goal of a believer is not earthly recognition but eternal life in Christ. This requires an ongoing commitment to live out His word, to resist temptation, and to remain steadfast in faith despite the challenges of the modern world.

As Christians, we are ordained with a profound biblical responsibility to speak life into one another. Every believer is called to carry a message of hope, encouragement, and truth, bringing life not only to children but to everyone we encounter. Our words have the power to uplift, strengthen, and inspire, reflecting the love and grace of God. A single verse or word of encouragement can have a profoundly positive impact on someone's life, offering them the reassurance they need to persevere.

As Deuteronomy 31:6 reminds us: **"Be strong and courageous. Do not be afraid or terrified because of them, for the Lord your God goes with you; He will never leave you nor forsake you."**
This promise is a powerful reminder that God's presence is constant, providing strength and courage in every situation. By sharing such truths, Christians become vessels of God's love, offering comfort and encouragement to those in need.

Words of wisdom from the Kingdom of God:

You have a wonderful sense of humor, just like Sarah's smile! God has filled your heart with joy, and those who have heard the news will rejoice with you. "*Your happiness is contagious and brings light and laughter to those around you* **(Genesis 21:6).**

I love talking to you because you're a good listener and a true friend. You embody the wisdom of James 1:19: *"Everyone should be quick to listen, slow to speak and slow to anger"*.

I know I can trust you completely and share my thoughts without hesitation.

Your generosity is truly inspiring. Like Barnabas, who was known as the "**Son of Encouragement,**" you have a gift for uplifting others.

Romans 12:7-8 speaks of this gift: "**If it is to encourage, then encourage.**" I always leave our conversations feeling better, blessed by your kindness and encouragement.

I cherish the peace that comes with your presence when you're here with me. **Your ability to patiently wait on the Lord and remain calm, even when others around you are plotting wicked schemes, you are truly inspiring (Psalm 37:7).**

Being near you fills me with a deep sense of calm. Your presence brings peace to my heart, and you teach me the importance of waiting on God. For this, I am deeply grateful.

I have never encountered anyone with a heart as generous and selfless as yours. You have consistently demonstrated that you are willing to sacrifice everything for the people you love, and I believe God will reward you for your faithfulness **(John 3:16).**

You are the one person I've always trusted and felt comfortable confiding in, sharing my secrets. Your friendship means a great deal to me, and I have cherished it since we met. **I want you to know how much I appreciate you (Proverbs 17:17).**

Deuteronomy 31:6 "**Be strong and courageous. Do not be afraid or terrified because of them, for the Lord your God goes with you; he will never leave you nor forsake you.**"

We all need those words of affirmation: You comfort me. I know you've been through trials and are now comforting others with the hope and strength you've found through those experiences. I'm grateful to God for doing this in your life. I'm glad you're here, and don't forget that God will never abandon you **(2 Corinthians 1:3).**

Through intentional, thoughtful words, a faithful community can create growth, healing, peace of mind, mutual encouragement, and a sense of purpose in our children's lives. Just as athletes need support and guidance to stay on track, every Christian needs a positive word to encourage and uplift them. Our children, in particular, rely on their parents' words to strengthen their minds and point them toward God's truth.

Parents are called to use their words not only to guide their children, but also to build them up in love, offering prayers that bring life, protection, and blessings. This practice will help keep the next generation on track, equipping them to run their race of faith with strength and resilience in today's fast-paced, technological world.

*"**Praise be to the God and Father of our Lord Jesus Christ, the Father of compassion and the God of all comfort**"*.

He promises to be near, to walk beside us in every trial, and to give us the strength we need to stand firm. Whatever our circumstances, we can rest assured that God's love will never waver and that his faithfulness is unshakeable.

You are never alone, for He is always with you, guiding, protecting, and loving you unconditionally.

As a child of God, you are called to love others with the same love he has shown you. Your identity as a citizen of his kingdom implies the responsibility to represent his character in everything you do. Just as he has comforted you, you must extend that comfort and love to others.

This is the heart of the Christian faith: loving God and loving people. Your life is a testimony to the transforming power of his love. Your life no longer belongs to you, and by loving those around you, you show them the way to His eternal kingdom.

Psalm 23:1
The LORD is my shepherd; I shall not want.

HEAVENLY CITIZEN

CHAPTER TEN

Our citizenship is in heaven. And we eagerly await our savior, the Lord Jesus Christ. (Philippians 3:20)

Jehovah Rapha: The God Who Heals

I Am a Citizen of Heaven: Blessed and Fully. Trusting in His Kingdom Alone. The Lord reveals himself under the name Jehovah Rapha, "*the Lord who heals*", which draws our attention to the fact that healing is part of his fundamental nature. This name was first uttered in **(Exodus 15:26),** where God promised the Israelites that if they listened to his voice and obeyed his commands, he would protect them from the diseases that afflicted Egypt. *He offered not only physical healing, but emotional and spiritual restoration to those who walked in faith and obedience.*

His words still resonate today: "***For I am the Lord who heals you***". To receive his healing, we must have faith, believing that he is willing and able to restore what is broken.
Faith doesn't mean the road will be easy. It is often in suffering that God's presence becomes most real. Job is a case in point.

This servant of God was a righteous man, but God allowed Satan to test him. In **Job 2:1-7,** Satan questioned Job's integrity, saying he would curse God's name if he lost his health.
God allowed affliction, but set limits on his life. Job could not be killed. As a result, Job was struck with painful sores from head to toe, so severe that he scratched himself with pottery shards to find some relief. Despite it all, Job clung to his faith in the Lord. His story draws our attention to the fact that no believer is immune to suffering, but that God accompanies us in the wilderness and will restore our suffering in due course.

The God Who Heals: Heavenly Father

Jehovah Rapha, the God who heals, hear our prayers. I come before you today with a heart full of faith, confident that you are both willing and able to restore what is broken in me. I declare that I am a citizen of Heaven, blessed and fully satisfied in Your Lord. As you have said, "***For I am the Lord who heals you***".

I trust that Your healing power is at work in my life right now. Keep my faith strong, Lord, so that I may always turn to You for restoration and peace. In Jesus' name, Amen.

In the New Testament, we see this healing ability again in the story of the woman with a flow of blood. For twelve long years, she suffered, her condition worsening despite medical help. But when she reached out in faith to touch the hem of Jesus' garment, she was instantly healed. Jesus said to her: **"My daughter, your faith has healed you. Go in peace and be delivered from your suffering" (Mark 5:34).**

The miracle didn't happen by touch alone, but by an intentional touch filled with faith. Like her, and like Job, your miracle is on the way for me and my family, Lord.

Trust Jehovah Rapha, for even in suffering, he works, restores, strengthens, and heals. If you listen carefully to the voice of the Lord, your God, and follow His commandments by doing what is right in His sight, He promises to protect you from the sufferings and diseases that once afflicted the Egyptians.

In your case, it could be cancer, kidney problems, drug addiction, or any other afflictive disease, but there is no disease or condition that God cannot heal. Jehovah Rapha, the Lord who heals, has the power to restore and bring healing to all areas of life.

Whether it's a physical illness, an emotional struggle, or a spiritual battle, God's healing is available to all who turn to him in faith and obedience. No matter how serious the situation, nothing escapes his ability to heal or transform. *Trust his promise, for he is the God who heals, and he is faithful to bring restoration to his loyal servants.*

When you dedicate all your hope and life to Christ, you are no longer just a citizen of this world, *but you become a citizen of the heavenly world, with Almighty God at its head, as the head of your spiritual government.*

This means your identity is now rooted in God's kingdom, and your purpose is aligned with His divine plan. Your values, thoughts, and actions are transformed to reflect God's will, and you are called to live in accordance with His righteousness.

As a member of this heavenly community, you are part of a vast family of faith, comprising approximately *2.9 billion people*; the love and grace of Jesus Christ unite *your place of worship*. You are no longer alone; you have the body of Christ, the Church, to walk beside you in faith, encouragement, and service.

Your life no longer belongs to you because you have surrendered it to the Lord. This does not mean that you lose your individuality, but rather that your life is now guided by God's will, rather than by your desires. You can no longer do as you please; He promises to take care of you, provide for your needs, and strengthen you in times of trial.

However, he also calls you to be a good steward of the body and life he has given you. This means taking care of your physical health, protecting your heart and mind from sin, and being diligent in your walk with him. Faith requires action and obedience to God's word to ensure that you remain under his protection and in his grace.

As a citizen of heaven, you will receive the blessings that accompany a life devoted to God.

These blessings are not only material but also spiritual in nature. A peace that passes understanding, a joy that circumstances cannot shake, and the assurance of eternal life with Christ. For without him, no one will go to heaven. Paul said Acts 4:12. "**There is salvation in no other, for there is no other name under heaven given among men by which we must be saved**".

Jesus is the only way! While on earth, you will experience God's provision, guidance, and favor, but the greatest reward is the promise of an eternal home in his presence. Your faithfulness to Him allows you to share in the riches of His kingdom, and as you walk in obedience and trust, you'll see His promises come to fruition in your life.

By listening to His decrees and laws, as a citizen of heaven, you will experience His healing and care, for He is the Lord who can heal you. His faithfulness to those who follow his instructions; they are spared from evil, receive his healing, and the blessings of his protection.

The solicitations and seductions of this world often pull believers in all sorts of directions, leaving us scattered, weary, and sometimes far from the standards we know God has set for our lives. Yet one reassuring truth remains: God knows us intimately, far better than we know ourselves. Even before we were conceived, He knew every detail of our being, our strengths, our struggles, our impulses of obedience, as well as our moments of doubt.

He discerns what lies in the heart, beyond our visible actions. Even when the pace of life becomes frenzied and disorganized, our worship is not limited to a specific religious building or a fixed schedule. As believers, we can always honor God in our hearts, through our thoughts, in a quiet space for a few minutes, or in a personal prayer.

True worship flows from a heart aligned with His Spirit, whether in the silence of a morning commute, while driving alone, in traffic jams, or on the train, in the silence of a night prayer, or in our daily thoughts to Him. In spirit and truth, we can live a life of worship even amid the demands of our day. Prepare your heart and mind to meet God, because tomorrow he will do something extraordinary for you.

How many times have you dreamed of starting something big, a business, a project, or a courageous action that could change your life?

But you've let doubt or other people discourage you from doing it. You start with enthusiasm, imagining the success and impact it could bring, but as time goes by, hesitation sets in. You question yourself, you analyze every detail, and before you know it, the passion disappears.

The idea came from God and set your heart on fire, but you let it become another "if and only if". Lost in fear and uncertainty. Doubt makes you believe that you're not ready, that you're not capable, that you don't have enough intelligence, or that the time hasn't come yet.

One day, while I was on vacation, someone turned to me and said, "I know God wants you to write this book. I'm not a book reader, but I can't wait to read it". Her words reminded me that this was not simply a personal desire, but a call placed in my heart by God. That moment gave me the strength to overcome my doubts and finally put my faith into action.

The truth is, if we keep waiting for the perfect moment, if we keep waiting for the ideal opportunity, if we keep putting it off, hoping for the right moment, if we keep putting it off, waiting for the right moment, we may never take the step that will lead us to a breakthrough; the right moment is now.

I know you'll encounter more than your share of Bible verses and quotes throughout this book. But I hope that as you read, you'll also encounter passages you may have overlooked or forgotten, and realize how essential these holy words are to our lives. By bringing them to light, you'll not only enrich your faith, but you'll also be equipped to share them with other believers in need. **Philippians 1:6** "*Being confident that he who began a good work in you will carry it on to completion in the day of Christ Jesus.*"

God will never abandon you because of your doubts, but it's your faith that will serve as the cornerstone of your journey. Faith doesn't mean you won't be afraid; it means you trust God enough to move forward despite every negative dirt road that lies in your path.

When Peter stepped out of the basket onto the water, it wasn't his strength that kept him afloat, but his faith in Jesus **(Matthew 14:29-31).** As soon as he focused on the wind and waves, doubt engulfed him. But Jesus didn't leave him there; he reached out and picked him up. In the same way, God will always be there to catch you, but you have to take the first step in faith. Don't let doubt silence the call God has placed in your heart. Go ahead, trust Him and let your faith be the foundation that keeps you standing and taking your first step.

Nothing is hidden from him. He sees all Christians, in our private moments as well as in our public lives. While we can deceive others, we can never deceive God. Whenever we appear before Him, we are fully known. Galatians 6:7 The apostle Paul said that God cannot be mocked, that his justice is certain, and that he sees every action and every choice. Jesus asked *every Christian to pray with sincerity, humble their heart, and seek His forgiveness.*

But have you ever felt spiritually dry, lost all motivation to keep going, no matter how much you pray, fast, worship, or read His Word? Do you feel like your soul remains thirsty despite your best efforts? ***Yes, I do too***.

I've been there. Feeling spiritually deserted means experiencing a period of emptiness, exhaustion, or estrangement from God, during which prayer becomes meaningless and devoid of purpose. Your worship lacks passion, and your faith seems stagnant. You may feel like you're wandering in a desert with no water, no strength to carry on, just an overwhelming sense of disconnection.

This dryness often stems from trials, unanswered prayers, unconfessed sins, or simply the weariness of life. Doubt and discouragement make it hard to move forward. Yet even in those moments, you kept the faith, knowing that God would never abandon us. Just as rain eventually falls on parched ground, His presence will renew our hearts to greatness.

The prophet **Daniel 2:21** says: "*He changes times and seasons; he deposes kings and sets up others; he gives wisdom to the wise and knowledge to those with understanding.*"

The following words are addressed to you, yes, to you who are reading this very moment. A cloud, as small as a man's hand, rises from the sea: "*By your patience I will give you answers*".

My life hasn't been the same since I learned how the Lord shows up for the people he loves. **Hebrews 12:6** The Lord chastens him whom he loves, and chastens all whom he takes for sons.

It was the same for the prophet Elijah, when he prayed to God to send rain, the drought having persisted for three and a half years.

James 5:17 Elijah was a man of the exact nature as us: "*he prayed earnestly that it might not rain, and no rain fell on the earth for three years and six months.*"

The Lord asked him to go up Mount Carmel to look at the sea. The prophet told God six times that there was nothing. Then the Lord said to him! Go again. Each time, he saw nothing. It's only on the seventh that the clouds form and the rain comes; when the Lord asks us to look again, it's because he'll be by our side in the fire. God will undoubtedly carry you out of the water on his shoulders.

The patience of believers is a strength, an unwavering perseverance in faith that allows us to wait on God, even in seasons when God is silent and still. How many times have you waited for a blessing from him, whether great or small, not knowing if that day would come, only to discover that his timing was perfect?

The right husband or wife, a baby, a job, healing, a breakthrough; just when you were ready to give up hope, the answer was closer than you thought. Sometimes the key is not to give up too soon, because God's blessings often arrive just when we need them most.

I know you can be disappointed and denigrated, that it's tough for you sometimes, or most of the time, and that life isn't fair. Your life has dried up more than seven times already, and you haven't seen where your hope came from.

If you read 1 Kings 45, you'll understand that there are clouds with wind, and there will be heavy rain to address your problems. Keep the faith and see how God's mighty hands will give you respite. He will water your problems, not only yours, but also those of your children and grandchildren, because of your faith.

Isaiah 44:3 *"For I will pour water on the thirsty land, and streams on the parched ground; I will pour out my spirit on your offspring, and my blessing on your posterity."*

Psalm 24:1

The earth is the LORD'S, and the fulness thereof; the world, and they that dwell therein.

HEAVENLY CITIZEN

CHAPTER ELEVEN

"Rejoice, people of Zion, exult before the Lord your God, for he gives you autumn rains, because he is faithful. He sends you abundant rains, autumn rains, and spring rains, as before." Joel 2:23 says:

The Citizenship of Christian Parenthood

After **27** years of following the Lord since my baptism, my journey began with my grandmother, who nurtured my love for Him. It's been a long journey, sometimes lonely and challenging, but filled with priceless grace and blessings. I know you, too, have faced difficulties, but over time, we realize the strength God has built within us, not only for ourselves, but also for our families and those around us.

People often say that "life is short", but for those of us who walk in faith, every moment, every hour, and every second is a gift of grace from God, granted to us until the day we join him eternally in his kingdom.

No matter where you live on earth or what faith you follow, whether Christian, Muslim, Hindu, Buddhist, or Zoroastrian, we are all of the same kingdom and possess the same citizenship. From nation to nation, tradition to tradition, culture to culture, we invoke God under many names: **Yahweh, Jehovah, Elohim, Adonai, El Shaddai, Hashem, Allah, Vishnu, Waheguru, Ahura Mazda, Zeus, and many others**. Although our expressions of faith may differ, we are part of a greater spiritual community, united; we are longing toward the same divine direction.

No terrestrial nationality or passport can give access to the kingdom of God. Although people must identify themselves by their nationality, culture, and passport to enter another country, the faithful citizenship that counts is that of heaven. The only condition of entry is faith in Jesus Christ. No good deed, no religious ritual, no personal effort can replace the saving grace that comes from faith in him. Jesus said it clearly:

John 14:6:
"I am the way, the truth, and the truth. No one comes to the father except through me."

His sacrifice on the cross paid the price for our sins, giving every Christian the only valid passport to eternal life, with no expiry date. No matter how righteous a person may appear, their works will never be enough to earn them a place in heaven. The only way to enter this kingdom is through the saving blood of Jesus Christ. Jesus is the only way, the only condition to receive the actual passport to heaven, and for all of us to become citizens of God's eternal kingdom.

Salvation is not based on merit, status, or works, no matter how righteous a person may be. Whether pastor, bishop, deacon, apostle, prophet, evangelist, or president, no position can justify a place in heaven. The only way in is through the blood of Jesus Christ, who gave his life so that we could be redeemed.

It is by God's grace, received through faith, that we are saved. When we place our trust in Christ, we gain faithful citizenship in God's eternal kingdom, where earthly divisions no longer matter and only his love and mercy remain.

This divine passport is not earned through your applications and fees, but is received as a gift through the gift of faith. Just as a traveler must present the necessary documents to enter a foreign country at the airport, a person must place their trust in Jesus Christ to enter heaven.

Those who accept Jesus as their Savior are granted a new identity as children of God, and they receive citizenship in God's kingdom. In him, there will be no division of race, nationality, color, or earthly status, no sin or evil, no death or suffering, no sickness, no darkness or long night, no hunger or thirst, no sorrow or tears, no curses or consequences of sin, no war or violence, no lies or deceptions.

Jesus Heals Everything: From Sin and Sorrow to Life of family and friends, and Resurrection

Held by the Hands of the Healer

This powerful song by **King David calls** every believer to cherish the countless benefits of knowing and trusting in the Lord. Mercy and compassion are at the very heart of God's nature. He is neither distant nor indifferent; he made his ways known to Moses, and he is intimately involved in the restoration of his people, Israel. He reaches into the depths of our distress with healing in his hands and hope in his heart.

Jesus revealed this healing nature in action; he is the great physician of our souls. He touched the untouchable, lifted the broken, and even raised the dead. **He gave new life to the widow's son in Nain, awakened Jairus' daughter, and raised Lazarus from the grave after four days.**

These were not simply miracles of divine power, but revelations of divine love. It's a testimony to Christians that it's never too late for God to intervene. He sees you in your suffering and responds with holy compassion. His healing goes beyond the body, transforming the heart, renewing the mind, and restoring the soul.

On July 13, 1996, *the enemy attacked my life. Psalms 103:2-3 Let all that I am praise the Lord, that I may never forget the benefits he lavishes on me. He forgives all my sins and heals all my diseases.*

My testimony

I was involved in a catastrophic car accident that left me unconscious and broken. When I finally woke up in a hospital bed a few days later, both my ankles and my right wrist were broken. My ribs and back were severely bruised, and the left side of my face was badly damaged. I was still in high school at the time, but everything came to a halt.

I wasted two whole years going in and out of hospitals and clinics. It was a painful period of failure and uncertainty. The doctors didn't know if I would ever walk again. I spent four long years fighting to regain my health and rebuild my life, step by step. Despite the trauma and isolation, I sought healing in many places, through doctors, counsellors, friends, and family who helped me greatly, but nothing could give me back the confidence and purpose I'd been robbed of.

Only Jesus could do that. Only He could reach into the broken pieces of my life and begin to rebuild me. He didn't just heal my body; He redeemed my soul. I am forever grateful to Jesus, my Savior, my Redeemer, my unfailing Friend. He saved me then, He sustains me now, and He will forever be the One who carries me through.

We are genuinely grateful to the many Christian doctors and caregivers God has placed among us, those who work with integrity and compassion, seeking not just profit, but purpose.

They make a difference in our families and communities. However, we must never forget that the only permanent healer resides in the heart of every believer, keeping them at peace and providing a rest that the world cannot offer. And as we experience his touch here and now, ultimate healing awaits us all in the kingdom of heaven.

The God who heals, forgives, and makes all things new has secured eternal victory through Christ.

The same Jesus who healed them still heals today. Whether we're emotionally wounded, physically tired, or spiritually dry, in our feelings, our flesh, and our faith, he sees you.

Where our soul aches, our body breaks, and the spirit longs, His mercy flows. In our emotional battles, physical burdens, and spiritual warfare, in anxiety, affliction, and apathy. His presence is there now. His work of restoration in every faithful person today is a preview of the complete renewal to come. Until we return home with our heavenly passport in hand, we live in faith and hope, securely held by the hands of the Healer.

He will wipe every tear from their eyes. There will be no more death or mourning or crying or pain, for the old order of things has passed away.

Heavenly Father,

Thank you for being the God who heals, the Rapha who forgives and restores. I praise you for your mercy and compassion, for seeing me when I'm broken-hearted and for never pushing me away.

I thank you for the healing that comes from your presence, the healing of my body,

You have healed my spirit and my soul. Lord, I place in your hands the fragile areas of my soul, those still marked by pain. I surrender every scar, every weight, every tremor of fear, sure that your gentleness has the power to restore all.

Jesus, you are the doctor of my heart. You put your hand on the wounds that no one else could reach.

You snatched me from death; without you, I would be gone. Do that miracle in us again today. Wake what is fading. Strengthen what falters. Bring your peace to stormy places. Teach me to rest in your promise: you are near, and nothing is beyond your power.

Holy Spirit, fill me with hope as I wait for the full redemption you have promised. Remind me every day that your healing power is not only for the past, but also for the present and the future.

Until the day I see you face-to-face, please help me to walk in faith, covered by grace, and held by the hand of Jesus, the ultimate healer. In Jesus' name, I pray, **Amen.**

God's healing identity reveals His profound love and unwavering desire to see His creation flourish. It is through this loving nature that He invites us to bring our wounds and brokenness before Him in prayer, knowing that He possesses the power to restore and renew our health. His healing touch extends not only to our souls but to all who are broken-hearted.

In this assurance, we find peace and strength, trusting that His care will mend the deepest parts of us, bringing restoration and wholeness to every area of our lives. On our knees, we call your name, Lord, before we say a word, you already hear our prayer. I appreciate your grace; it is sufficient to safeguard our family.

In the Book of Revelation, God grants the apostle John an extraordinary vision, transporting him to the heavenly realm to witness the glory, majesty, and divine mystery of the eternal kingdom. The apostle John, exiled on the island of Patmos, receives a vision from God.

This vision is rich in symbolic images and prophetic messages concerning our future home as believers, the end times, and the ultimate triumph of good over evil. John was in the Spirit when he saw these extraordinary things in heaven (Revelation). In Revelation 4, the apostle John gets a glimpse of the throne room of Paradise, a sacred moment when the veil between earth and eternity is removed.

The Lord, in His mercy, transported the apostle John, also known as John the Beloved, one of Jesus' twelve disciples, by the Holy Spirit into His very presence, allowing him to witness the glory, majesty, and adoration surrounding the eternal throne. For a time, John became a heavenly tourist, walking the courtyards of our future home while still clothed in mortal flesh. Although he had to return to earth, he was the only human whom the Lord gave this experience. He took with him a message of admiration and hope for generations to come.

As of 2025, more than 2.9 billion Christians will read his words and cling to this divine insight into what lies ahead. The day is drawing near when we will join the great assembly around the throne, no longer as visitors, but as citizens of the celestial, worshipping the Lamb who sits on the throne for eternity.

Brother John describes a throne surrounded by a different army of angels, with 24 elders seated around it. In front of the throne is a sea of glass, with four living creatures worshipping God, saying: **"Holy, holy, holy is the Lord God Almighty"**.

The apostle John sees a scroll with seven seals that no one can open except the Lamb of God (only Jesus Christ). The Lamb takes the scroll, takes charge and authority to reveal and implement God's plan for the world. This is the same Jesus who came and died for our sins, but this time, no one can approach his presence except the one who holds the passport of faith, acceptance, and baptism.

Brother Nic had to learn the truth the hard way by having the privilege of meeting Jesus in John 3:3.

Jesus said to Nicodemus:

"Truly, I say to you, no one can see the kingdom of God unless he is born again: Truly, I say to you, no one can see the kingdom of God unless he is born again'; no one can enter the kingdom of God unless he is born of water and the Spirit."

In the heavenly vision John saw, the twelve elders symbolize the twelve tribes of Israel, representing the continuity of God's covenant relationship with his faithful people, i.e., all who hold that the Lord alone is the way, the truth, and the life.

These elders, seated around God's throne, also represent the faithful of the Church, as well as all faithful citizens who have accepted Christ as their Savior, particularly the twelve apostles, who are the foundation of faithful Christian communities. As members of the heavenly council, they stand in awe of God's glory, submitting to his eternal authority. Their actions represent a posture of adoration and reverence, acknowledging that God is the Creator of all things and affirming His supreme worth and holiness forever.

Angelic beings and the heavenly council play a crucial role in John's divine vision, as devoted worshippers who continually honor God. In Revelation 4:10-11, we see the elders casting their crowns before God's throne, demonstrating their humility in recognition of God's sovereignty. They proclaim, **"You are worthy,**

you are holy", our Lord and only God, to receive glory and honor, and all power belongs to you.

You created all things, and by your will, they were made perfect; all creation exists for your purposes. The worship of elders serves as a reminder of your eternal authority and the centrality of your will over all things.

John has seen the new heavens and the new earth (Revelation 21), for the old ones have disappeared. He describes the new Jerusalem, a city of incredible beauty, descending from heaven. God will dwell with his people, and there will be no more pain, tears, or death.

My advice is to live with an open mind and great hope that our lives won't end there. Paul said that people are destined to die once and be judged for permission to enter God's kingdom:

Philippians 3:20-21 *"But our citizenship is in heaven. From there we eagerly await the Savior, the Lord Jesus Christ, who, by the power that makes him lord over all, will transform our lowly bodies to resemble his glorious body."*

God wants all His faithful believers to live a good and happy life here on earth, filled with peace, purpose, and love. He has sent us the Spirit as a teacher to guide us in cultivating virtues and adventures, building meaningful relationships, and finding joy in every little daily blessing. A life of trust in God that gives inner contentment, even when life is complicated.

Our faith in Him gives us hope and strength by following His ways, showing kindness, practicing gratitude, and seeking justice. Believers can experience the fullness of life He expects of them, find His love and grace in what they do. "This is the day that the Lord has made**; let us rejoice and be glad.**

Psalm 118:24 Paul speaks of the transformation believers will undergo, receiving glorified bodies like Jesus' in heaven. Because of the difficulties you've encountered on earth in the few years you've been here, you need to keep the faith, no matter what challenges you experience in your life:

Physical health problems, mental and emotional health, social and relationship problems, economic and financial problems, work and career problems, school and learning problems, **F.A.I.R., discrimination, procrastination.**

The Bible emphasizes the importance of working diligently and with a servant's heart, illustrating how God desires us to work together in unity and with a shared purpose. Colossians 3:23 reminds us that whatever we do, we should do it wholeheartedly.

This perspective elevates the significance of our daily tasks, regardless of their size or scope. When we adopt a mindset of seeking intelligence through the word of God, it transforms everyday activities into acts of worship, bringing glory to God in everything we do, by working with excellence and humility.

I once heard a pastor explain it like this: when we reach heaven, the angels will reveal to us many blessings we missed during our time on earth. These blessings were delivered to us, but because of our position at that time, whether it be in our faith, mindset, or physical state, we were not in the right place to receive them.

The truth is, God is never behind in answering our prayers; He is always timely and faithful. However, our ability to receive His blessings can be hindered by our spiritual readiness. It is essential to align our hearts and minds with His will so that we can fully experience the abundant life He desires to give us.

In Isaiah 64:1, the prophet is passionately pleading for God's intervention, calling for a powerful and visible demonstration of His presence. He longs for God to tear the heavens open and come down in a mighty way, shaking the mountains before Him.

Isaiah's cry reflects a deep yearning for divine intervention and a desperate need for God's power to be evident in his life and the lives of his people. This heartfelt plea reminds us that, even in our struggles, we can approach God boldly, asking for His intervention and trusting in His ability to move mountains on our behalf.

It is in these moments of desperation that we can experience God's most significant acts of mercy and power.

Heavenly Abba

You who dwell in unapproachable light, yet draw near to those who are broken-hearted. Open the heavens and come down for me and my family.

Let the mountains tremble once more before you. Just as Isaiah cried out in desperate hope, I cry out to you, O Lord.

Shake what needs to be shaken in my life until only You remain. Your glory, your truth, and your unconditional love.

In quiet times, in exile and vision, my home is yours, O Lord.

He who walks among the candlesticks and speaks with a voice like raging waters.

You are faithful and true. You are my Lord, my Savior, and my Redeemer. O Holy is thy Name, be glorified, I worship thee, O Lord.

Do not reveal yourself in part, but in power. Let our eyes see, our ears hear, and our hearts burn with worship songs again to exalt your majestic name.

Let your Spirit fall with fire and mercy. Awaken the dead, heal the broken, open all eyes to read your words. And call sons and daughters to the light of your glorious kingdom.

My spirit is crazy to love you, O Lord. My heart beats fast as I sing your praises. I long for you, my Lord and my God

I pray and say thank you, I bring the Amen to all your teachings.

Let every tongue confess, let every knee bow, that Jesus Christ is Lord, to the glory of God, the Father. In the name of our Lord Jesus. **Amen.**

I dedicate this prayer to all those who await God's presence, who long to see his glory revealed in their lives and families. May he tear open the heavens and descend with power and mercy. May you accept Jesus Christ as your Lord and Savior at this very moment.

***(Your name and loved ones ...)* To:**

Vilus, Donald, Gerda, Mirline, Guerline Enude, Carline, Luc-Junior, Isaiah Jean Pochette, Ninide, Frederick, Quesnel, Mazou, Macda, Croilnor, Ms. Georges, Price, Martine, Jason.

Tuyikorere, Kanimba, Musabyimana Umutoniwase, Umutesi, Mugabutsinze Kanimba Kuli, Diane, Oda, Alodie, Shillinglaws Leandre, Pierre Richard, Sophia, Clarita Venor, Daril Julien, Mario Jeune, Fenet, Manex.

Denis Percy, Jude Dorcemond, Rose, Beatrice Marjorie, David, Herline, Gregory Nathie, Harouna, and Ali Dawas. Roserne Noel, Levania Prospere.

Psalm 27:1

Gabriel Marcelin

The LORD is my light and my salvation; whom shall, I fear? The LORD is the strength of my life; of whom shall I be afraid?

HEAVENLY CITIZEN

CHAPTER TWELVE

The King said, I see four men loose, walking in the midst of the fire, and they have no hurt; and the form of the fourth is like the son of God. Daniel 3:25

The Lord will fight for you; you need to Stand Still God Will Stand with You in the Fire, because the Battle Belongs to Him.

The Lord fiercely protects those who walk righteously before him. The Bible is full of evidence that God does not abandon His faithful in times of trial; in fact, He comes even closer to them. One of the clearest examples is found in the story of Shadrach, Meshach, and Abednego.

Although they were thrown into a fiery furnace for refusing to bow down to a false god, the golden statue erected by King Nebuchadnezzar of Babylon, the Lord himself entered the fire with them. Not only were they not harmed, but God's presence was so evident that even their enemies were forced to recognize His power.

It's the same God who walks with you today. No trial is too hot, no accusation too strong, and no difficulty too profound to keep him from standing by your side.

When you're misunderstood, wrongly accused, or attacked for your loyalty, resist the urge to defend yourself with your strength. At some point, silence will come in handy. God sees the heart and knows the whole truth of every situation. You don't have to carry the burden of explaining your innocence; He is your defender and judge.

What matters most is your attitude before him: remain humble, remain faithful, and trust that he will bring you justice in due time. Your vindication may not come immediately, but it will come, and when it does, it will be undeniable that it was the Lord who fought for you.

Let his presence in the fire assure you that you are never alone and that your righteousness is never in vain. Isaiah 43:2 "**When you walk through the fire, you will not be burned; the flames will not engulf you. For I am the Lord your God...**"

Heavenly Father

Lord, thank you for being our protector and defender in every trial. When I feel the heat of life's storms, I won't be afraid because you're here with me.

Just as you were with Shadrach, Meshach, and Abednego, I trust you to justify me and carry me through this situation with your faithful hand.

I will be patient and wait for you as my holy advocate. No one has ever defeated you, but in you alone I place my trust. In Jesus' name, **Amen**

Have you ever found yourself in a toxic situation at work, in your family, or in your environment that leaves you unsure of what to do? Have you ever found yourself in such a toxic environment, whether at work, with family or friends, the people you should trust most, that you don't know what to do? It's the kind of pressure that makes you want to run away, stop everything, throw in the towel, or quit.

At times like these, you're on the verge of losing all respect, the confusion can seem overwhelming, but the Bible offers a powerful reminder: *"The Lord will fight for you; all you have to do is stand still in silence"* **(Exodus 14:14).** Silence amid chaos isn't weakness; it's confidence in the action of self-mastery. Sometimes our silence is not a sign of surrender, but a weapon of wisdom.

Proverbs 17:28:
"Even fools pass for wisdom if they keep silent, and for understanding if they hold their tongue".
Jesus invites you to keep silent and trust God to fight the battle on your behalf.

You may feel the urge to leave, to escape from what seems unfair or unjust. Although God sometimes speaks to your spirit to move forward, it's not always He who urges you to leave. Before you take that step, ask yourself, "Is this what God wants for me, or is it discouragement that's trying to get me to leave?" The enemy often uses opposition and tension to push believers out of the places where they've been called to influence and shine.

If you've been faithful, done the right thing, and are still under pressure, it may be a sign that you're exactly where God has placed you for a purpose. Trials don't just come from enemies, but also from friends, colleagues, and even strangers; don't let that discourage you.

In these moments, guard your heart and your words. *"**Lord, set a guard over my mouth; watch over the door of my lips**"* **(Psalm**

141:3). Not all situations require you to defend yourself; some require you to remain silent. God's power far exceeds anyone's plans. ***"He will command his angels to protect you in all your ways"*** **(Psalm 91:11).**

The attacks may seem relentless, but so is God's protection. He is not distant from your pain; he sees everything. He honors the faithfulness you show in private and the tears you shed in silence.

So, stand firm. Keep your eyes fixed on the one who never fails. Let God fight the battles that are beyond your strength, and trust Him to deliver justice in due time. His timing may not always match yours, but His justice is certain. In the end, you'll see that no weapon formed against you will prosper. You'll bear witness that God defends the righteous, lifts the

humble, and completes what He begins. And in that victory, you'll not only be vindicated, you'll shine.

Heavenly Father
My soul belongs to You, O Lord

I come before You with a humble heart, seeking Your divine protection over my life and my circumstances. You are my refuge and my strength, my ever-present help in times of need. I place my trust in You, knowing that Your presence shields me from all harm, physical, emotional, and spiritual.

Lord, surround me and my family with Your unfailing protection. Guard our souls, our health, and our relationships wherever we go, for You are the ***great I AM***. Grant me wisdom, understanding, and discernment so that I may walk in Your will and reconcile all things in my path to You.

May Your presence go before me, beside me, and behind me, guiding my every step. Thank You, Father, for Your unwavering love and faithfulness. I trust that You are always with me, now and forever. In Jesus' mighty name, I pray. **Amen.**

"Every word of God is pure; He is a shield to those who take refuge in Him." (Proverbs 30:5)

God's commitment to his people at every stage of life. When he says, even to your old age and gray hairs, *"I am he; I am he who will sustain you. I have made you and I will carry you; I will sustain you and I will rescue you."* **Isaiah 46:4**

He assures us that his presence and provision do not diminish over time. Unlike the people you know and support who may waver or fade, God's love remains steadfast and his strength unchanging. He is the same God who walked with you in your youth, and will continue to carry you in your old age.

This verse reflects the heart of a faithful Father who not only guides you through life but also supports you in it. It speaks of his personal involvement and constant care, from your first breath to your last.

This promise is compelling in a world where age is often seen as a burden rather than a blessing. I remember growing up in a time when respect for elders wasn't optional; it was ingrained in our culture. You couldn't whistle at an adult, and they were addressed with titles like "***Mister John" or "Mrs. Hannah".***

It was a way of honoring the wisdom and experience that come with age. However, today we live in a culture where youth is often idolized and respect is frequently linked to status, wealth, or education. Older people are usually neglected, rejected, or disrespected.

Young people feel free to say or do whatever they please in the presence of their elders, without question. Yet God's word remains unchanged over time. **Leviticus 19:32** says: "***Stand up in the presence of the aged, show respect for the elderly, and revere your God. I am the LORD.***"

Disrespecting the elderly isn't just bad manners; it's dishonoring God. Whether you feel able or tired, energized or exhausted, God's promise remains the same: "***I will carry you, I will sustain you, I will save you.***"

His role in your life does not diminish with age. While the world may try to silence or sideline the voices of older generations, the Lord approaches with compassion and strength. His grace never wanes, and you'll never reach an age where His love is far away.

At every stage of life, from youth to gray hair, God remains your refuge. His hands are still strong enough to hold you. His heart is still fixed on you. And His power still works through you. That's the beauty of belonging to a God who never tires, who never overlooks your worth, and who promises to be your faithful support for the rest of your life.

The peace of prayer is the quiet assurance that, no matter the storm around you, God is listening and already at work on your behalf. Every time you kneel in prayer, you step into a divine conversation where God's peace is waiting to envelop you.

It's incredible to realize that the Creator of the universe listens with loving attention to every word, every sigh, and even the silent cries of your heart. When we fully believe in Him and trust His will above our own, we begin to seek His guidance before despair, hopelessness, or sadness can take root in our homes.

Prayer becomes more than a routine; it becomes a refuge. And in that sacred place, God begins the work of transforming your heart, lifting your spirit, and strengthening your mind to face whatever lies ahead.

A renewed mind opens the door to a new direction, where God's purpose replaces confusion and His strength enables every step forward. Faith in Christ isn't meant to be passive; it's a call to get up every day with purpose and power. When you hold fast to faith, you are not alone.

The Lord will walk beside you, and His strength will accompany you throughout your life.

So let go of your old patterns and move forward with a renewed attitude. As my mother used to say, 'If you see how, you can do it.' But if you don't know how, my son, let the Lord take care of it and move on. No trial is too overwhelming, no setback too great, because His protection surrounds you and His Spirit energizes you. It's a memorable visit. Every time the Spirit of the Lord visits you, something changes, something moves, and something better will happen.

Your faith is a shield that protects your heart from fear, your mind from doubt, and keeps you rooted in God's promises, no matter what storms you may be going through. Life will inevitably bring storms, but God never wants you to face them without armor.

As **Ephesians 6.11 13** reminds us:

"Put on the whole Armor of God, that you may be able to stand firm against the wiles of the devil. For we wrestle not against flesh and blood, but against principalities, against powers, against the rulers of this dark world, against evil spirits in heavenly places." Therefore, take up all the weapons of God, so that you may be able to withstand in the evil day, and stand firm after overcoming everything.

"Your faith is your arrow, repelling doubt, silencing fear, and allowing you to focus on the promise, not the problem. Every challenge becomes an opportunity for God to reveal His strength in you."

He will never let you fail in the fire or be shipwrecked in the storm. Persevere, even when you're tired, knowing that your dedication is not in vain. God's purpose for your life doesn't change just because the winds howl louder; it becomes clearer when you trust him through every storm.

God's first institution is the Christian family, established as the foundation of love, unity, and His covenant relationship with humanity. The Christian family is not the product of government, policy, public law, or cultural power; it is a sacred institution, ordained by God before the foundation of any government.

In the union of Adam and Eve, God established a pattern of love and a covenant that reflects His divine nature. Long before kings reigned or laws were written, the Christian family was created to bear His image and fulfil His plan on earth.

It is the backbone of spiritual and moral stability, a living symbol of God's eternal purpose. When a family honors God, it becomes a powerful force for good, training generations to walk in truth and grace. This is why a man leaves his father and mother and is united to his wife, and they become one flesh.

Heavenly Father

Your grace is sufficient for me and my family. Lord, help me never to take Your grace for granted. Keep my eyes fixed on You, and remove anything in my heart that doesn't honor You. Let me walk daily in the fullness of Your love. **Amen.**

My Grace Is Sufficient for Your Family

"My grace is sufficient for you, for my power is made perfect in weakness." **(2 Corinthians 12:9)**

Beloved family of God, hear these words: **My grace is sufficient for your family.** You may sometimes feel that the challenges of life are too significant, that the burdens of responsibility are too heavy, or that the pressures of society threaten the unity of your home. Yet I remind you today that My grace is more than enough. Where your strength ends, Mine begins. Where your resources run dry, my abundance flows.

I am the backbone of your spiritual and moral stability, the unshakable foundation beneath your household. The storms may rage, the winds may howl, but the house that is built upon My Word shall not fall. For I am not only the God of the individual; I am the God of families. Your family is not an accident of history, nor merely a social arrangement; it is My first institution, established in Eden, blessed by My hand, and designed to reflect My eternal purpose for My Kingdom in heaven.

Your home was meant to be a sanctuary of love. Love that is patient and kind, love that bears all things and endures all things. This love is not born of human will alone but flows from My Spirit. When you forgive one another, when you choose kindness over anger, when you speak life instead of criticism, you are building your household on the foundation I have laid. Remember: just as Christ loved the Church and gave Himself up for it, so you are called to love within your family.

A family that abides in My love becomes a living testimony to the world. In a culture where selfishness and division are common, your home shines as a light set on a hill. Do not underestimate the power of such a witness. Even the smallest acts of love within your home ripple outward to touch lives far beyond what you can see.

Prayer as a refuge

Prayer is not merely a routine or a duty; it is your refuge. In prayer, you come into My presence, and I come near to you. In that sacred place, I begin the work of transforming your heart, lifting your spirit, and strengthening your mind. The weight you cannot carry alone is lifted as you kneel before Me.

Stand up in prayer in My presence to intercede for your family. I hear you, and I will answer you. Pray not only for provision, but for protection, wisdom, and unity. Pray for the next generation, that they may walk in My truth and not depart from it. Your prayers are incense before My throne; they rise, they are seen, and they are answered in My time and according to My will.

Generational Blessing: I will be your God and the God of your family, from generation to generation, for four generations. The failures of man do not break my covenant; My faithfulness endures. What you sow in prayer today, your children and grandchildren will reap in blessing tomorrow. Do not think that your quiet moments of intercession are unnoticed. Even when you see little change, trust that I am working in the unseen.

I am He; I am He who will sustain you. I made you, and I will carry you. I will sustain you and rescue you. Do not fear for your children, for I hold them in the palm of My hand. Even when they wander, I pursue. Even when they falter, I restore. My love is stronger than rebellion, and My mercy is greater than sin.

I have commanded My angels to guard you in all your ways. My heavenly hosts surround your family. You do not walk alone, though your eyes cannot see the multitude of guardians I have placed around you. They encamp around those who fear Me, delivering and preserving them. In moments of danger, I send them forth. In times of confusion, I whisper peace. Trust not in your own vigilance alone, but in My ever-present protection.

The Power of **Silence**

Keep silence in My presence, and you will see My mighty hand at work in your family. Too often, your heart grows restless, and your tongue speaks more than your spirit hears. Yet in the stillness, I reveal Myself. Silence is not emptiness; it is fullness. It is the space where my voice resounds most clearly. When you learn to wait quietly before Me, your anxieties lose their grip, and My peace takes its place.

Be still, and know that I am God. Do not rush ahead of My timing, nor lag in fear. Walk in step with My Spirit. In silence, I strengthen your patience. In silence, I refine your faith. And in silence, I remind you that your family is held securely in My hands.

Your family is more than a household; it is a living symbol of My eternal purpose. When you gather at the table, when you bow in prayer, when you forgive and reconcile, you are declaring to the world that I reign. Each day you live faithfully within your home, you participate in My Kingdom on earth as it is in heaven.

Let your home be a sanctuary of My presence, a refuge for the weary, a school of love, and a testimony of faith. Let your children see in you the example of discipleship, humility, and courage. And let your neighbors know the beauty of the gospel lived out in your family.

Proverbs 10:19
"Sin is not ended by multiplying words, but the prudent hold their tongues."

Final Word to Paul and to you now.

Beloved, never forget: **My grace is sufficient for your family.** You do not walk alone. I am your sustainer, your refuge, your protector, and your God. From this generation to the next, I will uphold you. I have made you, and I will carry you. Be silent before Me, and you will see My hand at work. Lift your family to Me in prayer, and I will answer. Trust in My promises, for they are sure and everlasting.

"But the Lord is faithful, and He will strengthen you and protect you from the evil one." **(2 Thessalonians 3:3)**

Psalm 28:7

The LORD is my strength and my shield; my heart trusted in him, and I am helped: therefore, my heart greatly rejoiceth; and with my song will I praise him.

HEAVENLY CITIZEN

CHAPTER THIRTEEN

Living Fearlessly Under God's

Protection and Provision.

How to Live with Purpose, Provision, and Peace in God's Kingdom.
When you become a Christian, you take the first step into the Lord's grace. But this is not the end of the journey; it is the beginning. As God's children, we are called to grow in the knowledge and understanding of His Word. Scripture reminds us:

"***My people are destroyed for lack of knowledge***" **(Hosea 4:6).**

To live in victory, you must seek wisdom and truth from God's Word, for it is the foundation of your life.

Being a Christian doesn't mean you are called to live in poverty or accept a life of constant lack of blessings. ***Poverty is not proof of holiness, nor is misery a sign of true faith.***

The Lord is your Father, and as your Father, everything that belongs to Him is also given to you through Christ.

The Bible declares, "***The Spirit himself testifies with our spirit that we are God's children. Now if we are children, then we are heirs, heirs of God and co-heirs with Christ, if indeed we share in his sufferings so that we may also share in***

his glory." **(Romans 8:16–17).**

This inheritance isn't limited to heaven alone; it also influences how we live on earth. As Paul states:

"***For all things are yours; whether Paul, or Apollos, or Cephas, or the world, or life, or death, or things present, or things to come; all are yours; And ye are Christ's; and Christ is of God***" **(1 Corinthians 3:21-23).**

Therefore, open your eyes and embrace the Lord's Word as the law of your life. God has already provided for you in Christ. He has promised not only eternal salvation, but also wisdom, peace, protection, and provision for your daily walk.

Jesus said, "***I am come that they might have life, and that they might have it more abundantly***" **(John 10:10)**.

As you grow in knowledge and faith, you will discover that your identity as a child of God is not one of lack but one of abundance, purpose, and divine inheritance.

As a child of God's kingdom, you are protected by His divine hands, empowered by the Holy Spirit, and called to live with a kingdom-aligned purpose that reflects His glory in heaven.

God watches your faith through your struggles; He defends, protects, and strengthens those who walk with Him. Just as he sent an angel to shut the lions' mouths for Daniel, he always sends protection to those who trust him now.

It is essential that we first seek to know the Lord honestly and receive His wisdom, for spiritual ignorance can lead to avoidable suffering, even among those who profess to believe in Him.

"**My people are destroyed for lack of knowledge, because you have rejected knowledge**, **Hosea 4:6**".

Christians are not called to live in misery or want, although this was sometimes once seen as a sign of piety. While Scripture teaches us to be thankful in all circumstances, it also reveals that God delights in providing for His people and bestowing upon them an abundance of blessings.

As Paul says in **Philippians 4:12-13**:

"*I know how-to live-in humiliation, and I know how-to live-in abundance. In everything and everywhere, I have learned to be satisfied and to be hungry, to be in plenty and to be in want. I can do all things through him who strengthens me.*"

Contentment isn't a lack of money; it's the peace of knowing that God is our source, whether we're in abundance or need. Throughout the Bible, we see many faithful servants of God entrusted with great wealth:

"*Abram had become very wealthy in livestock and in silver and gold*" **(Genesis 13:2)**.

"*After Job had prayed for his friends, the Lord restored his fortunes and gave him twice as much as he had before.*" **(Job 42:10)**

Joseph of Arimathea, a wealthy man and a prominent member of the council, waited for the kingdom of God because he was also a faithful follower of Jesus. He dared to ask Governor Pilate for Jesus' body and prepare the tomb for his burial **(Matthew 27:57-60)**.

Joseph of Nazareth, a carpenter, son of Jacob and husband of Mary, was already dead when Jesus was crucified.

"***King Solomon was richer and wiser than all the other kings of the earth***" **1 Kings 10:23**.

Christians are called to live with open hands, ready to give, bless, and serve others with what God has given them. Wealth, in and of itself, is not an evil; it's a tool.

As 1 Timothy 6:10 reminds us, *"the love of money is a root of all kinds of evil"*.

The problem is not having money, but being ruled by it. God is not against wealth, but He is against greed, selfishness, and putting one's trust in riches rather than in Him. When wealth is received with gratitude and managed wisely and generously, it becomes a powerful instrument for good in God's kingdom.

God has given us a kingdom identity and, as citizens of heaven, we are not meant to live in spiritual or material poverty. If you're reading this, perhaps this is God's message: rise above the patterns that hold you back, reject the lies that belittle you, and walk boldly in the truth that you are His beloved child, called, chosen, and covered by grace to accomplish great things. Consider Joshua's bold prayer to God: he asked for the sun to stand still, and it did.

As a testimony in **Joshua 10:13, "The sun stood still, and the moon stopped, until the nation took vengeance on their enemies."**

This miraculous moment wasn't just about cosmic power; it was about God's faithfulness to His people. When His servant prayed, God responded immediately and mightily.

After Moses' passing, Joshua stepped into leadership with unwavering trust in God's power to fight for His people. That same access to divine intervention is available to us today. As believers, no obstacle is too significant when we lean on the Lord.

You can count on it; He will show up for you.

2 Thessalonians 3:3 "But the Lord is faithful, and he will strengthen you and protect you from the evil one."

Jesus commands an army of angels, ready to fight on behalf of His people, in Matthew 26. This call to heaven reveals that an army is at His disposal, more than twelve legions of angels, which is about 72,000 heavenly soldiers.

You are not supposed to see how God fights your battles to keep you alive with your natural eyes, because most of the time the struggle comes in from the spiritual world, and God is handling everything coming your way to destroy you personally.

The battle is not yours to fight when you choose to walk by faith, not by sight. In the situation described in **2 Kings 6:16-17**, the prophet Elisha reassures his fearful servant by revealing a powerful spiritual truth:

God's protection is far greater than any visible threat.

Surrounded by an enemy army, the servant could only see danger with his natural eyes, and he was afraid. However, when Elisha prayed for his eyes to be spiritually opened, he could see how the Lord conducted His business to defend His faithful servants.

In that moment, God allowed him to see the unseen: a vast heavenly army of horses and chariots of fire encircling them. This passage reminds us that we are never truly alone; even when circumstances seem overwhelming, God has angelic forces fighting on our behalf in the spiritual realm. Faith allows all Christians to see beyond what's visible and trust in the power and presence of our unseen Defender.

We are not here to fight with our strength but to stand firm and keep our faith as a weapon, knowing that God and his angelic army will protect us. Just as David proclaimed:

1 Samuel 17:47 *"The battle is the Lord's." We, too, can find peace in the assurance that victory belongs to Him*."

The Lord will reveal Himself to you in due time; this is the unshakable promise to those who wait with patience and faith. Though the seasons may feel long and the waiting may stretch your soul, God's timing will not disappoint you. When you pray to Him with a heart that longs for His immediate presence, He will not hold back.

When you seek him with sincerity, you'll experience the fullness of his power and peace. In his presence, there's clarity, comfort, and the divine assurance that he's doing everything for your good.

To be a citizen of God's kingdom is to live with purpose, now and in eternity. Here on earth, your life carries the weight of God's call; you are not without purpose, but anchored under His sovereign dominion. The Lord holds full authority over your life and family, guiding every step with an eternal perspective.

Your hope lies not in temporary results, but in eternal security found in Christ. There is a coming kingdom where every tear will be wiped away and God's dominion will be fully revealed, and as His child, you are already part of that promise.

This citizenship comes with both privileges and responsibilities. As Paul stated:

"You are no longer strangers and foreigners, but fellow citizens with the saints and members of God's household" **(Ephesians 2:19).**

And again, ***"Our citizenship is in heaven, from which we eagerly await a Savior, the Lord Jesus Christ"*** **(Philippians 3:20).**

Live as if you belong to heaven. Walk in love, pursue righteousness, speak the truth, and serve with humility. Let your daily life reflect the kingdom you represent, becoming a light that draws others closer to the King.

Heavenly Father

Lord, thank you for calling me a citizen of your kingdom. You have approved my heavenly passport and given me access to your Holy Spirit to guide me and my family. Please help me to stay patient and faithful, as I wait for you to act on my life. Draw me closer to your presence and teach me to live with purpose, rooted in your truth.

May my life represent your love, justice, and mercy, and may I always walk in humility and faith.

I trust that you control my life and that of my family.

Keep my eyes fixed on you, O eternity.

In Jesus' name, **Amen.**

Paul is educating us that our faithful citizenship is not of this world but in heaven. As believers, we belong to God's kingdom, where Jesus reigns as our Savior and King. This heavenly citizenship gives us a profound hope that eliminates all earthly struggles.

While we live in this world, we eagerly await Christ's return, knowing that He will fulfil His promises and bring His kingdom to completion. Our identity is not defined by worldly status, but by our place in God's family, which is secured through faith in Christ.

I am one hundred percent certain that you remember that Jesus said, "***No one comes to the Father except through Me.***"

Because of this, we are no longer strangers or outsiders in God's kingdom. We are fellow citizens with His people, united as members of His household. This truth calls on us to live with purpose, reflecting the values of His kingdom, love, righteousness, and faithfulness.

We are not isolated individuals living in this world by ourselves, but part of a divine family, called to encourage, uplift, and serve one another. As we walk in this truth, we embrace our heavenly identity and eagerly anticipate the day when we will dwell fully in His presence forever.

Christian families must establish an open channel of communication with the Lord, allowing each member to share their thoughts, emotions, and deepest concerns with Him freely, without fear of judgment.

Encouraging this openness not only deepens individual faith but also strengthens family bonds, an environment of trust and compassion anchored in God's love and guidance.

While our relationships are valuable, they are also fragile. The trust placed in each other can be passed along, sometimes leading to disappointment or betrayal. However, when we put our trust in the Lord, we embed ourselves in His unwavering promise:

"Never will I leave you; never will I forsake you." **(Hebrews 13:5).** With this assurance, we can boldly declare, *"The Lord is my helper; I will not be afraid."*

In this divine relationship, families will find true comfort and the strength to overcome life's challenges, knowing that God's counsel and care will sustain them through every trial.

To avoid misunderstandings and build emotional support in your life, it's essential to cultivate a habit of closeness with God. One practice that has helped me is to imagine that the Lord is there, beside me, when I pray. He silently listens to my thoughts, concerns, pain, or joys.

It may seem unusual to you, but feeling his presence near you made it natural to talk to him about whatever was on my mind, wherever I was. These moments became a spontaneous opportunity to share everything, the struggles, the gratitude, and even the tears.

Society often says that men don't cry, but that never stopped me. I wept freely before the Lord, knowing that he understood my heart perfectly. In prayer, I found the freedom to be myself, to complain when I was tired, to be afraid or happy, to laugh sadly even when I felt joy, and to express gratitude for his presence constantly.

I thanked him for writing my name in the book of life, granting me salvation and redeeming my soul as a citizen of his kingdom. These conversations with God are not mere formal prayers; they are raw, honest exchanges that deepen my faith in the Lord. In embracing this intimate connection, I found strength, comfort, and the unshakable assurance that I was never alone.

These types of honest conversations have made me strong, and I've never had to worry like others. God can calm the storm around you and your family right now. You'll need to establish a routine that will maintain stable communication with him. Stop praying as if the Lord were far away.

Paul said, "**God did this for you so that you would seek him and perhaps reach out for him and find him, though he is not far from any one of us.**" **(Acts 17:27)**

God's omniscience is beyond our comprehension, perfect and infinite in every way. He possesses complete knowledge of all things, past, present, and future, without any limitations or constraints. Unlike us, bound by time and space, God's understanding transcends all boundaries.

He knows every event, every intention, and every possibility, no matter where or when it occurs. His awareness spans across all of existence simultaneously, never missing a single detail, and nothing ever surprises Him. This perfect knowledge speaks to His divine nature, His wisdom, and the immeasurable scope of His understanding.

Furthermore, God's omniscience extends to the very core of each person. He understands the innermost thoughts, desires, and emotions of every individual, far beyond what is visible or outwardly expressed. Nothing can be hidden from Him, as His knowledge penetrates the depths of our hearts.

This ability to know and understand us entirely is both humbling and reassuring, as it reveals God's intimate awareness of our lives, our struggles, and our joys.

His perfect knowledge isn't just intellectual; it is deeply relational, as He knows us in ways we cannot even fully comprehend.

After many years of serving the Lord, I have come to understand His knowledge more deeply: God not only knows what is happening externally in everyone's life but also the most profound thoughts, secrets, motivations, and what is in every heart.

He knows the true intentions of every being. Nothing in all creation escapes His knowledge; no one can deceive the Lord. This is all the more reason to confess the truth to Him in every prayer.

Every time you pray, talking with Him and singing to Him can strengthen your relationship with Him. These moments of peace and reflection will bring you great benefit, I assure you. They will relieve your burdens and grant you a peace that the world cannot offer.

His omniscience is a characteristic of His nature, and his unfathomable wisdom surpasses all knowledge, placing Him at the pinnacle of our existence. This makes Him the top priority on our prayer list. Families can benefit significantly from outside support, whether it's advice from relatives, encouragement from trusted friends, or comfort from support groups. This means inviting the Lord into our lives, allowing Him to heal and restore all the broken pieces of our lives.

The Spirit of the Lord is a divine protection that covers you, a sacred shield of strength that protects you from all evil and the forces of the enemy. It is an unshakeable force that accompanies you at every step, surrounding you with grace and power, ensuring that no weapon formed against you prospers. In times of trial, it is your only refuge, guiding you safely through life's storms and protecting you from the dangers that lurk in the shadows.

This heavenly barrier stands firmly between you and evil, watching over you from all sides.

This divine protection is not just a shield, but a promise from Jesus, the unshakeable assurance that you'll never be alone in your struggles, because the Almighty is always behind you. The Lord will protect you from unseen dangers, and the Spirit will give you wisdom and discernment along the way.

The spirit is the living assurance that you are never alone in reaching your goal.

In life's most difficult moments, the Almighty will stand by your side, and you will feel his faithful presence. Rest in the truth that, whatever the obstacles, the Lord's presence will bring you the peace, strength, and victory that will always be yours. Isaiah 41:10 "Fear not, for I am with thee: be not dismayed, for I am thy God: I will strengthen thee, and help thee: I will uphold thee with my right hand gloriously."

Psalm 30:5

For his anger endureth but a moment; in his favour is life: weeping may endure for a night, but joy cometh in the morning.

HEAVENLY CITIZEN

CHAPTER FOURTEEN

*O*ne generation commends your works to another; they tell of your mighty acts. Psalm 145:4: God's Blueprint: The Sacred Legacy of Parental Love. We will be faithful to our mothers, Fathers, and Grandparents, the healers of souls and Hearts.

***L**et no harmful words come from your mouth.* Instead, speak words that are uplifting and helpful, building up everyone around you. Let your words carry grace and encouragement, so others may hear them and see the light of the Lord shining through your life.

Every soothing word spoken to your children should be a blessing, an encouragement, and a healing to their souls. A relationship of love and compassion must be established very early in the child's life, building trust that will lead them to rely on you as their primary source of comfort and guidance.

God's design for Christian education was given to Abraham, a covenant to raise his eight sons according to God's word, to train them with good moral guidance and teach them the kind of conduct that would please the Lord. From the day your children are born until the day they leave to start their own families, you are their steward and the only person they can truly turn to for all their needs and troubles.

The Lord said:

"For I have chosen him, so that he will direct his children and his household after him to keep the way of the Lord by doing what is right and just, so that the Lord will bring about for Abraham what he has promised him." (Genesis 18:19)

1 Corinthians 4:2: *The apostle Paul explains that faithfulness is an essential quality and a requirement of a steward. A child's loyalty and trust in their parents can never be fully measured; all the more reason to continue showing your children how much you love and trust them.*

Let them know that they are a gift from God to you, and how proud you are to have them. Compliment them when they do good things in life, and encourage them to believe that their actions matter, their efforts are seen, and that they are competent, by God's grace, to become everything He created them to be.

Though my children are grown now, I continue to cherish every opportunity to express my love for them, with hugs, kisses, and words that affirm their value.

No matter how many years pass, they remain my beloved sons and, in my presence, they are still the respectful, tender boys I've prayed for since their birth. It's a sacred reminder that a father's love, like our Heavenly Father's, doesn't fade with time; it deepens, strengthens, and continues to nurture long after childhood has passed.

The inherent value and uniqueness of each person, created by God as a being made in God's image, means that each individual reflects aspects of their character, but diversely and distinctly, while being made admirably and wonderfully.

Psalm 139:13-14 says: "***You formed my inward parts; you knit me together in my mother's womb. I give you thanks, I am fearfully and wonderfully made.***"

Your works are marvelous, my soul knows, it echoes deep within me. "**Wonderfully made**" are the right words, for there is no other way to describe the divine work of God's hands.

We all know, whether we admit it or not, that no technology, no scientific breakthrough, can come close to replicating what God has designed. The human soul, the breath of life, the intricate beauty, and the complexity of our being; these are beyond the reach of human invention. We are living, breathing testaments to a Creator whose craftsmanship is beyond comprehension.

All this means that our children can sometimes stray from your instruction, step away from their purpose; as a parent, you'll need to keep the faith and pray for them. You must hold fast to your faith and pray for them. The level of forgiveness you need to maintain is an open door they can turn to and run back to whenever they're in trouble.

The Bible states that Luke was the closest companion of the apostle Paul, and Luke recounts the story of a father in **Luke 15:20-24** who eagerly forgives his wayward son when he returns home with humility and courage.

When a rebellious son is returned with humbleness and repentance, it leads to a joyous celebration. Jesus teaches that God deeply cares about restoring the fallen, healing the sick, and the paralyzed of the mind, with a place for every Christian to run back to. We should share the same sentiment whenever that happens.

The parable of the lost sheep illustrates God's interest in every individual. Just as a shepherd leaves the ninety-nine to find the one that is lost, God relentlessly pursues those who have gone astray, demonstrating His unwavering love and grace over every Christian.

God endows each person with unique abilities, roles, and purposes. As the Bible teaches:

1 Corinthians 12:4-11:
We have been given different gifts according to the grace that has been bestowed upon us.

Within the Christian family, mothers, grandmothers, and grandfathers serve as the best spiritual caregivers, offering wisdom, love, and guidance grounded in faith. In most cases, when children are away from home, some will always run back to Grandma or Grandpa for love and affection.

Just as God knows the number of hairs on our heads, He cares for us with an intimate, unfailing love. This same kind of tender care is what parents show to their children.

The best doctors aren't always found in hospitals; they're often found at home, in the form of mothers and fathers who mend emotional wounds and heal brokenness with genuine love, patience, and experience because they are the best people for children to trust and listen to.

Parental comfort and hope in Christ

It starts with Mom and Dad, whose tender hands, countless hugs and kisses, and effective remedies bring comfort that no one else can understand. Their care, warmth, and soothing voices make them the first trusted healers and doctors in a child's life.

And for those lucky enough to have had a grandparent, their wisdom and unconditional love offer another form of healing. Through their stories, smiles, and gentleness, they reconcile the heart and uplift the soul. With years of lessons, kindness, and grace, their embrace becomes a refuge, a proper place of restoration when we're weak, even when we're in trouble and need to come home.

If we are always allowed to return to our parents as trusted sources of healing and comfort, imagine encountering Jesus not just at church, but also down the street, in the supermarket, at home, at work, in your car, wherever you are. He is always present, allowing you to recognize that while others may care, no one can truly heal your heart like He can. You can always return home to him.

Jesus, our healer

Jesus did not come to earth by chance, but by divine will. He deliberately left heavenly splendor to enter our broken world, bringing with him hope, healing, and offering his life for our salvation. Whether he walked the roads of Galilee or sat at the right hand of the Father, his power remains intact.

The same Jesus who opened the eyes of the blind, raised the dead, and calmed the storm is still at work today, wherever you are. His ability to heal knows no borders, times, or limits. All he asks is that we believe.

As Jesus said:

***"Jesus said to him, 'If you can! All things are possible to him who believes.* (Mark 9:23.)**

Sincere faith and silence before God

Sometimes we share our hearts or plans with those who seem to be friends, only to feel betrayed or misunderstood. That is why I have learned to talk to them as if my life belongs to another family, my address, my family, or every real issue of my life can only be trusted to God alone.

I am open to answering every question and giving a reasonable answer to everyone curious enough to ask, but my real life belongs to only one person. But even then, keep in mind that no one can override God's plan for your life. In moments of disappointment, stand still and surrender to God; in the quiet, let your faith speak louder than your words. "Instead of defending yourself, draw closer to him. Silence the noise and close your eyes, abandon all hurt and confusion. Jesus continues to speak, to heal and to guide.

When you keep the faith, believing wholeheartedly that only Jesus can intervene in your situation, that no friend, no doctor, not even money can bring you the answer, he will certainly show up for you.

Faith is not just believing in what God sees; it's having the certainty that he will act.

Faith that heals. Take the example of the centurion who approached Jesus in Capernaum, seeking to recover his paralyzed servant who was suffering terribly. When Jesus offered to come and heal him, the man responded with humility and bold conviction:

He said he was not worthy for Jesus to enter his house. Yet he believed that a simple word from Jesus would be enough to bring healing.

His faith was so strong that it moved Jesus. And just as the centurion believed, the servant was healed. It's not your status, but your faith that will bring healing.

This same powerful faith was evident in another man who came to Jesus, desperate for healing for his dying son. He begged Jesus to go before it was too late. But instead of following him, Jesus told him, "***Your son will live***." Without hesitation, the man believed Jesus' words and went home.

As he approached his house, his servants came to meet him and told him some astonishing news: his son had been healed at the very moment Jesus had declared.

This miracle, recounted in **John 4:46-54**, reveals the unrivalled authority of Jesus' word. Just as God created the world in the book of Genesis, Christ's word continues to be animated by this same divine power to heal, restore, and breathe life into even the most desperate situations.

The apostle Paul affirms this truth in **Colossians 1:16-17:**

"***For in him all things were created that are in heaven and on earth, visible and invisible, thrones, powers, dominions, authorities. All things were created through him and for him***."

He is before all things, and all things subsist in him. e. This means that nothing in our lives is beyond his reach or control. When Jesus speaks, all creation listens. And when we respond to his word with faith, as this father did, we make room for the miracle prayer **for grace and the faithful education of children.**

Heavenly Father

I thank you for your inexhaustible love and for all the sacrifices you have accepted so that I may walk in your truth.

Support me, O Lord, so that my words will always be edifying to others, especially children, to bring encouragement, healing, and grace, as you commanded in **Ephesians 4:29.** Teach me to be a faithful guardian of the precious souls you have entrusted to me.

Make me a guide with a love that resembles your heart, a compassion that exemplifies your mercy, a truth that never fails, a sense of humor that never fails, and a truth that never fails, even when it's hard.

May my children sense, through my words and actions, that they are deeply loved, and know that they are a priceless treasure from you.

May they grow up knowing that my presence is a refuge for them; a place of security, attention, and unconditional welcome.

Make me an attentive and intentional parent, rooted in Your Word, so that my home may be a symbol of heavenly peace and my heart the image of Your character. I ask this in the mighty name of Jesus, **Amen.**

The family is the mirror of God's heart.

Faith is the bridge between the promises of heaven and the realities of earth. Faith transcends geographical location, ethnic nationalities, and artificial religions; it is found in a heart that relies on the word of Jesus.

The centurion man said to Jesus:

"Just say the word, and my servant will be healed," and his faith was honored, and healing was achieved **(Matthew 8:8-10).**

The nobleman in John chapter 4 believed Jesus' promise without seeing proof, and his son lived. In both of these stories, miracles were achieved not by touch or ritual, prayer in a church service, fasting to ask God to perform miracles, or any other form of magic, but by trusting in the word of Jesus.

The word of God is the roadmap for everything if we learn how to put it into a faith-based practice. In parenting, too, this faith becomes vital, as we commit our children's hearts, destinies, and future goals to God, even if we can't see the outcome with our naked eyes, but the Lord will give answers in the invisible realm.

The divine plan for the sacred inheritance of parental love was created for a specific reason. The family is not a human invention; it is God's holy design. When a parent loves as God loves, they create an atmosphere that encourages the implantation of grace and spiritual growth.

Our world may be blurring the lines of family importance, but God's design never changes. Faithful mothers, fathers, and grandparents have the sacred calling to love profoundly and intentionally. Their love becomes heaven's healing touch on earth, building homes where souls are nurtured and hearts are healed.

In the very beginning, Adam and Eve were charged with perpetuating the first legacy of love. They were the first parents called to care not only for creation, but also for the souls of their children. From the beginning, the family was to be the first church where worship would be learned, the first school where wisdom would be taught, and the first hospital of healing where wounds would be bound in love.

Homes were to be holy places where God's presence resided and blessings were passed down from one generation to the next through faithful living.

A parent's sacred mission is to love in a way that reflects God's own love. That means showing restorative compassion, not crushing criticism. It means offering mercy instead of judgment, and speaking life instead of condemnation. Parents have the divine privilege of shaping a child's vision of God.

When children see love in their homes, they are more likely to believe in the love of their heavenly Father. They are more likely to realize great gifts of talent. This legacy of love has eternal significance; it sows seeds that can bloom long after we've been gone for generations.

Fathers, in particular, are called to shepherd their families with strength and tenderness. They are not only providers of material resources, but also spiritual
  guides.

David said in **Psalm 103:13:**

"As a father has compassion on his children, so the Lord has compassion on those who fear him."

They have to keep pointing their children in the right direction. A father's constant example, his humble prayers that children have never seen, and his protective presence become anchors in the storms of life.

Mothers carry a sacred power in their role as caregivers and a special love that only the Lord can understand.

Isaiah 66:13 As a mother comforts her child, so I will comfort you, making a direct connection between God's comfort and a mother's embrace. A mother's whispered prayers and gentle words often resonate in her child's adult life, reminding them of her grace and genuine love.

Her love is usually the first glimpse of God's mercy a child will encounter after birth. Faithful mothers are more than guardians of physical needs; they are cultivators of the mind and soul, faithful teachers and true friends. Their influence is felt deep in the child's heart, becoming an unshakable foundation of love.

Thank You, Lord, for the faithfulness of every mother, father, and grandparent.

Heavenly Father

We come before you with grateful hearts, honoring the divine plan you established from the beginning. Lord, you are the author of the family, you conceived it, and you sustain it from the start. The sacred heritage of parental love was never man's idea, but yours, a holy mission woven into the very heart of creation.

Thank you, Lord, for entrusting mothers, fathers, and grandparents with this sacred responsibility: to love as you love, to lead with compassion, and to build homes where your grace dwells, hearts are healed, and godliness is taught.

Help us never to forget that our homes are meant to be a sanctuary, a holy ground where your presence dwells, where worship begins, truth and love are passed on as precious heirlooms from generation to generation.

Lord, in a world that often alters the meaning of family, remind us that your purpose never changes. Strengthen every parent who feels tired.

Renew every grandparent who prays in quiet faith. May your Spirit fill every home with peace, purpose, and your divine presence. May we never take lightly the privilege of shaping souls and planting seeds that will blossom into eternal fruit.

Heavenly Father,

Renew the strength, tenderness, and steadfast love of all fathers. May their prayers, expressed or silent, build spiritual walls of protection around our families. May they lead not only by giving, but also by being present, gently guiding their children to You. And Lord, bless every mother with renewed strength and great joy.

May her words be healing water, and her hands an extension of your comfort. As you comfort us as mothers, may each mother reflect your mercy, patience, and grace. May her faithfulness be a lasting fragrance in your presence. Help us not to make her weep, let her be proud.

Teach us all, Lord, to love intentionally and eternally. May our homes become living testimonies of heaven's healing? Allow us to raise children who know not only our love, but also Yours. Allow us to sow seeds of justice that will bear fruit long after we are gone.

In every home, may your name be honored. In every generation, may your love be known. And in every heart, may your Spirit richly indwell each faithful family forever. We ask this in Jesus' precious name, *Amen.*

Psalm 31:15

My times are in thy hand: deliver me from the hand of mine enemies, and from them that persecute me.

HEAVENLY CITIZEN

CHAPTER FIFTEEN

Are there generational wounds in your family that need healing? Generational Wealth: Building a Legacy That Lasts.

Ask God to reveal to you the areas of your family where He desires to bring restoration. True healing begins with humility and a heart willing to surrender.

Through your daily prayers, intentional acts of love, and the power of forgiveness, you can become the vessel God uses to break generational cycles of pain and usher in a new legacy of blessing and great wealth. That's why I love all my family members, because I don't believe there are people more loving than my family.

This mentality is like believing that God has chosen your family specifically for you. However, you don't have to inherit the generational curses of your ancestors, nor be bound by their poor manners, lack of knowledge, or discipline. Instead, ask the Lord to help you break the chain and allow you to pass on your freedom to your offspring:

Good health, spiritual favor, divine protection, deliverance, victory over sin, and great wealth.

How you choose to live today will determine how you are remembered tomorrow and the kind of inheritance your children will inherit. Ezekiel 18:20 "The one who sins is the one who will die. The child will not share the guilt of the parent, nor will the parent share the guilt of the child. The righteousness of the righteous will be credited to them, and the wickedness of the wicked will be charged against them."

You're not out of the woods yet. As long as you breathe, you have a reason to act. You are a bridge between what has been, what can be, and what the Lord will do. When you choose to love faithfully, even when it's hard, you lay the foundation for a legacy that heaven celebrates.

Generations may never know your name, but they will feel the impact of your obedience. Your legacy will not be defined by perfection; your children, grandchildren, and great-grandchildren will tell your story. It's because of your persistence in trusting God and living out of His love that your children, grandchildren, and great-grandchildren will tell your legacy.

The Bible makes this clear:

Psalm 103:17 "*But the LORD's lovingkindness endures forever for those who fear him, and his mercy for their children's children.*"

When you live in Christ, your spiritual DNA (Deoxyribonucleic Acid) changes. "*If anyone is in Christ, he is a new creation. Old things have passed away; behold, all things have become new*". **(2 Corinthians 5:17).**

What has been passed on to you, such as addiction, anger, fear, or rejection, sickness, and poverty, must not continue to be chained from your parents to you and your children. Through Jesus, every generational curse is broken and ceases to exist. He carried the weight so that you and your family can walk in freedom and blessing.

Your prayers are not empty; they are a form of spiritual warfare. "The prayer of a faithful person is powerful and effective" **James 5:16.** Your intercession can shift the atmosphere of your entire household. Don't underestimate what God can do through a heart that is praying. Keep standing in the gap. Continue to declare truth over your children and grandchildren. Keep trusting the One who restores, renews, and rewrites family stories.

God will use your breakthrough to establish a legacy of faith that stretches into eternity.

A woman approached Jesus, pleading for the healing of her demon-possessed daughter. At first, Jesus replied that his mission was mainly for the Jews, but the woman's faith moved him. Thanks to her persistence and faith, Jesus declared that the demon had left her daughter, and she was instantly healed, even though Jesus was not physically present **(Matthew 15:21-28).**

You and I, who are faithful Christians in Jesus Christ, must stop following the so-called prophets who, everywhere today, exploit our people by demanding money in exchange for miracles.

True faith in Jesus requires no manipulation, no fuss, and no humiliation. When Jesus healed, he did so with love, compassion, and authority, never for personal gain or to put on a show for the congregation to applaud, as we see in the story of Balaam and Balak **(Numbers 22-24).**

All the false prophets and apostles, prophecies, and false miracles will be displayed before us so that we can see that the God we follow never shouted at people, pushed them to the ground, or demanded gifts for healing. Instead, he spoke, and miracles happened.

The Bible warns against false prophets who deceive for profit **(Matthew 7:15, 2 Peter 2:1-3).** We must trust in Christ alone, knowing that his grace and power are freely given to those who are not healed.

Similarly, when Jesus' friend Lazarus died, he was not present at the time of his death. Yet four days after Lazarus was laid in the tomb, Jesus called him back to life, demonstrating his power over death **(John 11:1-44).**

These miracles show that Jesus' power is not limited by time or distance. Just as he healed and restored lives then, he is still able to do so today. No situation is too severe for him to redeem. Ask him for forgiveness, healing, and restoration, while humbling yourself. His love and grace are always available, waiting for those who come to him in faith.

All the steps required to receive his help are simple. You don't need to pay money, travel great distances, or ask someone else to act on your behalf to pray for you; you don't need a prophet or special mediator to pray over you or to lay hands on you.

All you need is a sincere heart, ready to reach out to Jesus in faith. He hears your prayers wherever you are, and his power is just as real today as it was when he walked the earth.

Jeremiah 29:12 Then you will call on me, and come and pray to me, and I will hear you.

Jesus gave every Christian direct access to God's royal presence. Imagine arriving in a foreign country for the first time. What documents do you need? A passport, a visa or entry permit, and a travel ticket. The authorities need to know who you are and where you're from. In the same way, when you present yourself before God, you need to recognize yourself as a citizen of His kingdom.

This begins with identifying yourself in prayer, following the example the Lord has set for us, addressing Him as ***"our King."***

Heavenly Father.

I thank you for our faith, which is the key to accessing the kingdom of heaven through prayer. As a citizen, you can ask God to enter your heart and heal your soul of doubt. By praying, you accept your place in the community of the faithful and consecrate your life to Him as a member of His royal house.

This implies a change in your way of thinking, which becomes more positive, progressive, and spiritual. From now on, you will be eager to seek more knowledge, you will seek his intelligence, and your mind will find everything in the Bible, as Solomon said in **Proverbs 18:15:**

"***The mind of a prudent man acquires knowledge, and the ear of a wise man seeks knowledge***".

The decisions we make and the atmosphere we create around us can, in some cases, pave the way for illness and even death. Wisdom born of faith, on the other hand, makes a climate conducive to a believer's spiritual life as a citizen of the Kingdom of God.

Thanks to prayer and faith, much suffering can still be alleviated and transformed by the intervention of Jesus. Just as he once gave sight to the blind, hearing to the deaf, speech to the mute, and walking to the lame, his healing power is still alive and accessible. The healing of the blind man at Bethsaida remains a powerful testimony*: Christ is still at work, restoring hearts and repairing what seemed lost.*

These stories remind us that healing is possible, right where you are, right here, right now. Spiritual breakthroughs and miracles become reality when we exercise our faith. But the key lies in asking, as **James 4:2** points out: "***You do not possess, because you do not ask.***"

Brothers, let us raise our voices to Him today. Present him with your requests, and you'll see how he acts, step by step. Be convinced that God is willing to honor your faith, manifest his power, and meet your needs.

God heals not only bodies, but souls, too. He knows our frailties, especially when we go through illness, emotional breakdowns, the loss of a loved one, or major upheavals. In such situations, it may be natural to turn to doctors, hospitals, or even the often-restrictive administrative systems. Yet above it all, we can always place our trust in the power of God.

The story of the woman who had been suffering from blood loss for twelve years **(Mark 5:25-34)** is a powerful testimony to His compassion. She was not only healed by her faith but also honored by Jesus for her boldness.

A simple touch of her garment was enough to transform her life. In the same way, when the Spirit of God moves on earth, your faith can call upon Him and provoke divine intervention. It's in this momentum that your breakthrough can happen.

The two most significant revelations of my life came after long years of waiting. The first came after 19 years of persevering prayer and fasting. During this season of waiting, I experienced periods of limitation, discouragement, and even despair.

But I never thought of giving up, because my life no longer belonged to me: I had placed it entirely in the Lord's hands. I firmly believed that He would show up on my behalf. And during this period of waiting, He strengthened my faith, making me stronger and more enduring. Then, at the moment He had chosen, He opened the long-awaited door, bringing the breakthrough for me.

The second promise was delivered after 25 years of waiting. God had prepared me and placed me at the right time, in the right place, in the correct country, the proper city, and above all, alongside the right person.

Then, suddenly, **everything changed**.

He renewed my life, and the blessings I'd been waiting for so long began to manifest. God's timing is always perfect; He knows precisely where and when we need to be positioned to receive the miracles, He has planned for us.

How many times have we doubted, weary from waiting, not knowing that our breakthrough might be just a few steps away? God often acts when we least expect it, but it's never too late.

Heavenly Father

I come before you, Lord, approaching in faith, convinced that you hear my voice. I surrender myself to your perfect timing, for you are never too late. You probe my heart long before my lips open, and you already know my needs. You have prepared the answer to my prayers: to restore my soul, ease my struggles, and grant me your peace. I know you will intervene, for in you alone rest my hope and trust.

Another striking example of Jesus' power is the healing of the man with the paralyzed hand on a Sabbath. Jesus said to him, "Stretch out your hand", and immediately it was fully restored **(Matthew 12:13)**.

This moment speaks to me deeply, for it reveals that

Jesus doesn't look at our religious labels - whether Christian, Muslim, Jew, pastor, or simple believer - what he looks at is the faith of those who approach him with trust.

Jesus' healings went far beyond the body. They touched the soul, brought forgiveness, and restored humanity to wholeness. Through these miracles, Jesus called hearts to faith, and many witnesses to his grace chose to believe and follow his light.

Even today, we pray in Jesus' name for healing, relying on his inexhaustible compassion and divine authority. We ask him for restoration not only for our afflicted bodies, but also for our broken hearts and wounded souls. And with firm faith, we proclaim that you, Lord Jesus Christ, heal, renew, and raise. We pray in the name of Jesus. **Amen.**

Generational Wounds: "I am Alpha!

Let us be honest: not every inheritance passed down is godly. Some families carry wounds that span decades, broken relationships, no one remains married in the family, cycles of anger, addictions, or spiritual oppression. These patterns are often unseen chains, binding generations to pain instead of freedom. The good news is this: through the blood of Christ, every generational wound can be healed. What was broken can be restored. What was cursed can be redeemed.

Are there places in your family story that still need healing?

Do you feel the weight of struggles that did not begin with you, but were handed down to you?

Bring them before the Lord. His Spirit is mighty to deliver and free you, and His Word declares that *"if the Son sets you free, you will be free indeed"* (John 8:36).

When you choose to walk in obedience and faith, you open the door for God to use your breakthrough as the foundation for a new legacy. Instead of chains, you pass on freedom. Instead of silence, you pass on worship. Instead of despair, you pass on hope. God delights in turning wounds into testimonies that glorify His Name.

Paul said in **Colossians 2:14-15:**

Jesus canceled the charge of our legal indebtedness, which stood against us and condemned us; He has taken it away, nailing it to the cross with His blood. And having disarmed the powers and authorities, he made a public spectacle of them, triumphing over them by the cross.

Warnings Against False Prophets

In your pursuit of healing and legacy, beware of false prophets. Scripture warns repeatedly against those who claim to speak for God while deceiving people for their own profit. These men and women may appear spiritual, but they function more like magicians, luring people with empty promises and manipulations.

Do not let your heart be misled. You are the sons and daughters of the living God. You do not need a false prophet to stand between you and your father. In Christ, you have direct access to the royal presence of God Himself. His Word is living and active, and His Spirit dwells within you.

Be patient and wait. Stop rushing to hear a man's voice when the Lord is whispering to your own heart. Learn to be still in His presence. Jeremiah 29:12 promises: *"***Then you will call on me, and come and pray to me, and I will hear you***."*

What greater assurance do we need? The God who made the heavens bends His ear to listen when you pray.

Jesus Christ has given every believer direct access to the throne of God in heaven. No mediator is required, no false prophet is needed. You can come boldly before the Father, because the blood of Jesus has already opened the way.

Imagine arriving in a foreign country for the first time. What documents must you present? A passport, a visa, perhaps an entry permit, and a travel ticket. Without them, you would be turned away at the border. In the same way, Jesus is your eternal passport into the Kingdom of God. His cross is your visa, stamped with the seal of forgiveness. His resurrection is your travel ticket, ensuring that the gates of heaven are open before you. You belong there, not as a stranger, but as a child of the King.

Create A Legacy of Faith for Your Family.

Your Kingdom inheritance is not only for you; it is designed to overflow into the lives of your children and grandchildren. Let every generation in your family line rise to praise His works. Let the story of God's faithfulness be told again and again until it echoes into eternity.

Build your home upon the promises of God. Teach your children to pray. Model patience, humility, and obedience. Refuse the lies of false prophets, and listen for the still small voice of the Lord. The choices you make today will shape the generations yet to come.

Beloved, you are heirs of His promise. You are citizens of His Kingdom. You are living witnesses that His Word is accurate and His mercy endures forever. Stand firm, hold fast, and pass on a legacy of faith that will never fade.

Psalm 32:7

Thou art my hiding place; thou shalt preserve me from trouble; thou shalt compass me about with songs of deliverance.

HEAVENLY CITIZEN

CHAPTER SIXTEEN

The king, his servants, and his Kingdom.

All our being will rest upon His shoulder.

Jesus came to them and said: Matthew 28:18:
"All authority in heaven and on earth has been given to me. The King's words about his Kingdom: Our whole being will rest on his shoulder.

The King's words about His kingdom are the foundation of true faith. Jesus Christ, the King of kings, constantly spoke to His disciples about the Kingdom of God. His words were not merely suggestions but divine truths that reveal the nature, purpose, and destiny of the Kingdom. In John 18:36, Jesus clearly states:

"***My kingdom is not of this world. If it were, my angels would be fighting to prevent my arrest by the Jewish leaders. But now, my kingdom is from another place***."

His teaching distinguishes His kingdom from earthly dominions, emphasizing its spiritual reality and divine origin.

The first mission of the King:

Jesus' primary mission was to explain the Kingdom of God and demonstrate its power through many miracles. Wherever He went, He preached repentance and entering the Kingdom. The first words He spoke in His ministry were:

"***Repent, for the kingdom of heaven is at hand***" **(Matthew 4:17).**

The Lord asked us all to repent, not about religious rituals, big screens, or social media, but about a change of heart and mind to align with the principles of God's rule. The miracles, healings, and deliverances performed by Jesus were signs of the Kingdom's presence, confirming that He had come to restore what was lost.

The kingdom and the end of time

The end of the world is not hidden from Christians who follow the instructions and read the Bible, unlike any other book, but rather to seek knowledge of God and His kingdom; it has been revealed through the prophecies and teachings of Scripture. Jesus himself spoke of the signs of the end times and the fulfilment of God's plan.

He made it clear that history is moving towards a definitive climax when His reign will be fully realized.

In **Matthew 24:14**, the Lord proclaimed: "***This gospel of the Kingdom shall be preached in all the world for a witness to all nations; and then shall the end come.***"

So, it's clear that Kingdom preaching is at the heart of God's plan for all Christians.

The Kingdom message was often obscured by teachings that emphasized personal blessings, healing, and prosperity. While these are essential aspects of God's goodness, they were not the King's fundamental focus. Jesus taught that no one can see the Kingdom of God unless they are born again.

"***Most assuredly, I say to you, unless one is born again, he cannot see the kingdom of God.*** " **(John 3:3).**

This means that understanding and entering the Kingdom of God requires a spiritual transformation, not just an intellectual or religious experience. Reading this message with an open heart will change one's state of mind to find descriptive information about the Kingdom.

If you are reading this book, you are among the blessed Christians who have the opportunity to receive the true gospel of the Kingdom. Many have heard fragments of the message, but few have sought to understand the complete revelation of what Jesus came to establish.

The Kingdom is not just a distant promise; it is a present reality, accessible to all who seek this knowledge. The teaching of repentance and new life as a Christian is not about conforming to religious traditions, but about accepting the divine order established by Jesus. We are God's resource for seeking Kingdom knowledge from the source that is God's word.

The Bible is filled with teachings and revelations about the Kingdom, and those who diligently seek will find the truth. As ambassadors for Christ, we must live by Kingdom principles, demonstrating love, justice, and faith.

The Kingdom of God is not just the teaching we receive, but what we become in Christ. May this book transform your life and bring you closer to the reality of God's eternal Kingdom.

Understanding Our Heavenly Citizenship: Because our citizenship is in heaven, our priorities, affections, and attitudes should reflect the values of the Kingdom of God rather than the fleeting concerns of this world.

Jesus calls his disciples to:

"***Seek first the kingdom of God and his righteousness, and all these things will be added to you***" **(Matthew 6:33).**

Confidently, that everything else will be provided according to His will. This heavenly perspective shapes our way of life, guiding our choices, our relationships, and our daily walk with Christ.

Rather than being consumed by worldly pursuits, we are called to invest in eternal treasures, sharing the Gospel wherever we are, loving others selflessly, and growing in our faith, openly identifying ourselves as Christians.

Living with a heavenly mindset doesn't mean we neglect our earthly responsibilities; instead, it means approaching them with a higher purpose in mind.

Colossians 3:2 exhorts believers to:

"***Set your minds on things above, not on earthly things***".

This mindset enables us to endure trials with hope, knowing that our present circumstances are temporary compared to the glory that awaits us (Romans 8:18).

As citizens of heaven, we are Christ's ambassadors on earth, representing His love and truth to all who will listen in a fallen world. Our faith in Jesus gives us peace and assurance, enabling us to live with joy and confidence, eagerly anticipating the day when we will dwell forever in his presence.

The presence of Jesus Christ offers an unmatched power that every Christian can rely on, shining like a beacon of hope in a world darkened by sin, brokenness, addiction, cybercrime, violence, poverty, hunger, and war. While this fallen world is filled with chaos, suffering, and moral decay among nations and governments, Christ's authority remains firm.

His power continues to provide peace, healing, and redemption to all who trust in Him. In John 16:33, Jesus reassures His followers: "In this world you will have difficulties. But take courage! I have overcome the world." His victory over sin and death through the cross proves that no evil force can defeat His sovereign reign. Although the world promotes fear, division, and despair, Jesus offers restoration, unity, love, and eternal life to those who seek Him.

As believers, we are called to walk in His power, standing firm in faith and hope, shining His light amid darkness. But not a hair of your head will perish **(Luke 21:18).**

Our Heavenly Citizenship: Living as Citizens of God's Kingdom.

The blood of Christ signed our heavenly citizenship with love and purpose. Unlike earthly passports, ours accesses have no borders; no human can touch, stamp, see, or enforce their laws upon them. The government established by the Lord grants us unlimited access across the heavens through faith, prayer, and worship.

Our heavenly citizenship, sealed by the blood of Christ, is a love affair with a divine purpose, knowing no borders. Unlike earthly passports, it cannot be seen or stamped. Established by the Lord, this eternal kingdom grants us unlimited access to the heavens through faith, prayer, and worship.

The Christian life is not one of discouragement, but of hope, as we await the fulfilment of God's promises. On the cross, Jesus surrendered his soul into the hands of the Father, declaring in:
Luke 23:46: *"Father, into your hands I commend my spirit."* He trusted only one to keep it. No government had access to this passport. Our bodies will return, but our souls live forever with Christ in his kingdom; that's why it's so important to be part of this kingdom.

Everything he had planned to accomplish has come to pass. *Did he need to do it? No!* He rose from the dead and opened the doors of heaven's embassy, inviting every one of us to apply for our own passport.
As Paul declares in **Romans 10:9:**

"If you confess with your mouth the Lord Jesus and believe in your heart that God raised him from the dead, you will be saved." No complications, no fees, no middlemen, no long queues, no cancellations, and no travel visa refusals. Your salvation comes through verbal confession and sincere belief. Confessing with the mouth acknowledges Jesus as Lord, declaring his authority and divinity, and then you're a saved Christian. Acquiring basic biblical

knowledge to strengthen your faith is your passport to the kingdom of heaven.

Through this simple act of faith, you receive the greatest passport, one granting you access to the very presence of God.

"So then, you are no longer strangers and foreigners, but fellow citizens with God's people and members of His household." **Ephesians 2:19**

When we fully commit ourselves to living a life of faith, we are no longer strangers and outsiders, but part of God's family. Our identity shifts from uncertainty to belonging, and we can assert ourselves in the assurance of His promises. Before coming to faith in Christ, it's easy to feel lost or uncertain. Still, these words of encouragement are designed to awaken in you a curiosity that will open your heart and mind to the transformational knowledge of God's kingdom.

Every Christian is a curious person, paying attention to everything God has said so as not to miss out on His blessings. In His truth, there is no disappointment, because no one can deceive our Lord or anything. With certainty, we can trust that He will guide us wisely.

As believers, the Holy Spirit continually guides us, warning us at every step to ensure that we walk by God's will. God's throne is in heaven, and the earth is His footstool, emphasizing His sovereignty over all creation. Artificial structures or boundaries do not limit him; He is the Creator of all things, and His word is always accurate.

What He promises, He will surely fulfil, and His faithfulness is unshakeable. Knowing this, we can move forward with confidence, knowing that God will always do what He says He will do.

This spiritual heritage belonged to God's chosen people, and you and your family have inherited this citizenship through Christ's sacrifice on the cross, which fully paid for everyone with His life.

Now you and your family are part of something greater than what this world can offer. We are the people of God's kingdom, not as second-class members, but as full citizens, no longer under the control of any country and enjoying all the rights and privileges of God's family.

Paul said, "**Let every person be subject to the governing authorities. For there is no authority except from God, and God has instituted those that exist.**" **Romans 13:1**

Heavenly Citizenship

Our heavenly citizenship is a divine gift that defines who we are and where we truly belong. Unlike earthly nations with their borders, visa restrictions, and customs controls, God's kingdom knows no boundaries and welcomes all who place their faith in Christ.

Our identity is not based on our birthright, nationality, or achievements, but on God's grace and our acceptance of Jesus as Lord. Through him, we have the privilege of being called children of God, heirs to an eternal inheritance that cannot be taken away from us.

This citizenship comes with great responsibility. As ambassadors for Christ, we are called to show His love, grace, and truth in a world that does not recognize the creative power of the Lord. Although we live among the temporary systems of this world, our allegiance is to a higher authority, the King of kings.

We must walk in faith, defend justice, and share the good news, inviting others to enter the eternal kingdom. Our words, actions, and choices must be guided by the principles of heaven rather than those of this world.

Despite the trials we may face, our heavenly citizenship gives us unshakeable hope. Earthly problems are temporary, but our future in God's presence is eternal. Jesus Himself assured us in

John 14:2-3:

"*In my father's house are many mansions: if it were not so, I would have told you. I go to prepare a place for you. And if I go and prepare a place for you, I will come again, and receive you unto myself; that where I am, there ye may be also.*"

Only the Lord holds the key to your life safely in His hands, beyond the reach of any force. No one can take you away from him. "*I give them eternal life, and they shall never perish; no one can snatch them out of my hand. My Father, who has given them to me, is greater than all; no one can snatch them out of my Father's hand.*" **John 10:28-29**

Whatever happens in this life, your soul is safe? You will return home one day, but until then, enjoy every moment and cherish every moment spent here on earth with your family. Your heavenly identity grants you the privilege of standing before an ambassador, Jesus Christ, surrounded by angels in a divine community without equal.

We are a chosen people, a royal priesthood, a holy nation, a people belonging to God, that you may declare the praises of Him who called you out of darkness into His marvelous light. **(1 Peter 2:9)**

The teaching of the apostle Paul

Twelve disciples walked with Jesus, but one of them turned away, leaving eleven faithful witnesses to the power and divinity of the Lord. These men did not live easy lives; they lived transformed hearts. They saw Jesus' command disease, calm storms, forgive sins, heal a paralytic, heal a man with leprosy, give sight to two blind men, heal a mute demon-possessed man, and conquer death.

Their lives are undeniable proof of Christ's victory over all forms of struggle. The Lord gifts you with education, intelligence, and reasoning, tools designed to guide your moral compass and help you seek the more profound truths of Christ's mission.

The questions you carry in your heart for so long are the very ones that these eleven disciples asked Jesus directly for us. And through His Holy Spirit, they recorded all of the answers from Jesus for us.

This knowledge should lead you to a greater awareness: Jesus has authority over every aspect of life, over medicines, laws, wealth, and the very systems of this world's governments. Suppose you are seeking the truth, and I believe you do, by reading this book on heavenly citizenship, written by a simple servant, Gabriel Marcelin, who has an extraordinary spiritual message.

In that case, your soul is already drawn to the eternal kingdom where the Lord awaits to meet you. But to obtain your passport to the kingdom, you must turn your heart to God and confess with your mouth that Jesus is Lord. In doing so, you will receive the key to your new home, a new faith, and a new identity.

"Therefore, if anyone is in Christ, he is a new creation; old things have passed away; behold, all things have become new."

2 Corinthians 5:17. Whatever your difficulties, let the power of Christ, through the Holy Spirit, begin to transform your life from within.

Psalm 34:7

The angel of the LORD encampeth round about them that fear him, and delivereth them.

HEAVENLY CITIZEN

CHAPTER SEVENTEEN

*L*iving as Citizens of Heaven Paul's Teaching

on Faith and Perseverance

Paul's Teaching on Faith and Perseverance

Paul often wrote to believers that choosing to follow Christ would involve challenges. Godly living requires standing firm in the faith despite the trials of this world. That's why he taught Timothy to endure trials with wisdom and perseverance.

Like Timothy, we will face trials of faith, and we must stand firm, relying on God's strength to overcome them. Christian families are not exempt from difficulties, but through every trial, the Holy Spirit remains our guide, dwelling in our hearts to strengthen us with faith, wisdom, and confidence in God's promises.

***"Who can separate us from the love of Christ*?**

Tribulation, distress, persecution, famine, nakedness, danger, the sword? As it is written: *"For your sake, we face death all day long; we are regarded as sheep to be slaughtered. No, in all these things we are more than conquerors through Him who loved us"*.

Romans 8:35-37

Living as citizens of heaven requires an eternal perspective. Families must focus on the hope of eternity rather than the concerns of this world. Paul encouraged believers to turn their hearts toward the eternal rewards found in a relationship with God. He advises us to seek the things of heaven:

"If then you have been raised with Christ, seek the things above, where Christ is seated at the right hand of God. Set your minds on the things above, not on the things of the earth". **(Colossians 3:1-2).**

Our faith calls us to align our lives with the priorities of heaven, confident that God's promises are far greater than anything this world can offer. As followers of Christ, our priorities should be anchored in eternal realities rather than being consumed by the fleeting pleasures and pursuits of this world.

His own life was a testament to this truth; he did not chase temporary success or material possessions but pursued something far more precious: the eternal reward of knowing Christ.

This does not mean we must reject all earthly joys, but rather that our hearts should be focused on what is truly worthy: our relationship with God and the inheritance He has prepared for us.
Being a Christian does not mean passively waiting for blessings to fall into our laps without effort. God calls us to work diligently,

stewarding our time and resources wisely while keeping our eternal hope in view. Enjoying life on earth is a good and natural part of God's design, just as we will experience joy in heaven.

However, our ultimate fulfilment does not come from temporary pleasures but from the deeper riches found in Christ. Every success, every moment of joy, and every blessing should draw us closer to Him, shaping our hearts to long for His kingdom above all else.

Paul prays in **Ephesians 1:18** that "***the eyes of your heart may be enlightened so that you may know the hope to which He has called you, the riches of His glorious inheritance in His holy people***."

This is the perspective we must embrace, living with gratitude for today while keeping our hearts fixed on eternity. Our true inheritance is not in the things we accumulate or accomplish in this world but in the everlasting glory we will share with Christ. When we prioritize the eternal, we live with a sense of purpose that transcends temporary struggles and fleeting joys, knowing that our true treasure is found.

Peace be with you! The Kingdom Revealed, Living in the Reign of the Risen King. The invisible kingdom of God is not a concept or a dream; it is a spiritual reality, unveiled by the resurrection of Jesus Christ.

On the morning of the resurrection, Mary wept before the tomb. Looking inside, she saw two angels sitting where Jesus' body had been laid, one at the head and the other at the foot **(John 20:12),** the two heavenly messengers.

This moment was more than divine comfort for his confusion; it was a powerful glimpse of the glory of the Kingdom.

The Kingdom of God operates beyond the physical realm.

This is where death is defeated and the angels confirm the reality of salvation: for every Christian, ***Christ is risen***.

No one can judge, condemn, or kill the Messiah. He holds the kingship over all situations and all lives, and has become the only way to heaven. He was no longer in the tomb.

He had risen, and the Kingdom had begun to manifest itself in the life of every believer, both those living today and those who died in faith before his return.

Thanks to the resurrection power and eternal truth of Jesus Christ, citizenship in this Kingdom becomes a reality for all Christians of faith. Redemption and forgiveness of sins are no longer promises; his sacrifice fulfils them.

Forgiveness of sins: the supreme advantage

One of the most significant advantages of Christians enter the Kingdom of God through faith in Jesus Christ, which is the complete forgiveness of sins. Indeed, even Christians who are in churches preaching the gospel are apostates. When a Christian citizen places their trust in the risen Lord, their past is erased and they are made new.

Colossians 1:13-14 says: "*For he has delivered all Christians from the dominion of darkness, and has transported us into the kingdom of the Son he loves, in whom we have redemption, the forgiveness of sins.*"

This means we no longer live-in guilt, condemnation, or shame. Jesus' blood has blotted out all sins before God, bringing peace where there was once separation and hostility, with new life and a new beginning.

As citizens of His Kingdom, we recognize that Jesus is the ultimate ambassador who has granted every believer a heavenly passport. Thanks to him, our true home is not in this world, but with him.

As Jesus answered Pilate, "*My kingdom is not of this world*"
(John 18:36).

The Jewish leaders thought that their power over Jesus had ended at the cross. But the King remained in the city for another forty days and forty nights after his first return to teach us about his kingdom. He revealed himself and prepared the disciples for the coming of the Holy Spirit. He explained to them that they would not be abandoned.

He said, "*But the Comforter, the Holy Spirit, whom the Father will send in my name, will teach you all things and remind you of everything I have said to you (John 14:26).*

But you will receive power when the Holy Spirit comes upon you, and you will be my witnesses in Jerusalem... and to the ends of the earth."

He taught them the Kingdom of God, not in theory, but as the resurrected, living, and glorified King.

Jesus entered the room where the disciples had gathered to share their thoughts on his words, saying that he would rise again after three days and that no one had ever done such a thing before. The eleven disciples were gathered when the great Master appeared before them to say: **'Peace be with you.'**
He began to teach them the excellent task that lay ahead of them and the price they would have to pay; he wanted them to fully understand that they had been chosen precisely for this reason. He revealed his resurrected body to them, showing them his hands and his side, not only as proof of life but also as a declaration of his reign.

The Kingdom of God shattered their fear, giving them peace and replacing despair with joy. And to bear witness to this, they would not only carry their cross and die to spread the news, but through their sacrifice, all who believe in this truth: "**yes**," you and I, and yes, you too, will inherit a place in His kingdom.

Jesus did not just bring a message; he was the message. The living proof, the incarnation of divine love, authority, and eternal life. At that moment, he sealed the heavens on the passport of every believer, a mark of love and identity for each worshiper.

All our worship and praise will not be in vain today and for eternity. When his mission on earth was accomplished, ***the King ascended to heaven from the Mount of Olives*** (Acts 1:9-12):

The breath of the Holy Spirit

After he had said this, he was taken up before their very eyes, and a cloud hid him from their sight. *They were looking intently up into the sky as he was going, when suddenly two men dressed in white stood beside them. 'Men of Galilee,' they said, 'why do you stand here looking into the sky?'*

This Jesus, who has been taken up to heaven from among you, will come in the same way as you saw him going to heaven. He ascended to heaven and sat at the right hand of God, leaving behind a legacy of hope, power, and the promise of his return for believers.

When Jesus breathed on His disciples and said, "*Receive the Holy Spirit*" **(John 20:21-23),** He equipped them to carry the message of the Kingdom to you and your family. Jesus said to them again, "*Peace be with you! As the father has sent me, I also send you*". He told them that if they forgive anyone's sins, they will be forgiven; but if they do not forgive others, neither will they be forgiven. He told them that this would be a sacred mission.

The disciples were transformed from faithful servants into ambassadors of the Kingdom. The Lord said to them:
"And behold, I am with you all the days, until the end of the world."

They were entrusted with the ministry of forgiveness, reconciliation, healing, and spiritual authority. The presence of the Holy Spirit is the mark of the Kingdom in the life of a believer, something that every Christian will experience at some point, empowering them not only to live righteously but also to bring the influence of heaven into a broken world.

This divine breath was not only for them; it was for all of us today, in the name of Jesus. The Holy Spirit is another profound blessing that empowers, teaches, comforts, and heals all Christians who believe. Jesus said, "*Receive the Holy Spirit.*" He also told them, "***You will receive power when the Holy Spirit comes upon you***" **(Acts 1:8).**

This Spirit enables Kingdom citizens to overcome anything the world can throw at them, to walk in truth, and to grow in Christlikeness. The Holy Spirit is the very presence of God dwelling within us, a full payment of glory here in each of us, to help all Christians make the right decisions and keep the right company **(Ephesians 1:13-14).**

Through Him, we have divine access to God's wisdom, peace, and supernatural strength in all circumstances.

The peace, purpose, and joy of the Christian family is believing in Jesus, who brings us into a life of lasting peace, divine purpose, and true happiness. Jesus said: "*Peace I leave with you, my peace I give unto you: not as the world giveth, give I unto you. Let not your heart be troubled, neither let it be afraid.*" **(John 14:27).**

Unlike the peace of the world, this peace is founded on God's sovereignty. It's a calm that holds even in storms; have you ever lost your peace in a situation beyond your control? I can't count the number of times the Lord has had to save me. Please share your story in the comments.

Paul's ministry was characterized by relentless suffering, both physical and emotional, as he remained steadfast in proclaiming the Gospel of Jesus Christ. He faced extraordinary trials for the sake of Christ: he was flogged, stoned, imprisoned, and continually lived under the shadow of death.

Can we truly comprehend the harsh realities of the ancient law of the almighty God?

How would they treat you to say the name of Jesus, let alone to write all of these books about heavenly citizenship for Christians? If those in authority opposed a leader's message, imagine how far they would go to silence Paul. What would they do to you?

He recounts in **2 Corinthians 11:24-25**: *"Five times I received from the Jews the forty lashes less one. Three times I was beaten with rods, once I was stoned, three times I was shipwrecked, I spent a day and a night in the deep."*

These are not isolated events but a life marked by continuous persecution. Yet, Paul never backed down. His commitment to the Gospel was rooted in the supernatural origin of his calling. In **Galatians 1:11-12**, Paul clearly states that the message he preached did not come from any human source or was not taught by a person. He boldly says:

"I want you to know, brothers and sisters, that the gospel I preached is not of human origin. I did not receive it from any man, nor was I taught it; I received it by revelation from Jesus Christ."

This divine revelation equipped Paul with both the authority and the resilience to endure unimaginable hardships. Just before his death, Paul was executed by beheading in Rome during the reign of **Emperor Nero (Nero Claudius Caesar Augustus Germanicus).** He was a ruler whose governance grew increasingly violent and unstable. Historical accounts suggest Nero orchestrated the deaths of his mother, Agrippina, and his wife, Octavia, among many others.

For the very Gospel you're reading about in this book, Paul sacrificed his life. In his final days, he wrote with powerful clarity and conviction:

"For I am already being poured out as a drink offering, and the time of my departure has come. I have fought the good fight, I have finished the race, I have kept the faith." **(2 Timothy 4:6-7)**. A new way of life with eternal security. When someone enters the Christian faith and becomes part of the Kingdom, they experience a transformed lifestyle and an infinite promise. **Romans 12:2** Paul said:

*"**Do not be conformed to this world, but be transformed by the renewing of your mind.**"*

Living in the Kingdom means learning heavenly values from the Bible: love, humility, truth, justice, and mercy. But it's not just about the present, it's also about the future. Jesus promised:

*"**My Father's house has many rooms... I am going there to prepare a place for you**"* (John 14:2-3).

Eternal life is not a vague hope; it's a secure home. **1 Peter 1:4** assures us that believers have "an inheritance that cannot perish, spoil, or fade. This inheritance is kept for you in heaven. No one can steal it, and nothing can destroy it.

Before ascending to heaven, Jesus gave what is known today as the Great Commission: 'All authority has been given to me in heaven and on earth.' *Go therefore and make disciples of all nations.* **(Matthew 28:18-19).**

The King delegated the work of the Kingdom to his people. Discipleship isn't optional-it's Kingdom strategy. By teaching, baptizing, and obeying Jesus' commands, we don't just grow churches, we grow the Kingdom on earth. Every believer becomes a living temple, bearing the divine presence within them. God's reign is not extended by military conquest, but by love, service, and the proclamation of evangelical truth, echoing the character of the risen Christ.

The authority to manifest Heaven on earth is given to every believer who refuses to wait for the Kingdom's arrival passively. As Jesus declared, **"As the Father has sent me, so I am sending you,"** we are his representatives, ambassadors of Heaven. He was commissioned to embody his Kingdom through both word and action.

When we pray, **"Your kingdom come, your will be done on earth as it is in heaven,"** we do not speak idle hopes, but declare our mission.

As citizens of God's Kingdom, we are carriers of healing, justice, grace, and truth.

In a world of brokenness and darkness, we shine as beacons of hope, showing love through our actions and speaking words that give life. Christ is risen and reigning even now. Until he returns in glory, we are called to reflect his light and expand his rule here on earth.

Jesus' instruction: Powers for mission before his ascension, on one occasion, while he was eating with them, he gave them this command: *"Do not leave Jerusalem, but wait for the gift my father promised, which you have heard me speak about.* ⁵ *For John baptized with water, but in a few days, you will be baptized with the Holy Spirit."* **(Acts 1:4-5).**

He knew that his disciples would need the divine presence to fulfil their heavenly mission. The Kingdom could not advance solely through human effort. "He said, **'You will receive power, and you will be my witnesses**" **(Acts 1:8).**

This promise was given not only to the apostles but also to all believers today. The Holy Spirit is the driving force behind the Kingdom movement. Thanks to Him, we speak with boldness, love with conviction, and live with purpose. As citizens of heaven yet still living on earth, we walk empowered by the Spirit, proclaiming the message of our risen King until He returns to reign forever.

King Jesus, the King of kings, was truly alive. After his resurrection, the King remained in town for 40 days to provide irrefutable proof that he had physically risen from the dead. **Acts 1:3** says:

"After his suffering, he showed himself to them and gave many convincing proofs that he was alive. He appeared to them over forty days and spoke about the kingdom of God."

These appearances dispelled doubts, strengthened faith, and confirmed that Jesus had truly conquered death. **John 6:38***"For I have come down from heaven, not to do my own will, but the will of him who sent me."* **John 3:13***"No one has ascended into heaven except he who descended from heaven, the Son of Man."*

and live with purpose. As citizens of heaven yet still living on earth, we walk empowered by the Spirit, proclaiming the message of our risen King until He returns to reign forever.

King Jesus, the King of kings, was truly alive. After his resurrection, the King remained in town for 40 days to provide irrefutable proof that he had physically risen from the dead. **Acts 1:3** says:

"After his suffering, he showed himself to them and gave many convincing proofs that he was alive. He appeared to them over forty days and spoke about the kingdom of God."

These appearances dispelled doubts, strengthened faith, and confirmed that Jesus had truly conquered death. **John 6:38**"*For I have come down from heaven, not to do my own will, but the will of him who sent me.*" **John 3:13**"*No one has ascended into heaven except he who descended from heaven, the Son of Man.*"

The teacher, who had never attended school, prepared his disciples for their exams over the course of forty days. He then continued to teach them about the kingdom of God. He opened their minds to understand the Scriptures **(Luke 24:45),** helping them see how the law, the prophets, and the psalms all pointed to him.

He gave them their mission, known as the Great Commission, and told them about the coming of the Holy Spirit, who would empower them to spread the word to all nations. It was a time of spiritual training and preparation that transformed the disciples from uncertain followers into bold witnesses and ambassadors of heaven. Jesus used this time to lay the spiritual foundations of the early Church. He comforted and restored those who had failed, each one of us, especially Peter, and united his disciples around a common mission.

His presence after his resurrection gave the disciples courage and showed them that he was faithful to his word. Although they had dispersed when he was arrested, they were now gathered around a common purpose and goals. Jesus was preparing them to become the leaders of a global movement that would later become the Gospel, intended to save all Christians.

After his ascension, Jesus was exalted as king and ruler over all creation. **Philippians 2:9-11** states,

"*God exalted him to the highest place and gave him the name that is above every name.*" From heaven, he intercedes for us **(Romans 8:34)** and prepares a place for his people to live as citizens of his Kingdom while remaining on earth. Today, as his disciples, we live with a heavenly perspective. Jesus answers a question about the coming of God's Kingdom by saying, "People won't know, *'He's here! Or he's there! Because the Kingdom of God is among you.*"

Heavenly Father,

Our Father who art in heaven, hallowed be thy name. Thy kingdom come; thy will be done on earth as it is in heaven. I lift all Christians throughout the world, for they are yours, called by your name, redeemed by your mercy, and by your blood shed on the cross. Father, protect all those who follow Christ. Protect them by the power of your name.

Sanctify us by your truth, for your Word is truth. As we go out into the world to proclaim your Word, keep us separate from the world for your purpose, clothed in righteousness, filled with grace, so that we may shine your light, bear witness to your love, and reveal your glory in a world thirsting for hope, in the sacred name of Jesus, **Amen.**

Psalm 37:4

Delight thyself also in the LORD; and he shall give thee the desires of thine heart.

HEAVENLY CITIZEN

CHAPTER THIRTEEN

The LORD is my shepherd; I shall not want.

When I walk through the valley of the shadow of death, I will fear no evil: for thou art with me. (Psalm 23)

The Lord Is Our Shepherd

Divine Protection from the King of Kings in the Wilderness. When facing life's trials and difficulties, one truth remains certain: our faith should remain firm. God consistently governs every Christian's life. His protection is steadfast, even when discouragement causes you to doubt your dreams and purpose here on Earth.

When these challenging moments come your way, remember who you are and, more importantly, who holds your life in His hands. You don't need to explain your struggles to anyone or seek approval from the world. Our most outstanding advocate is alive, Jesus Christ, who stands as your defender. He is your shield, fortress, and refuge, providing unwavering protection to those who trust in Him.

The foundation of God's defense lies in His sovereignty. As Christians, we must accept the fundamental truth that God's power is unlimited and his authority extends over all creation. He is subject to no limits and bound by no circumstances. By trusting in His sovereignty to abandon our fears and anxieties, we are convinced that nothing happens outside His sight. Even in our weakest moments, God's strength sustains us, and his plans for our lives stand steadfast.

Psalm 91 is a powerful recitation of Moses crying out to God for the protection of his people. Those who abide in the secret place of the Most-High shall rest in the shadow of the Almighty. I will say of the Lord. 'He is my refuge and my fortress, my God, in whom I trust. He will deliver you from the snare of the deceiver and the peril of the pestilence.

He will cover you with his feathers, and under his wings you will find refuge; his faithfulness will be your shield and rampart. This psalm assures us that when we place our trust in God, he becomes our refuge.

His presence shields us from harm; His truth guards us from deception, and His love keeps us firmly grounded, steady through every storm. No matter the trials we face, God remains our steadfast protector. His unwavering faithfulness watches over our lives and families, both individually and personally.

When we hold fast to our faith amid adversity, Paul reminds us to walk with the quiet confidence that God will act on our behalf.

As the Lord declares in **Isaiah 54:17**:

"No weapon formed against you shall prosper, and every tongue that rises against you in judgment you shall condemn."

This promise reminds us that although the enemy may plot against us. God's defense is impenetrable; His protection and mighty hands are always near: *"The Spirit of the Lord will rest upon him, the Spirit of wisdom and understanding, the Spirit of counsel and strength, the Spirit of knowledge and of the fear of the Lord"* **(Isaiah 11:2).**

The Book of the **King, chapter 20**: The word of the Lord came to Isaiah with these messages: Go back and tell Hezekiah, leader of my people, "Thus says the Lord, the God of the earth:" Thus says the Lord, the God of David your father: I have heard your prayer, I have seen your tears. I have listened to your prayer; I have seen your tears. Behold, I will heal you. On the third day, you shall go up to the house of the Lord.

How many times has the Lord revealed Himself to us, only for us to forget Him, turn our backs on Him, and wait for us as a father should, to take us back into His loving arms?

Isaiah 30:18 *"Yet the Lord desires to show you mercy, and he will rise to show you mercy; for the Lord is a righteous God. Blessed is all who wait for him."*

2 Kings 20:6 *"I will add 15 years to your life, and I will deliver you and this city from the hand of God. I will rescue you and this city from the king of Assyria; I will defend this city for my own sake and for the sake of my servant David."*

What do you think of these words: The Lord said, "I will wait for you, I will defend you, I will show you mercy, I will have compassion on you, I will deliver you, I will not judge you, and because all the judges of the world, do you know what I will do: I will add 15 more years to your life after healing you, to show death that I am the Lord?

These are not ordinary words, as you will surely agree. How many of these words has the Lord already spoken to you, or spoken on your behalf? As you read this book, has there been a moment in your life when the Lord has revealed Himself to you? From the smallest to the most remarkable miracles, the Lord has worked in your own life!

God said to Moses, *"When people ask you who did this? When your family asks, 'What happened to you?' When a colleague asks you what's going on to get you so excited*? When it seems like everything's going wrong, all the bad news, all the illnesses, all the personal and family problems. I want you to remember these words Moses spoke:

He said, "*You shall say to the children of Israel,* **I AM** *he who sent words to you*" **(Exodus, chapter 3, 14).**

Hezekiah's thoughts at that moment mirror the feelings many of us have today. Faced with an unexpected incurable illness, he believed there was no hope left and that his world was falling apart. Yet, it was precisely during this moment of despair that the prophet Isaiah arrived with good news from the Lord, not from the best doctors or anyone else on earth, but from the King of kings himself. King Hezekiah was to return to the temple on the third day. One could almost hear the anguish in Hezekiah's voice, the weight of his suffering having erased all his royal qualities and principles.

Have you ever found yourself in a place where discouragement made you feel as though you had lost control, where hope seemed distant or out of reach?

The community of believers has had many encounters with the Lord. Our stories are too long to tell, and our blessings too numerous to count. The Christian community is where we can share even the smallest blessings and describe how God has revealed Himself to each of us. When God told Isaiah, "Take a lump of figs," and he applied the figs to the ulcer, the wound was healed; not in a few days, not the next day, but suddenly and completely.

The king was suffering from a painful infection, probably deep folliculitis, a condition that affects the hair follicles in areas such as the groin, armpits, or neck. This infection caused intense discomfort and plunged Hezekiah into a state of distress.

Hezekiah turned to God's prophet Isaiah and asked him, "What will be the sign that I will go up to the house of the Lord on the third day to ask Him to heal me?" This moment was a profound expression of faith, as Hezekiah placed his trust in God's healing power. He understood that even in the face of physical pain and uncertainty, faith in God's ability to heal and deliver could lead to transformative results.

The Christian community is that sacred place where we come together to worship God and express gratitude, even for the smallest blessings we receive. It is here that we can openly share how God has revealed Himself in our lives, often in unexpected ways.

These personal experiences strengthen our faith and bring us together, because they all reveal the power of divine love and God's supernatural help in our lives.

A powerful example of this truth appears in the story of King Hezekiah, when the Lord instructed the prophet Isaiah to "take a lump of figs" and apply it to the king's ulcer. Miraculously, the king's ulcer was healed. This seemingly simple act carried deep meaning. The figs had been there all along, but they remained ineffective... until the Lord infused them with His healing power.

Isaiah responded to Hezekiah's request for a sign by saying:

"This is the sign you will receive from the Lord: The Lord will do what he has said: Behold, I will turn back the shadow of the degrees that was lowered in the sundial of Ahaz by ten degrees.' And the sun returned ten degrees backward, by which it had descended.

This unique sign was not only a demonstration of God's power, but also an invitation for us to participate in his plans. God has designed a unique relationship with each of us, enabling every Christian to participate actively in the blessings He offers. God said to Paul that His grace is sufficient for him and his abundance is unconditional. However, he often calls us to take steps of faith, perseverance, and trust that shape our character and strengthen our bond with him **(Isaiah 38:8).**

Paul discusses this in his letter to the Hebrews, stating, "**Faith is the assurance of things hoped for, the conviction of things not seen**." By involving us in the process, God deepens our faith and helps us see the beauty of His timing. Our blessings are not just gifts to receive, but part of a journey where our obedience, actions, and hearts align with His perfect will. He invites us to participate in fulfilling His divine plan for our lives. This partnership with God makes blessings even more meaningful, as they are not only for our benefit but also part of a larger story.

Hezekiah's request for the shadow to move backward instead of forward highlights a profound truth about human nature; we often find it hard to believe in miracles when they seem too easy. Jesus doesn't need to physically touch, appear in bright light, or show a fiery sign to demonstrate His power; His word alone suffices.

If you believe, you can receive your miracle because faith is the key that opens His blessings. Throughout the Gospels, numerous examples demonstrate that people were healed simply by believing, as seen in the case of the centurion, who said, "**Lord, just say the word, and my servant will be healed**" **(Matthew 8:8).**
When confronted with something extraordinary, we might think it has to be difficult to be real. But God often defies these false expectations, working in ways that seem impossible to us. His power isn't limited by human logic, nor does He need to struggle to do His will.

Again and again, He shows that our role is not to question but to trust. When we have faith, He moves in ways beyond our understanding, proving that what seems impossible for humans is effortless for Him.
One of the most powerful examples of God's intervention is the story of Daniel in the lion's den. Despite the threat of death, Daniel remained steadfast in his devotion to God, refusing to bow to the decrees of an earthly king.

His punishment, a night in a den of deadly lions, was meant to demonstrate the king's dominance, but it only revealed God's supreme authority. Instead of becoming prey, Daniel experienced divine protection as God sent an angel to shut the lions' mouths. His rescue was not due to his strength but to God's faithfulness. Just as He did for Daniel, God defends those who stay faithful to Him, proving that no earthly power can stand against His will.

The king knew that Daniel was innocent, that he had not broken any laws, except for praying to his God. However, the king had a reputation to uphold and a decree to enforce, to ensure that no one would dare pray in the name of the Lord. Yet God not only preserved Daniel's life but also sent divine intervention, causing the lions' mouths to be closed.
This miraculous act made it clear that Daniel was under God's protection, a protection like no other. No matter how strong the opposition, when God's hand is on his servant, no weapon formed

against him can prevail. Although we face struggles, battles, and opposition, the ultimate victory belongs to God.

He is not a passive observer of our challenges; he is a mighty warrior actively fighting on behalf of all Christians. Paul is asking the faithful community to hang on. If God is for us, who can stand against us?

God's defense is not limited to the physical or emotional; it also encompasses the spiritual. He provides the strength to endure and the faith to overcome. Even when the odds seem insurmountable, we can count on Him to fight for us.

The apostle Paul, in 2 Timothy 4:17:

Said this on his own experience of God's protection: «But the Lord stood by me and strengthened me, so that through me the message might be fully proclaimed and all the Gentiles might hear it. «

Despite imprisonment, opposition, and hardship, Paul found that in every circumstance, God remained by his side, strengthening him to fulfil his mission. Defense is available to every family today. No matter the circumstances, we can be confident that God is not playing politics with our lives; he offers to protect all who believe in him. However, this knowledge should also inspire a response of trust and faith.

We are to walk in the assurance of faith, the kind described in **Hebrews 11**: "*Faith is the substance of things hoped for, the evidence of things not seen*." We can trust that God will act in His perfect timing for our family.

Divine Protection from the King of Kings in the Wilderness

Every believer knows the reality of the wilderness. It is the place of testing, the season of uncertainty, the stretch of road where resources seem scarce and the future unclear. Yet it is also the place were God's faithfulness shines most brightly. The wilderness is not meant to destroy you; it is intended to reveal the strength of the King who walks beside you.

When you find yourself in the wilderness, remember this unshakable truth: your protection does not rest on your own ability or the shifting circumstances around you. **Your defense lies in the**

sovereignty of God. He who rules the heavens and the earth holds your life securely in His hands. The trials you face are not random; they are under His watchful authority. Nothing touches you that He has not already measured, and nothing formed against you can prevail.

The Promise of Protection

Scripture declares with power: *"No weapon that is formed against thee shall prosper; and every tongue that shall rise against thee in judgment thou shalt condemn. This is the heritage of the servants of the LORD, and their righteousness is of me, saith the LORD."* **(Isaiah 54:17).**

This is not a distant hope but a living promise. The weapons may be formed, but they will not succeed. Words of slander may rise, but they will fall under God's judgment. Accusations may be spoken, but the verdict of heaven is clear: you are defended by the King of Kings.

God Himself says, *"***I will defend you. I will show you mercy***."* Mercy is not weakness; it is the strength of love shielding you from the full weight of what you deserve. Mercy is God's fortress around His children, His way of declaring that nothing will separate you from His care.

Walking in the Assurance of Faith

Because of this promise, we are called to walk in the assurance of faith. Faith does not demand proof; faith trusts the character of God. We do not need to see to believe. Like Abraham, who *"did not waver in unbelief but grew strong in faith, giving glory to God"* (Romans 4:20), we are called to take God at His word, even when our eyes cannot see the evidence.

To trust the Lord with your life is to anchor yourself in His sovereignty. It is to confess with confidence that the worldview around you no longer shapes you. You belong to Him. You are not defined by fear, culture, or the shifting opinions of society. You are determined by the covenant love of the King who purchased you with His own blood.

The Wilderness as a Place of Encounter

The wilderness is not merely a place of scarcity; it is a place of encounter. Israel wandered in the desert for forty years, but their story was not one of abandonment; it was one of provision. Manna fell from heaven, water flowed from the rock, and the presence of God went with them in the pillar of cloud and fire.

In your wilderness, you will also find provision. God may not give you everything you desire, but He will always give you what you need. He may not remove every hardship, but He will never withdraw His presence. His protection is not always about removing the storm but about shielding you within it.

Confession matters. When you declare with your mouth that you belong to Christ, you are renouncing the world's claim upon your life. You are affirming that you are a citizen of a higher Kingdom, under the rule and care of the King of Kings.

This confession does more than mark your faith; it secures your perspective. You no longer see life as the world sees it: fragile, hopeless, uncertain. You see life as God declares it, protected, purposeful, and eternal. The wilderness is not your grave; it is your training ground. The dangers around you are not your destiny; they are the backdrop against which God's glory is revealed.

Therefore, rise each day with this confidence: you are covered by the shield of the Almighty. No weapon will prosper. No accusation will prevail. No wilderness will overcome you. God's mercy surrounds you; His sovereignty defends you, and His faithfulness sustains you.

2 Thessalonians 3:3:

"The LORD is faithful, who shall establish you, and keep you from evil."

You belong to Him. You are not of the world; you are His child, His servant, His heir. And because you belong to Him, you can rest in the certainty that the King of Kings Himself is your protector.

Psalm 40:1

I waited patiently for the LORD; and he inclined unto me, and heard my cry.

HEAVENLY CITIZEN

CHAPTER NINETEEN

"*I* AM THAT I AM"

Encountering the Eternal God: His Glory, His Protection, and His Final Revelation in Christ.

Exodus 33:11:
The Lord spoke to Moses face-to-face, as one speaks to a friend.

In a conversation with Moses in **Exodus 3:14**, God gave him his name: **"I AM THAT I AM,"** in response to Moses' question about His identity.

This profound statement provides deep insight into the nature of God. His existence is eternal, His sovereignty is unquestioned, and He is self-sufficient.

Moses' question opens a window for us to understand God better, highlighting His divine traits and power. It shows that He sought human relationships and guidance. His personal presence entered into His people's defense system and laws.

Moses stands as a central prophet for Jews, Christians, and Muslims, known as the one through whom God revealed His law and led His people. **Traditionally seen as the author of the first five books of the Bible, the Torah or Pentateuch**, Moses was the first prophet chosen to deliver God's message to Israel.

On Mount Sinai, God gave him the Ten Commandments, making him the mediator of the covenant and initiating Israel's sacred journey under God's law.

Sinai represents the starting point of covenant life, where God's will be given in written form. In contrast, Mount Nebo marks the end of Moses' earthly pilgrimage, where he was shown a vision of the Promised Land, but was not allowed to enter. Therefore, Sinai became the mountain of law given, while Nebo became the mountain of promise revealed, both a reminder of God's faithfulness and the cost of disobedience.

In **Exodus 33:18-20**, Moses makes a bold request, asking God to reveal His glory to him. God responds, *"I will cause all my goodness to pass in front of you, and I will proclaim my name, the Lord, in your presence. I will have mercy on whom I will have mercy, and I will have compassion on whom I will have compassion. But you cannot see my face, for no one may see me and live."*

In this encounter, God is not only speaking to Moses but also imparting profound truths that deepen our understanding of His sovereignty and mercy. This passage highlights that God's glory surpasses human comprehension, and His actions are determined solely by His divine will.

We come to see that God's nature is magnificently holy, merciful, and compassionate; yet his full glory exists beyond our ability to grasp or fully behold. Through this dialogue, we are reminded of the infinite depth of God's character, far greater than what we can perceive or understand. After sin, we can no longer see the presence of the Lord's glory and live.

In Exodus 33:20, God says to Moses: *"But you cannot see my face, for no one can see me and live."*

This statement reveals God's overwhelming holiness and majesty. His divine essence is so pure and majestic that the complete revelation of His glory would be too much for any human being to bear. This encounter highlights the significant disparity between God's infinite nature and his immortal existence in relation to humanity.

While God reveals aspects of His goodness and mercy, His full glory remains veiled, preventing us from being consumed by its overwhelming splendor.

His presence is so powerful, and yet, in his mercy, he chooses to reveal himself in a way we can bear. Just as he protected Moses by covering him with his hand as his glory passed by, God also protects us from what we're not yet ready to see. This confirms to us that while the enemy may plot against our families, God's defense is impenetrable. His protection surrounds us, and His blessings will continue to follow us for many generations to come. Even when opposition arises, God turns adversity into promotion, lifting us higher when we stand firm in faith.

Our spiritual battles

As we trust in God's protection and defense, we are called to strengthen our faith and pray for one another. Spiritual battles are won through unwavering trust in God, constant prayer, and obedience to His word.

Just as Moses sought God's presence and guidance, we too must seek him daily. Our confidence must be based on the certainty that God is our refuge and stronghold, that he protects us from evil and leads us according to his perfect will. No stratagem of the enemy can stand against the power of God's protection over his people.

The Bible says that God is eternal, not bound by the constraints of the past, present, or future. In **Revelation 1:8**, he declares, "*I am Alpha and Omega*", meaning that he encompasses all time and eternity. His divine nature transcends our limits, and His plans are perfect, unfolding according to His divine timetable.

When we trust in God's eternal nature and power, we find peace, knowing that He is always in control, orchestrating every detail of our lives for His glory and our good. God has your back.

Have you ever withdrawn from the noise and distractions of the world and found comfort in the realm of prayer with God?

Have you felt his presence envelop you, as if he were speaking directly to your heart, in words no one else can hear?

It's in these sacred encounters that the depth of God's intimacy is revealed, that the soul is nourished, and His voice resonates with peace, wisdom, and love. In these moments, the world fades away, your soul receives healing, and all that remains is the deep connection between you and your Creator.

The billion-dollar Question?

Every believer has millions of questions about how to pray and how to receive immediate answers from the Lord. Asking why, how, and when to pray is a natural part of the Christian journey.

You may be asking yourself similar questions, looking for the key to unlocking God's answers in your life.

However, in our desire for immediate answers, it's easy to forget that prayer isn't just about asking for quick results, but also about building a relationship with God. In this regard, he is the father. True prayer requires patience, sincerity, and a deep connection with God, allowing His divine plan to unfold within you.

In today's world, worshiping God has become an emotional experience, especially in churches or on TV, but it can sometimes lack the actual spiritual depth it should have. Everywhere, there are self-proclaimed prophets and apostles, all claiming to speak for God or to have received messages from God on your behalf.

However, Paul says in **1 John 4:1**: **"Dear friends, do not put faith in every spirit, but test the spirits to see whether they are from God, for many false prophets have gone out into the world."** The Bible warns all Christians to be discerning, as many who claim to represent God can lead us astray. Their end will be consistent with their actions; most of them will meet God himself, but it is our responsibility to test their words against the truth of Scripture and the guidance of the Holy Spirit.

Jesus is considered the last prophet, and God has sent no other prophet since his arrival. The Bible explains the completion of God's revelation through Jesus, the ultimate and final messenger.

In Revelation 22:18-19, it is made clear that no one is to add to or subtract from the prophetic message that has been delivered, indicating that the revelation of God's will was completed with the blood of him who will soon return.

The warning in these verses highlights the seriousness of modifying or adding to God's Word, as doing so could lead to serious consequences, and indicates that nothing else should be revealed. As you read this book, consider whether anyone claims to be a prophet or apostle.

No additional revelation or prophecy is required or permitted beyond what has already been revealed in the Scriptures. It warns against altering or extending God's message. As you read this book, consider whether anyone today identifies themselves as a prophet or an apostle.

Many people in various religious groups use these titles. Still, it's essential to ask whether their messages align with the complete and final revelation of God's Word through Jesus Christ and the apostles in the New Testament.

Moreover, at the Transfiguration, Jesus' appearance undergoes a radical transformation. His face shines like the sun, and his clothes become dazzling white, symbolizing his divine nature. The heavens open, the Holy Spirit descends upon him in the form of a dove, and a voice rises from the cloud to declare:

"***This is my beloved Son, in whom I am well pleased: listen to him***! (Matthew 17:5)

*God's divine affirmation places Jesus at the center of his revelation to over **2.9 billion faithful Christians and believers worldwide today**.*

At this moment, God commands us to listen to Jesus, signifying that He is the ultimate source of truth and authority. This reinforces the conviction that, after Jesus, there is no need for another prophet or revelation, since He fulfils and completes God's plan for all who accept this knowledge.

Jesus often withdrew from the crowds to pray alone, seeking solitude to connect deeply with His Father. In **Matthew 14:23**, we read that after feeding the five thousand, Jesus went up on a mountainside by Himself to pray. This moment of solitude was a need for spiritual renewal and communion with God, demonstrating that even the Son of God took time away from the crowds to be alone in prayer.

Jesus gave an example to find quiet moments in our lives to strengthen our relationship with God, away from the distractions of the world.

Moses often sought solitude to connect with God, especially during crucial moments. In **Exodus 34:28**, Moses went alone to Mount Sinai to receive God's commandments, spending forty days and nights in the presence of God.

This solitude was not only a time to receive divine guidance but also to strengthen his relationship with the Lord. Throughout his leadership, Moses regularly spent extended periods in solitude, showing how quiet reflection can bring clarity, guidance, and renewal during complex tasks.

Elijah, after his victory over the prophets of Baal in **1 Kings 19:9**, fled to a cave in the wilderness, where he met with God in solitude. In the stillness, God spoke to him not in the mighty wind, earthquake, or fire, but in a gentle whisper.

Elijah's time alone with God provided him with the strength and encouragement he needed during a period of despair. This demonstrates the power of praying alone in solitude, in moments of emotional and spiritual struggle, where God can speak to our hearts in the quietest of places and guide us toward victory.

King David, known for his intimate relationship with God, often withdrew to pray in solitude. In **Psalm 63:1**, he expresses his deep longing for God in a desolate place, saying:

"O God, you are my God, earnestly I seek you; I thirst for you, my whole being longs for you, in a dry and parched land where there is no water."

David's psalms reveal his consistent practice of seeking God in silence and solitude, reflecting a heart that yearns for God's presence. Similarly, **Daniel** was known for his consistent practice of praying alone.

In **Daniel 6:10**, he prayed three times a day in his room, continuing his practice despite the threat of persecution.

The apostle Paul also sought moments of solitude for prayer, as seen in **Acts 9:11**, where, after his conversion, he spent time alone in prayer. He frequently writes in his letters about praying for others in solitude, underscoring the importance of interceding for others in a private, intimate setting with God.

The Shepherd in the Valley

Psalm 23:4:
"Even though I walk through the valley of the shadow of death every day, I will fear no evil, for You are with me"

This verse speaks to the unavoidable reality of life that Christians face daily in the valleys, those dark, painful seasons of sorrow, loss, or confusion. But what transforms these valleys is not the absence of hardship, but the presence of the Shepherd.

God doesn't promise we will never walk-through trials; He promises that we will never walk through them alone. In these moments, His nearness becomes more than a concept; it becomes an anchor. The valley, though intimidating, is not a dead end. It's a passage, and our Shepherd is walking every step of the way beside us.

David's mention of the "rod and staff" further reinforces this image of God's care. These are not just tools of punishment, but also tools of protection and guidance. The rod is used to ward off predators and keep the sheep safe, while the staff gently guides and retrieves those that have wandered away.

In the valley, where shadows are long and threats seem close, these instruments remind us of God's constant watchfulness and gentle correction. The presence of the Shepherd is active, not passive; it is active, defending us, guiding us, and keeping us nearby. Even when the path isn't clear, we can trust the One who holds us securely.

Perhaps the most powerful truth in this verse is the assurance that our fears do not have the final word.

The enemy loves to whisper lies in the valley: "***You're alone***," "***You've failed***," "***There's no hope.***"

But the truth of Jesus' blood drowns out every lie: ***You are not alone. You are not forgotten. You are not without purpose.***

The valley is not the destination; it's a part of the journey that leads us closer to the heart of God. Every trial, every tear, every moment is filtered through the hands of a sovereign, loving Father who works all things together for the good of those who love Him. So, we walk on, not in fear, but in faith, because He is with us.

We are protected by the mighty hand of God.

He will cover you with His feathers, and under His wings you will find refuge; His faithfulness will be your shield and rampart." **Psalm 91:4**

There's a shift that happens when you begin to see God not only as a Shepherd but also as **a King**. Not just a caretaker, but **a ruler with absolute authority** over your life, He is sovereign over every storm, every struggle, and every spiritual battle in your life.

In the ancient world, kings defended their people with fierce determination. The honor of a king was wrapped in the protection of his territory. So how much more will **the King of Kings**, who calls you His child, cover you?

Psalm 91 is not a fairy-tale promise; it's a battle cry of divine assurance. The same God who delivered Israel, who closed the mouths of lions for Daniel, who walked in the fire with Shadrach, Meshach, and Abednego, is your protector today.

You are **shielded by His truth**, not by your performance. You are **guarded by His grace**, not by your strength. You are **covered by His covenant**, not by circumstance.

Isaiah 54:17 says:
"No weapon formed against you shall prosper."

This does not mean weapons won't form. They will. But it means they will not succeed in God's divine purpose for your life. The King has already declared the outcome: **Victory belongs to the Lord**. He covers not just your body, but your soul as well. He guards your peace. He defends your calling. He protects your identity as His beloved.

Do you trust God's protection, even when you can't see how He's working?

What "weapons" are in your life? Seems intimidating right now? Name them in prayer, and lay them at the feet of the King who fights for you.

Shepherd of my soul, King of all creation, in every valley and on every mountain, you are with me.

You are my refuge, my defender, and the One who holds my life in Your hands. When fear surrounds me, remind me of Your faithfulness.

When darkness falls, be the light that guides my steps.

I surrender every burden to You today, knowing that You are in control. Cover me with Your grace, surround me with Your protection, and lead me always in Your perfect will. In Jesus' name, Amen.

Psalm 46:1
God is our refuge and strength, a very present help in trouble.

HEAVENLY CITIZEN

CHAPTER TWENTY

*G*od's Partnership with Parents

How faithful parenting raises disciples, builds a godly legacy, and advances the purposes of God's kingdom. «Therefore, go and make disciples of all nations, baptizing them in the name of the Father and of the Son and the Holy Spirit, and teaching them to obey everything I have commanded you. And surely, I am with you always, to the very end of the age. » (Matthew 28:19-20)

Successful Parenting:

A parent who cares about the Kingdom is someone who faithfully raises their children through both teaching and setting a good example. Teaching God's ways requires more than just instruction; it requires setting a living example of faith, love, and justice. When parents embody divine principles through their own lives, they equip their children to fulfill God's will and live as citizens of His Kingdom.

Being a good parent is not limited to meeting physical needs; it involves shaping the child's character according to biblical values and preparing them to walk in obedience to God. "And you, fathers, do not provoke your children to anger, but bring them up in the discipline and instruction of the Lord." **Ephesians 6:4**

God's design for the education of children gives mothers and fathers the sacred responsibility of being their children's primary spiritual guides. This calling is not simply about managing behavior, but about guiding both the heart and mind of the child. Through daily interactions and intentional teaching, parents must instill in their children the wisdom necessary to navigate the real world. God creates children with remarkable intelligence and potential, but they need guidance to stay on the path of righteousness and success.

I had a conversation with a close friend who told me he let his kids choose their college degree. I asked him, "Is that wise?" He replied, "They should study what they like." I then asked him, "What if your child told you he wanted to major in theatre arts, art history, anthropology, philosophy, creative writing, peace and conflict studies, ethnic studies, dance, or geography? Would you take out a mortgage to finance your children?"

When a child finishes high school and decides to take a break, whether to work or travel, it's a decision that many parents support, in the hope that it will bring maturity and clarity. However, this temporary break can quickly become a permanent detour.

Once a child assumes financial responsibilities, such as paying for a car, and begins working full-time, the urgency of earning money often takes precedence over the long-term value of their education. What may start as a well-intentioned act of love and freedom can involuntarily become a trap, where immediate needs replace future aspirations, and college becomes a distant idea rather than a tangible goal.

As parents, our role is not to control, but to guide wisely. We need to help our children strike a balance between the short-term excitement of independence and the long-term impact on their future. It's essential to encourage responsibility while nurturing their vision. Love must include truth, foresight, and sometimes even a firm push to get them back on track toward their goal.

He returned the question and asked my opinion on the subject. I replied: "My children are a gift from God, and the Lord has entrusted me with the responsibility of guiding their lives to become faithful citizens of the Kingdom of Heaven.

Jesus solved practical problems. Be wise and seek to understand, for God, the source of all true wisdom, far surpasses the most significant discoveries of science.

"The beginning of wisdom is this: Get wisdom. Even if it costs you everything you have, acquire understanding" (Proverbs 4:7).

I told him that I've asked my children to be trained to do the same, to solve problems, serve others, and align their passions with purpose and economic values. I want them to look beyond the classroom and consider their calling, so they can live debt-free, provide for their families, and have the opportunity to help millions of others intentionally.

Because what you "*love*" won't necessarily help you pay your mortgage or raise a godly family. Seek first a purpose; provision is the fruit of faithful direction under the guidance of a Christian parent.

Through regular prayer, parents cultivate an environment where faith can take root and grow. Children learn to trust God, not only because they are taught, but also because they witness His presence in their parents' lives. When fathers and mothers surrender their parental role to God's wisdom, they become vessels through which He nourishes, corrects, and calls the unfolding generation of children into His eternal purpose.

The role of a parent is different from that of a mother or father. While biological parents bring a child into the world, sometimes another person, such as a grandparent, guardian, or other family member, or a godparent or godmother, takes the place of a parent. These people provide guidance, love, and discipline, acting as parents in the child's life.

As Paul says in **Ephesians 6:1:**
"Children, obey your parents in the Lord, for this is right."
Obedience to those who raise a child and have the responsibility of teaching them is essential to spiritual growth and maturity. However, the bond between a child and their biological parents remains unique because God has given them a special role in the child's life that is distinct from that of all other parents.

While anyone can play the role of parent in terms of advice and support, no one can ever truly replace a child's biological father and mother. That's why God commands children to honor their father and mother, rather than obey them.

Exodus 20:12 Moses said:
"Honor your father and your mother, so that you may live long in the land that the Lord your God is giving you."
Honoring goes beyond obedience; it requires deep respect, gratitude, and care. Even if a child is raised by someone other than his biological parents, he is called to recognize and honor the contract God has made with his parents, the role of his father and mother in his life, thus acknowledging God's purpose for the family and the importance of those who gave him life.

Honoring goes beyond obedience; it requires deep respect, gratitude, and care. Even if a child is raised by someone other than his biological parents, he is called to recognize and honor the contract God has made with his parents, the role of his father and mother in his life, thus acknowledging God's purpose for the family and the importance of those who gave him life.

At the heart of godly education lies the faithful and intentional transmission of biblical values. These truths enable children to discern and pursue both God's purpose and their unique divine vocation. This sacred transmission is accomplished by precept, educating children in the Word of God, and by practice, living these truths daily with humility, consistency, and love.

Parents are not only guardians of their children's physical well-being; they are divinely appointed shepherds of their minds and souls. As such, their example often has more authority than their words, shaping their children's understanding of faith, character, and obedience to God.

Bringing up children is therefore not an occasional task, but a covenantal responsibility between parents and the Lord. It requires surrendering to God's wisdom and understanding the pattern of righteousness in the rhythms of daily life. When parents abide in Christ and embody biblical truth, they lay a spiritual foundation that prepares their children to stand firm in the face of the world's trials and temptations.

Proverbs 1:8-9 exhorts:
"Listen, my son, to your father's instruction, and do not forsake your mother's teaching. They are an ornament to your head and a chain to your neck".

These verses remind us that parental instruction, when grounded in God's Word, is not just a guide; it's a crown of honor and protection for the soul.

The goal of a successful parent is not just to raise obedient or well-behaved children, but to raise respectful individuals who are secure in their identity in Christ and passionate about a life of purpose. Redirecting children toward success means more than enforcing rules; it involves pointing them toward God's truth, helping them build character, and encouraging them to pursue their unique calling to recognize their God-given talents, passions, and opportunities.

When children are raised with love, faith, and guidance, they grow into adults who make wise decisions, contribute positively to society, and live according to God's plan for their lives, which means they are less likely to get into trouble.

God's Partnership with Parents in Raising Faithful Families

God's partnership with parents is a profound and collaborative relationship. He has designed a guide for the growth and well-being of children. As part of this divine partnership, God has entrusted parents with the sacred responsibility of leading and training their children. Parents are often the first to initiate their children into faith, prayer, love, morality, education, instruction, self-respect, and respect for others.

We are called to influence our children and set them apart from the crowd through inspiration rooted in passion and destiny.
Christian parenting requires a sincere commitment to shaping children's character; at its core, it is a spiritual journey. The desire to see one's children succeed flows from love and devotion, embodying God's hopes for His children.

A parent's influence extends beyond words, as their actions, attitudes, and values leave a lasting impact on their children's lives.
Every child carries with them countless memories of the warmth, love, and guidance they received from their parents.

The stories, filled with moments of laughter, advice, and care, leave an indelible mark on their hearts, redirecting the way they see the world and face life's challenges. Whether it's a story whispered at bedtime in the soft glow of a nightlight or words of encouragement that resonate in moments of doubt, these memories become a foundation of strength and comfort.
Even as they grow up, they know that they are deeply cherished when they come home, and that their hearts are forever imbued with the love that first nurtured them. Adult children always have a place they'll forever call home for themselves and their offspring: their parents' house.

A Legacy of Love

By God's grace, I am honored to be responsible for caring for my mother, something I never take for granted. It is one of my greatest blessings to have her with me; she is still healthy, radiant, and wonderful. She is the heart of our family, our counsellor, and our source of comfort, always finding a way to bring joy to those around her. Her love flows through generations, and her grandchildren treasure every moment they share with her.
Since becoming a Christian, my mother has found profound joy in her faith. Witnessing her excitement about being part of God's kingdom is a true honor.

She embraces the promise of eternal life with great confidence, knowing that she is among **the 2.9 billion believers** destined for the Lord's heavenly kingdom. Her faith is a radiant light, guiding, inspiring, and strengthening all of us who are blessed to walk this journey beside her.

Some of my favorite memories with my mother are the stories she shares about my father, Elie Marcelin.

He was a remarkable man whose presence left a lasting impression. He was a gifted dancer, moving with a grace and rhythm that captivated everyone around him. I remember watching my dad dance with my mother in a quiet room, where the only music was the gentle hum of his voice.

It was their private melody, a tender moment more powerful than any song could be. Their love story began in middle school, leaving an incredible mark on all who witnessed their true love.

My father was a man of quiet confidence who carried himself with the strength and grace of a true gentleman. He naturally drew attention wherever he went, not through force, but through his presence. His smile was his most extraordinary charm, glowing with warmth and sincerity, capable of lighting up any room.

Although he spoke little, his gentle spirit and quiet wisdom left a lasting impression on my siblings and me. He taught us that true strength lies in kindness, humility, and understanding. He was our hero, the pillar of our family, a man we deeply admired, respected, and sought to emulate.

My father used to say, 'If my children fail, it will be my failure.

So, you'd better go out into the world and make me proud.' Those words were both a challenge and an inspiration, motivating us to strive for excellence and live by the values he had instilled so faithfully. They reminded us that our success was not just our own, but a reflection of our parents' heavenly love, guidance, and sacrifice.

His faith in us became a driving force, shaping our character and resilience. It was through his example that we learned how the divine calling of parenthood is not simply to provide, but to prepare children to carry forward a legacy of faith, integrity, and purpose.

Parenting is a divine calling that blends love, wisdom, and discipline into a beautiful adventure. When parents assume this sacred role with faith and grace, they create an environment in which children can grow into individuals who honor God, contribute meaningfully to society, and perpetuate the values they have been taught.

My father's confidence in us was evident when he encouraged us to explore the world and start our own families. He often reassured us by saying, "If God does not allow it, no one can harm you or touch a single hair on your head."

God is in control, and our parents prayed fervently for our lives. They often entrusted us with leadership roles within the family to test our strengths and develop our skills. While my brothers were more inclined to follow than to lead, I had a deep passion for leadership, even though I didn't always feel capable of it.

My experiences as a leader, guided by my parents' trust, helped shape my character, teaching me valuable lessons in wisdom, responsibility, and respect for others.

Parenting is an arduous journey, and God guides parents through His Word, teaching them never to stray from it. "Train up a child in the way he should go, and when he is old, he will not depart from it." Parents are called to seek God's will for their children, trusting in His sovereignty over their lives.

God's partnership with parents is not only about discipline and instruction; it is also about unconditional love, forgiveness, and patience. Together, this partnership creates an environment in which children can become the unique individuals God intended them to be.

Gratitude to Parents

Jesus emphasized the importance of honoring our fathers and ensured we understood the significance of this teaching. He reminded us that God's law requires everyone to "honor their father and mother," and that those who curse their parents face serious consequences.

However, the Pharisees had distorted God's commandment with their religious traditions, allowing people to neglect their duty to their parents under the pretext of spiritual offerings. They canceled out the very law that God had established, showing that empty rituals and selfish customs should never replace faithful obedience to God's word.

Jesus rebukes them and reminds us that honoring our fathers is not merely a suggestion but a divine requirement. When we fail to obey this commandment, we put ourselves at odds with God's will and expose ourselves to consequences in our lives. True honor is not only expressed in words, but also in deeds, showing that we respect and care for our fathers as God desires.

Jesus taught us not to let our traditions alter God's commandments. By honoring our earthly fathers, we ultimately honor our heavenly Father, thus aligning ourselves with His righteousness and blessings. Here is what will happen to you if you refuse to honor your father.

Proverbs 20:20 "*Whoever curses his father or his mother, His lamp will be put out in deep darkness.*"

Honoring one's parents is a fundamental principle embedded in God's commands. The Bible clearly states, *"Honor your father and mother, this is the first commandment with a promise, that all may go well with you and that you may enjoy a long life on earth"* **(Ephesians 6:2-3).**

This divine instruction reinforces that respecting one's parents is not only a matter of obedience but also a means of receiving God's blessings. When children show respect and gratitude to their parents, they align themselves with God's will, a life filled with wisdom, peace, and prosperity. Plus, you'll live longer.

Gratitude for parents is a powerful expression of love and humility. Acknowledge their sacrifices, patience, and unwavering support with a grateful heart. Children who honor their parents with words and actions cultivate deep emotional and spiritual growth. This respect strengthens family bonds and creates a foundation of love that extends beyond the home, influencing relationships in all aspects of life.

By appreciating and respecting their parents, children show God's love and grace, sincerely fulfilling His command. **Colossians 3:20** - "Children, obey *your parents in all things: for this is well pleasing unto the Lord.*"

The pursuit of wisdom is a daily endeavor for all who desire to walk in righteousness. Jesus encourages us to seek knowledge and understanding from God, as **James 1:5** says: "If any of you lacks wisdom, let him ask God, who gives to all generously and without reproach, and it will be given to him."

This verse reminds us that wisdom is a divine gift that enables children to honor their parents with discernment and love. By turning to God for guidance, children learn to manage their relationships with humility, patience, and respect, thereby living in accordance with His purpose.

Ultimately, honoring our parents reflects our obedience to God. It is not just about following a rule, but about embracing a principle that cultivates harmony, wisdom, and blessings. When children recognize their parents' sacrifices and teachings, they not only strengthen their family but also deepen their faith. In doing so, they fulfill God's commandment and experience the rewards of a life lived by His word, marked by longevity, favor, and divine protection.

Following one's parents' legacy is a profound act of honor, as it demonstrates respect for their wisdom and the life lessons they impart. Proverbs 4:1-*2 encourages children to "listen, children, to a father's instruction, and apply yourselves to knowing understanding.*

For I give you sound doctrine; do not forsake My law.

This verse emphasizes the importance of following parents' advice, whose wisdom serves as a foundation for meeting life's challenges. By adopting their teachings, children not only preserve the family heritage but also deepen their relationship with God, aligning themselves with His will.

Honoring this heritage strengthens family ties, fosters spiritual growth, and ensures that the values handed down from generation to generation continue to light the path of righteousness.

Psalm 51:10

Create in me a clean heart, O God; and renew a right spirit within me.

HEAVENLY CITIZEN

CHAPTER TWENTY-ONE

The Legacy of Wisdom

An Eternal Inheritance of Faith,
Family, and God's Love

Seeking the Wisdom of God

Jehovah is the ultimate source of all wisdom, healing, intelligence, and knowledge. He is a constant presence in our lives, just in His judgment, faithfulness in His promises, and holiness in all His ways. In times of doubt and confusion, children are encouraged to call upon Him, trusting that He will grant understanding and clarity.

As we seek His guidance, let His word become our lamp and light, illuminating our path and leading us toward righteousness. God's wisdom is not just for our benefit, but it is meant to honor Him and fulfill His divine will on earth.

The more we seek God, the more we come to know the depths of His love and the richness of His truth. His wisdom is far beyond our comprehension, but through His grace, we can understand and apply it in our lives. Unlike worldly knowledge that may fade or fail, God's wisdom is eternal, leading us on the straight and narrow path of righteousness.

By continually seeking Him, we align ourselves with His purpose, trusting that His wisdom will guide us faithfully through every circumstance.

A Legacy of Love, Gratitude, and Generational Wisdom

The foundation of a faithful Christian family begins with love, the kind of love that flows from the heart of God. The Bible tells us, "We love because He first loved us" **(1 John 4:19).**

Parents are called to embody God's unconditional and sacrificial love in the way they raise and guide their children. This divine love is not based on performance, but on presence, on being there, on being consistent, and on modeling a relationship with God that speaks louder than words.

When children are raised in this atmosphere of unwavering love, they grow up with a sense of belonging and a spiritual identity that anchors them in the storms of life.

Being a faithful parent is not a moment of staging; it is a journey of consistency. Just as God walks with us every day, we are called to walk with our children in the everyday moments that shape their hearts. From morning prayers to bedtime stories, from discipline to grace, every moment is a teaching moment.

Parents are the first and most powerful teachers of the gospel. When children witness faith in action, seeing their parents pray, forgive, serve, and trust God, they learn to do the same. Our mission is not only to pass on values, but also to instill a godly identity rooted in Christ.

Honor Your Parent

Gratitude and honor form the spiritual fabric of a healthy family. The Bible commands, *"Honor your father and your mother, that your days may be long in the land the Lord your God is giving you"* **(Exodus 20:12).**

This command is more than a call to respect; it is a call to blessing. When children honor their parents, they align themselves with God's divine order and open the door to His favor.

Yet honor is not one-sided; it flows both ways. Parents, too, are called to live in a manner worthy of that honor, leading with humility, gentleness, and truth. Gratitude then becomes a way of life as families learn to thank God and one another for His goodness in both trials and triumphs.

Creating a culture of gratitude and honor within the home begins with humility. Parents must be willing to apologize when they make a mistake and quick to forgive when their children stumble. This vulnerability promotes healing and builds trust. Confession and forgiveness are not signs of weakness; I did this all the time by telling my children I was sorry when I couldn't keep my promise.

Teaching children to honor God begins with showing them how to honor others, especially within their own family.

A home filled with mutual respect and gratitude becomes a reflection of heaven on earth. While the world measures generational wealth in terms of money and possessions, the Bible shows us a richer inheritance: wisdom, faith, and righteousness.

"A good man leaves an inheritance to his children's children" **(Proverbs 13:22),** and that inheritance begins with the fear of the

Lord. Teaching children to seek God's wisdom in their decisions, to be faithful stewards of resources, and to walk with the Holy Spirit lays the foundation that will bless not only their lives but also future generations.

This wealth cannot be stolen or lost, for it is acquired with integrity; it grows with every prayer, every act of obedience, and every seed of faith sown with love to bless millions of others. This wealth will be the preserved fruit of honest labor that will remain in the family for generations.

Faithful families truly change the world. When parents surrender their homes to God, when love is sincere, honor is mutual, and wisdom is sought before wealth, something powerful happens: generations are transformed. Your family is not just raising children; it is building a legacy.

And when God is your partner in raising your children, that legacy becomes eternal. May your home be filled with His presence, may your hearts be filled with His love, and may your children walk boldly in His truth.

We give thanks to God for the gift of our parents, for the father who gave us life and guided us, and for the mother whose love nurtured us in every season. As **Proverbs 23:22** reminds us, we honor their wisdom, not only in their youth, but especially when they are older, knowing that their experiences are treasures.

Colossians 3:20 calls every Christian to obedience and respect, not out of mere duty, but because it delights the heart of the Lord. Today and always, we choose to listen, cherish, and walk in gratitude for all they have done and continue to do in love.

Heavenly Father,

Thank you for the sacred gift of family and for entrusting us with the hearts and souls of our children. We recognize that the task of raising them is far too great to be undertaken alone. So, we invite you, Lord, to be our ever-present guide, our source of wisdom, strength, and peace in every season.

Teach us to love as you love unconditionally, patiently, and graciously. Please help us to remain present, consistent, and nurturing, even when we're tired. May our homes be filled with the light of your presence, and may our children see you clearly through the way we live, speak, and lead.

Create in us humble hearts where confession flows freely and forgiveness is offered generously. Show us how to cultivate a spirit of gratitude in our homes: gratitude for one another, for your daily provisions, and for the mercy you give so freely. May we learn to honor one another in the same way that we desire to honor you. We pray, in Jesus' name, Amen.

The Cry of a Newborn: From the Womb to the Kingdom of God.

"For we know that if our earthly dwelling, this tent, is destroyed, we have a building from God, an eternal home in heaven, not built by human hands." **2 Corinthians 5:1**

There is a sacred and safe place, a holy beginning ordained by God. Before birth, a baby knows only the warmth and calm of their mother, a divine refuge designed to protect them and nurture their growth. In this sanctuary, life continues effortlessly, in total dependence, but with everything he needs.

The mother's heartbeat becomes a soothing melody, and her body becomes a receptacle of love.

This small space represents heaven and earth for the child. Every gesture of attention from the outside world is a blessing from the Lord.

Whether it is a whispered prayer, a gentle caress, or a father's protective hand touching the belly, the baby usually moves with joy, just as when the Lord touches our lives. In this mysterious communion, hidden from human eyes, God is already at work, weaving a life with an eternal purpose.

David said in **Psalm 139:13**: *"For you formed my inward parts; you knitted me together in my mother's womb."*

But the womb, though safe, is not the final resting place. The child is unaware of the destiny that awaits him beyond this sacred space inside his mother.

For the baby, this is life in all its fullness.

The closeness of his mother, the shield of her presence, and the security provided by his father's vigilance create a complete world.

Yet God's plan is always greater than comfort. What appears to be an end is a sacred transition.

The child has no idea what the Lord has in store for him after a life longer than just nine months, from conception to birth. When labor begins, the pain intensifies to say goodbye. Both mother and baby cry out, then contractions set in, and the child has entered a new world.

It is not the child's will that causes birth, but the will of a higher power. The baby resists, but cannot remain in his mother's womb. The same God who formed life in the womb now calls him to leave that space, and no one else has the power to keep him inside.

What's the first thing every baby does when they enter this life?

They are crying. Would you agree that the same is true when each of us enters the kingdom after a short stay on earth? We feel so safe under the Lord's protection that we all want to live here for a few hundred more years! And in our case, not only do we have to leave, but our brothers and sisters also cry for us not to leave.

Unfortunately, no doctor, scientist, or technology will ever have the power to change this concept. However, all Christians believe that after the pregnancy of this life, the next birth will undoubtedly be better with the Lord in his kingdom.

When babies cry, it is not because they know what awaits them, but because they do not know what awaits them. They are afraid of the unknown. They have left the only place they trusted, without knowing that a greater love awaited them, in a new form. They thought that life might be over, when in reality, it is only the beginning.

How many of us, when faced with the end of something familiar, a job, a friendship, even a marriage, begin to cry out in fear? We panic, believing that loss means abandonment. But my brothers and sisters, listen carefully: **God never takes us away to forsake us.** He removes us only to place us under His loving protection.

Jesus said in **John 17:16**, *"They are not of the world, even as I am not of it."* Like a baby being formed in the womb, we, too, are being shaped in this world for a brief season. Our time here is short, but it is not without purpose. We are being prepared for another life, a life of greater possibilities. This earthly existence is merely the preparation for eternity.

The womb is not the final destination, and neither is this life the end. We are **citizens of another Kingdom**, and our time on earth is the **gestation of the soul**. Through joy and sorrow, trials and grace, we are being gently molded under the watchful care of our Heavenly Father.

We pray every day to complain why he wants us to die; however, when the time comes for each of us, we must leave here.

When our time comes, we will not be alone, just as doctors and nurses surround a mother giving birth, with the father holding her hands and being the first to have the baby in his arms. Likewise, the Lord will surround us during our transition with all the angels; heaven will not remain silent when a saint returns home, heaven will celebrate!

Psalm 116:15 David said:
"*The death of his saints is precious in the sight of the Lord.*" Why?
Because it is not an end, it is a birth into glory.
The Lord is at the gates, arms wide open, saying,
"Welcome home, my child. I have been waiting for you.

This section is reserved for those who believe in and accept Jesus as their Lord and Savior. If you do not know the Lord or if you know someone who does not have access to this actual knowledge and understanding, please share with them St. Paul's revelation in **1 Corinthians 2:9,** where he says:

"***What no eye has seen, what no ear has heard, what no heart of man mind has imagined, what God has prepared for those who love him.***"

Just as a baby cannot imagine the beauty of this world from its mother's womb, neither can we fully comprehend the glory of eternity. But it is real. And it will be ours.

Do not fear the contractions of this life. Do not fear the cry of departure. The same God who carried you in your mother's womb now holds you in the womb of this world, and He is preparing to deliver you to a place far from here, better than you can imagine.

> We do not want you, brothers, to be ignorant about those who sleep, so that you may not grieve as others do who have no hope.
>
> **1 Thessalonians 4:13**

A Letter to All Fathers and Mothers, you are worthy of the most beautiful poems our hearts can write. For your love, your strength, and your sacrifice. May you know heavenly peace, even amid earthly storms.

A Legacy of Love: A Poem for Mom and Dad

Daddy

From our first breath to our grown-up stride
 you stood like anchors, firm at our side.
A faithful father, a mother so true, in every season
 we looked up to you.
Dad, your hands bore the weight of care
 protector, provider, always there.
You taught us truth in quiet ways
 in storms of life, you never swayed.
A rock in a world that shifts like sand
 you held our hearts and minds with a steady hand.

Mommy

Mom, your grace was gentle and deep
Sowing love while the world was asleep.
Your prayers, though silent with every heartbeat
Lit the darkest nights with wisdom's heat.
You're my warrior cloaked in heaven's light
You battled softly, out of sight.
Together, you forged a sacred vow.
To lead with love, to kneel and bow.
Your unity, a divine covenant of marriage
Taught us to love by God's design.
We heard the Gospel in your voice
And learned to trust, to hope, rejoice.
Each lesson shared; each Scripture spoken.

Each song is sung through sleepless nights
a chain of grace, uncut, unbroken.
The late-night talks, the table grace
the stories, the tears, the warm embrace.
All formed the soul we carry now
your faith impressed upon our brow.
You are my angels, my true guardians.
I am a heavenly citizen because of who you are.
My heart and soul have no words to tell love.
I honor you both with heartfelt language.
May you receive blessings from my prayers.
Your legacy is not carried with shame, but love.
So, thank you, Dad, for standing tall
And Mom, for rising after every fall.
For holding us through joy and pain
for planting seeds that remain.
You didn't just raise sons and daughters
you raised disciples, living waters from heaven.
Now, as your living legacy, we take our stand
Holding truth in both heart and hand.
We'll raise our children in that same love
guided still by God above. A house of peace
a light that shines, a family walking in God's design.

« My people shall dwell in a peaceable habitation
and in sure dwellings, and quiet resting places. » **Isaiah 32:18.**
God establishes the Christian father as the priest of his home, tasked with guiding, praying, and offering his life in service for his loved ones.

You have always remained peaceful in the heart of the storm. Silent but attentive, your sure hands, your head bowed in prayer. You knew how to read my silences. Your presence never shouted, but it carried the sacred weight of discipline marked by the mercy of true love. Your steps have engraved the path on which we learned to walk, strengthened by your example and your faith. THANK YOU, DAD.

Our mothers are missionaries of divine love, serving their families with faith, gentleness, and sacrifice.

Your hands held a piece of paradise. You are the beating heart of our home, the quiet breath behind our wisdom, the respect with a divine personality. The invisible wings that carried us. Your prayers built the architecture of every cry that God has answered. Your arms are a sanctuary of grace and a tabernacle of love.

You watched over the doors of each of our steps, building around us a world of kindness. On our knees, you taught us to pray, to forgive, to believe.

Through your faithful love, you wrote the story of our lives, the one to which we always return from grace. No word, no ink can describe the depth of your love. Your advice still resonates in the silence of our hearts. We will always be your little one, your little treasure, and your seed of eternity.

With all our hearts, with all our souls, and to the ends of infinity, we say thank you, Mom, for your love that reflects that of God.

Heavenly Father

Our Father in heaven, hallowed be Your name. Your kingdom come; your will be done on earth as it is in heaven. Give us this day our daily bread. Forgive us our debts, as we forgive our debtors. And lead us not into temptation, but deliver us from evil. For yours is the kingdom, and the power is with me and my family.

When the storms of life surround me, be my anchor. When fear rises, be my peace. Thank you for never leaving my side, for being my strength, my refuge, and my calm. Teach me to trust You more, to rest in Your promises, and to walk by faith, not by sight. In Jesus' name, **Amen**

Psalm 61:1–2

Hear my cry, O God; attend unto my prayer. From the end of the earth will I cry unto thee, when my heart is overwhelmed: lead me to the rock that is higher than I.

HEAVENLY CITIZEN

CHAPTER TWENTY-TWO

T he House **God Built.**

Restoring the Altar of Family Through Faith, Love, and Generational Wealth.

«For he was looking forward to the city with foundations, the architect and builder is God. » **(Hebrews 11:10)**

Heavenly Citizenship:

When the world observes a strong family, it witnesses much more than just healthy routines or good upbringing; it sees the reflection of a strong man, a strong father, created by God Himself. The strength of the family starts with the strength of the one who kneels before the heavenly Father. At a time when the family altar has been demolished or forgotten, God issues a sacred call to rebuild.

This is not merely a cultural trend or personal choice. Still, a divine mission for all fathers, mothers, and grandparents to restore order in homes where God is worshiped, His Word rules with heavenly laws, and love flows in humble obedience.

We are a community of Heavenly citizens and faithful stewards chosen to build Kingdom families according to God's divine plan.

As part of the 2.9 billion believers who have placed their faith in Jesus Christ, I don't just identify as a Christian; I live as a citizen of heaven.

Philippians 3:20 reminds us:

"But our citizenship is in heaven, and we eagerly await a Savior from there, the Lord Jesus Christ."

This is more than theology; it's a mission. We are the ambassadors of the Kingdom of God, living in a world that is increasingly at odds with its truth. For parents, especially fathers, this means leading with courage, conviction, and Kingdom purpose.

Our families are not the product of public policies, cultural systems, or changing social trends directed by any earthly government. Yes, we respect the laws of the country we live in. We pay our taxes, our mortgages, and our bills; we follow the rules to the letter.

However, the laws of the Lord are not just rules; they are sacred missions of the Kingdom, holy directives directly from Heaven for our family.

When Jesus shows up, whether in the fire, the hospital room, the broken marriage, the wayward child, or the financial storm, no force in hell can override His decision. His plans are higher. His ways are better. His grace is unstoppable.

In a world quickly moving away from the truth, we are called to stand firm in the faith of the Disciples, building our homes on the rock, brick by brick, and sharing the good news of salvation with everyone we meet.

God's Design for Fatherhood

Brethren, *this is how your heavenly ideals come to life.*

God's plan for parenthood, and fatherhood in particular, is both intentional and sacred. He has entrusted fathers with a unique strength and calling to fulfil a divine mission.

This call goes far beyond simply providing or exercising authority; it is a mandate for spiritual direction. Fathers are charged with shepherding their homes, protecting, guiding wisely, and raising their children in partnership with the Lord.

This sacred role requires a heart of integrity, a spirit of humility, and a love in the image of the Lord. The home becomes a sanctuary, a place where faith is nurtured, Scripture is lived and taught, and grace is the foundation.

In a world that often encourages men to be passive or proud, godly fatherhood stands in stark contrast. Kingdom fathers walk by faith, like Abraham, lead with solid conviction, like Joshua, and love sacrificially, just as Jesus did.

When fathers live by God's design, they equip the next generation not only for success on earth but also for eternal significance.

From Brokenness to Restoration

I didn't grow up with this understanding. My childhood home lacked spiritual truth. I was raised in a
Godless environment filled with brokenness, confusion, and a lack of direction. Divorce and emotional wounds were all around me. Dysfunction seemed unavoidable.

At one point, I lived with two broken feet and two broken wrists, but I didn't make excuses. On the contrary, I lived like a soldier who had returned from the war broken and sustained by grace. A grace that was, and still is, more than enough. I never complained; I continued to live with resilience.

My determination to break the cycle of generational poverty drove me to seek God more in a way that would resemble a face-to-face conversation.

And it was in this broken place in my life that I met Jehovah Rapha, the Lord who heals.

When Jehovah meets you in your lowest valley, He begins a new chapter, rewriting your life story.

By choosing to follow Jesus, I not only saved my soul but also broke the generational chains I had inherited. Through the power of the cross, I became a new creature, and my home became the first generation of healing and restoration.

Today, I am a citizen of a place of redemption. I am forgiven and strengthened by the One who called me out of darkness. And if He did it for me, He can do it for you if you choose to hold fast to the faith. Your past does not disqualify you. God's grace redeems everything you entrust to God's care.

Living with Eternity in Mind

We don't raise children to survive in this world; we raise sons and daughters for the world to come. **The King is returning, and every act of faithful parenting pave the way.**

Living for the Kingdom means thinking beyond this life, **living with eternity in mind**. This is the purpose of Kingdom education. We're not here to impress the world but to prepare disciples for heaven.

In the valleys of life, our children must know that the Lord is their shepherd.

They need to see how we trusted the Lord when things didn't make sense, how we walked in peace during storms, and how we kept our eyes on the Lord when worldly distractions appeared. Our lives serve as their roadmap, and our obedience forms the foundation of their lives.

God does not ask parents to act alone. He is a partner to those who seek Him. He strengthens faithful mothers, equips loyal fathers, and rewards the wisdom of grandparents who sow seeds of prayer and truth.

God's plan for the sacred legacy of parental love is not a fantasy; it is His true purpose. Faithful parenting makes disciples.
Parenting builds legacies. It advances Kingdom purposes. Every time we pray for our children, breathe life into them, or model forgiveness, we are doing sacred work. We are building eternity.

Psalm 145:4 David said:
"One generation commends your works to another; they tell of your mighty acts." Your grace will endure forever.
Yes, there will be trials. But in **Exodus 14:14**, the Lord promises Moses:
"The Lord will fight for you, and you keep silent."

We may not always have the answers, but we do have God's presence with us. He walks with us through the fire. He defends our homes when we cry out. The battle is His. As fathers, we are not alone; we are citizens of the Kingdom, supported by the King of kings, called to raise families together.

Whether it's Christians seeking a fresh start or young families embarking on the journey of parenthood and faith, the path to parenthood is filled with mountaintop joys and deep valleys.
But no matter where we are, our focus must remain fixed forward, toward the open door of the Lord. The choices we make daily in raising children carry a weight that goes beyond the present; they echo into eternity.

Parenting is about much more than preparing our children for academic success, career stability, or even future marriage; it's about shaping hearts that beat for Christ, anchoring souls in the truth of His Kingdom, and building a legacy that spans generations.

The responsibility of parenting in faith is both humbling and sacred. It is a divine call to partner with Abba, not just to run a household, but to guide lives entrusted to us by Heaven. Every mother and father who dares to raise their family in the fear of the

Lord stands as a living witness to God's goodness and faithfulness, even amid the world's brokenness.

Heavenly Father,

Thank you for choosing me for more than just a role as a father. I am not only a parent but also an ambassador of the Kingdom. Although my upbringing lacked spiritual foundations, you, Jehovah Rapha, have healed my past and rewritten my future.

Please help me stand firm in your grace when culture presses against me. Strengthen my hands to guide, protect, and train my children in accordance with your eternal purpose. May my home shine with the light of Heaven, and may my children walk fearlessly, knowing their identity in Christ.

When trials arise, remind me that the battle is not mine, but yours. Use every ordinary moment of my fatherhood for your glory, so that our family's legacy is one of faith, truth, and everlasting love. In Jesus' name, **Amen.**

Marriage: The Foundation of the Sacred Mission

Marriage itself becomes the starting point for this sacred responsibility. Two become one, then become parents, and finally, grandparents and extended family influence. Each person has a role, a voice, and a divine contribution to building a godly home.

However, it all begins with parents who understand that raising a family is a form of spiritual warfare and stewardship. It takes faith to weather the storm, grace to cultivate unity, and courage to lead in a world moving away from the true God.

Fathers are called to lead with spiritual authority. They must guide their families in faith and obedience to God, provide spiritual instruction and loving discipline, and model godly character and humility within their homes.

As Paul declares:

"*If anyone does not provide for those close to him, and especially for those in his family, he has denied the faith*" **(1 Timothy 5:8).**

Provision isn't just financial; it includes spiritual guidance, emotional support, and unwavering presence. A godly father loves the mother of his children with sacrificial love, reflecting the heart of Christ to his entire family.

A Christian mother plays a sacred and divinely chosen role, blending the physical act of nurturing with the spiritual development of the heart. Her hands hold the future, and her words often become the first echoes of truth in her child's heart.

The Bible honors this responsibility, highlighting the influence of faithful mothers like Lois and Eunice, whose sincere faith transformed young Timothy into a man of God **(2 Timothy 1:5)**.

A mother's faith becomes a family treasure, passed down through daily teaching and her living example; a mother's dedication is a quiet yet powerful sermon of trust, love, and obedience to God that resounds louder than words.

A mother's love surpasses words, shown through actions, sacrifices, and a presence that words can never fully capture.

Long before a child learns to speak, they feel the warmth of a mother's hug, the comfort of her gentle touch, and the security of her constant care. Her love is evident in the sleepless nights, the silent prayers that never cease, the meals she prepares, the wounds she kisses, and the unwavering faith she has in her child's future. It's a living example of devotion that speaks directly from the heart, louder than any words or phrases.

It is a living testimony of devotion that speaks directly to the heart.

In contrast, the love of a Christian father reflects the heart of the heavenly Father himself. He sees that love isn't about permissiveness but about guiding and teaching his children to walk in truth and choose what is right. His discipline isn't fueled by anger but by purpose, motivated by a love that wants to see his children mature into godly disciples **(Hebrews 12:6)**.

He builds a home on a foundation of faith in action, where his sacrificial leadership and constant presence provide his children with a safe place to grow, fail, ask questions, and return home whenever they stumble. His children will always find rest in the strength of his arms and courage in the steadiness of his leadership.

They know they are not alone, for their father is with them; they trust him, and behind him stands the strong, unwavering presence of God.

Through their intentional love, Christian fathers instill in their children a profound sense of self-esteem and confidence, to the extent that no amount of criticism or bullying can shake them.
Above all, a Christian father teaches his children that they are dearly loved and wonderfully created by the Lord.

(Psalm 139:14). *"I praise you because I am fearfully and wonderfully made; your works are wonderful; I know that full well."*

A Christian father often says, *"I will lead you, correct you, protect you, and support you. You can always come back to me; I'm here, and I will always be here, because that's what my heavenly Father does for me."*

Through this devotion, he not only shapes his children's hearts for this life but also prepares them to

become citizens of the heavenly Kingdom. Together, mothers and fathers must create a strong unit, a home marked by prayer, peace, and the presence of God.

We must pray constantly for our children, for the Lord disciplines those He loves and chastises every son He receives, and we must avoid provoking discouragement. Above all, we must teach our children to love God with all their heart, soul, and strength, and to love their neighbors as well as themselves. This kind of education doesn't come from books or trends, but from a surrendered life grounded in Scripture and driven by the Spirit to love the Lord your God with all your heart, soul, and mind. A parent's words are always a blessing to a child.

It's a Kingdom call. Families established in God's design become salt and light in a world that needs renewal. They make disciples, preserve the truth, and become living testimonies of God's faithfulness. A Christian family is not perfect, but it is holy, set apart, and made possible by grace.
When a family follows God's design, it becomes a preview of heaven on earth. Let this be your inheritance: a home not built by human

hands but established by God; a generation enlightened by the truth; a house that lives not just for today but for eternity.

You're not just raising sons and daughters; you're raising citizens of heaven. And in the end, that's the house God is building; rock-solid, eternal, and filled with His glory.

The family is God's original model for portraying His image on earth. When fathers lead with humility and strength, when mothers raise their children with grace and wisdom, and when grandparents spread their heritage and blessings, the Kingdom advances, not only in churches but also around tables, in evening prayers, and in everyday love.

You may not come from a perfect family, but thanks to God's mercy, you can start one. Every act of obedience, every word of prayer, every choice to love even when it's hard, is the brick God uses to build something eternal. Your faithfulness in this generation lays the foundation for future generations. Heaven is watching. The world is watching. And your family is worth fighting for.

Heavenly Father,

Thank you for the sacred gift of family. Thank you for entrusting us with the lives of our children and grandchildren. We confess that we need your help, your wisdom, and your strength to build our homes on the rock of Christ. Restore what is broken.

Heal what is wounded. Renew the fire of worship, truth, and love in our homes. Please help us to lead not by our power, but by the power of the Holy Spirit. May our homes be places where your name is honored, your Word is spoken, and your love is poured out each day.

We ask that you bless our fathers and mothers abundantly and keep them in good health until the end of their lives. May the legacy we leave behind echo throughout eternity. In Jesus' name, Amen.

Psalm 84:10

For a day in thy courts is better than a thousand. I would rather be a doorkeeper in the house of my God than dwell in the tents of wickedness.

HEAVENLY CITIZEN

CHAPTER TWENTY-THREE

The Sacred Design of the Christian Family

The family unit begins with the understanding that the family is not just a human creation but a divine institution established by God Himself. From the beginning of creation, God designed families to reflect His nature on earth: His love and His authority. Within the family, children, parents, and grandparents each have a spiritual mission.

Christian families are not simply connected by blood; their shared identity unites them as citizens of the heavenly kingdom. This sacred purpose influences how we live, love, and lead in our homes. As ambassadors for Christ, families are called to mirror heaven's order and values on earth, raising children who know God, obey His Word, and walk in His truth.

Parents are called to be sanctified and to assume the responsibility of discipleship, not just the care of children. Their role is to teach, educate, and discipline with grace and truth, melding lives surrendered to Christ.

Children, in turn, are expected to obey and honor their parents, recognizing the authority God has placed in their lives for their protection and growth. Grandparents, often the spiritual pillars of the family, carry the mantle of wisdom and intercession.

Their experiences, prayers, and testimonies are essential threads in the fabric of generational faith. They help remind the family of God's faithfulness over the years, linking past victories with future promises. In God's plan, each generation plays an essential role - none is disposable, and all are necessary for the family legacy to thrive.

The time has come to honor our elders because in them lies the living memory of God's faithfulness and instructions. They are not burdens to be tolerated but treasures to be celebrated. When we honor our parents and grandparents, we uphold a kingdom principle that invites blessing and long life **(Ephesians 6:2-3).**

In a culture that often idolizes youth and dismisses age, the Church must rise and set a different standard, one that respects, listens to, and learns from those who came before us. The inheritance we receive is not earthly glory or wealth but a heavenly legacy of faith, obedience, and love. As Christian families, let us fulfil our sacred mission by walking in unity across generations to advance the Kingdom of God together.

The Lord Jesus is at your door.

We live in miraculous times; ***2.9 billion Christians around the world today are witnessing a powerful movement of God on planet Earth.*** *Billion believers following Jesus Christ, and the numbers are skyrocketing. The gospel of discipleship and the Holy Spirit is stirring hearts like never before.*

The souls who come to the Lord are awakened to the truth that eternal life can only exist through our Lord Jesus. As the Church grows, the light spreads into the darkness, and we celebrate that God is building His royal family in his kingdom on every continent, in every language, and across every generation.

In 2025, *over ten million Muslims converted to the Christian faith, including notable populations in Saudi Arabia, Iran, Iraq, Turkey, Jordan, Syria, Qatar, Palestine, Bangladesh, Pakistan, Indonesia, Albania, Kosovo, Bosnia and Herzegovina, and India. Let us rejoice in this spiritual awakening, knowing that every life turned to Christ resonates into eternity.*

We welcome them into the absolute truth of the mission for which the apostles and disciples laid down their lives.

Psalm 121:

"He who watches over you does not sleep. The Lord will keep you from all evil. He will watch over your life; the Lord will watch over your comings and goings, from now and forever."

These promises aren't far away; they're alive and active on you right now. Whatever path you take, the eyes of your heavenly Father are upon you. He is not a silent guardian, but a present and powerful protector, shielding you with his love and guiding you with his wisdom.

There is a direct line to the control room of the Throne of Heaven. It is not a physical phone, but a call of faith.

Jeremiah 33:3 This is the Lord's invitation to you: "***Call to me, and I will answer you, and show you great and hidden things that you do not know***".

This is the divine phone number of the office of Jesus Christ.

This number is available at any hour to meet the needs of Christians. Whether you pray for your marriage, your children, your health, or your future, Jesus listens. So do not hesitate to call on Him. Reach out to Him in faith. He is waiting for you to call, ready to respond with love, revelation, and healing.

Be reminded of the unshakable sovereignty of God in Isaiah 43:13, "From ancient days I am he. No one can take it out of my hands. When I act, who can reverse it?" What a powerful reassurance! Your life is not subject to fate or fear; it is held in the hands of the Almighty.

When God moves on your behalf, no force in heaven or earth can undo His plan. He is your advocate, your deliverer, and your defender. Trust Him boldly, for His authority is final and His love is fierce.

Hallelujah, you've nearly finished this book.

Congratulations, but it is only the beginning of your journey with Jesus. Return to these truths often to revisit Christ's words and let them nourish your soul. Share these writings and declarations with your friends and family.

Make your life a vessel of light and a witness, a church on the move wherever you go, for you are the temple of the living God, and the Holy Spirit of sanctification and power dwells within you. Shine like fire, immovable and filled with grace.

Receive this final blessing from the Lord Jesus and from my heart to yours: The grace and peace of God our Father and the Lord Jesus Christ be upon you and your family **(Philemon 1:3).** May His grace carry you through every storm, and His peace guard your heart in every season.

May your home be filled with love, may your days be guided by faith, and may your every step be ordered by the Lord. You are chosen, you are covered, and you are profoundly loved. Keep moving forward, embedded in Christ, until we all rejoice together in his glorious presence in his Heavenly kingdom. We are all from the same place, we have the same nationality, and we are Heavenly Citizens.

Heavenly Father,

Our Father, who art in heaven, hallowed be thy name. Your kingdom come; your will be done on earth as it is in heaven. We come before you with hearts full of gratitude and admiration. Thank you, Lord, for every reader you have brought to this message.

Thank you to the more than three billion souls around the world who turn their hearts to Jesus Christ. We rejoice in this abundant harvest and give you all the glory for the work you are doing in our generation. May your kingdom continue to grow, and may each of us remain faithful servants in your harvest.

Lord, we thank you for never sleeping or slumbering. You are our guardian, our protector, and the one who watches over our lives. Thank you for walking with us in every season, when we come and go, now and forever. We entrust ourselves to your unfailing stewardship and rest in the security of your presence.

Thank You, Jesus

Thank you, Jesus, for always being nearby. You have given us direct access to your throne through prayer, and we accept your invitation in Jeremiah 33:3 to call upon you. Whether we cry out for healing, for our families, for wisdom, or for peace, you promise to answer us with great and unfathomable things.

We will keep calling on you, Lord, and continue to believe. Father, we praise you because no one can overturn what you have declared. Since the beginning of time, you have been God, and your power has no rival.

When you act, no force can stand against you. Strengthen our faith so that we can rely on your promises and walk confidently in your will.

Thank you, Lord, for every word, every scripture, and every truth that has been shared. May these words take root in our hearts and bear fruit in our lives. May each reader become a shining light, carrying your Spirit and truth into homes, workplaces, and communities. May revival begin within us and spread through us. And now, Father, we speak blessing over each reader: ***"Grace and peace be to you from God our Father and the Lord Jesus Christ.***

May your grace sustain every Christian and your peace guide us. May our homes be filled with your presence, and may our lives be lived for your glory. We seal this prayer in the mighty name of Jesus Christ, our Lord and Savior. **Amen.**

A Letter to Every Christian and Faithful Follower of Our Lord Jesus Christ

Dear Readers,

From the **very first breath to the final heartbeat**, one truth stands firm and unshaken: everything must begin with the Lord Jesus Christ. **"For by Him were all things created, that are in heaven, and that are in earth, visible and invisible, whether they be thrones, or dominions, or principalities, or powers; all things were created by Him. "**

Him, and for Him." (Colossians 1:16-17)

"**In the beginning, God created the heaven and the earth**. «At the beginning of every relationship, project, business plan, marriage, engagement, desire for a child, job opportunity, life transition, or move to a new city or country, everything must start and finish with the Lord.

Before time was measured, before the stars were set in place, before the foundations of the earth were laid, **our Lord Jesus was there**. The Gospel of John echoes this eternal truth.

"I am Alpha and Omega, the beginning and the ending, saith the Lord, which is, and which was, and which is to come, the Almighty." Revelation 1:8

"In the beginning was the Word, and the Word was with God, and the Word was God...All things were made by Him; and without Him was not anything made that was made." (John 1:1, 3)

I made you, and you are mine.

This is not mere theological poetry, but the foundation of all reality. Jesus is not only pre-existent; he is present and powerful. As the apostle Paul proclaimed, he holds the keys to all things, even in those moments when you feel like you're falling apart.

"**Before the mountains appeared, before you formed the earth and the world, from eternity to eternity, you are God, from eternity to eternity, you are God.**" (Psalm 90:2)

He was not made. The Lord Jesus **is.** He has always been, and He will always be there forever.

So, whether you are in your journey, just beginning, struggling in the middle, or nearing the end, remember this: Start with Jesus. Stay with Jesus.

Finish with Jesus.

He is the **Alpha** and the **Omega**.

He is the **Author of all** and **Finisher of our story**.

He is the **Rock** that **never moves**, the **Light** that **darkness cannot overcome**. The **Way, the Truth**, and **the Life**. He is **the Living Water** that never runs dry, the **Resurrection** and **the redeemer of souls**, the **Risen Savior** who **conquered death** and **the grave.** His name is **Jesus.**

He is the One who writes your story and holds every page together. We trust you, Lord Jesus, to take the earth to Heaven. We are **Heavenly Citizens because of your sacrifice.**

Jesus, the Master Architect of All Creation

At the foundation of all reality stands Jesus Christ, **the Master Architect** who holds **every blueprint of creation**. Before the first stone of the earth was laid, before the stars were suspended in the heavens, and before time itself began to tick, *the Lord had already designed the universe with flawless precision. Nothing in creation is accidental or without purpose.* Every detail, every law of nature, every unseen harmony flows from His eternal plan. The cosmos is not a random explosion of matter, but the deliberate masterpiece of a Divine Architect who sees the end from the beginning.

Yet Jesus is more than a builder of galaxies and the orchestrator of nature's rhythm. He is also the Divine Strategist, the One who carries answers to every question. In a world marked by uncertainty and confusion, His wisdom remains unshaken.

Governments may rise and fall, philosophies may shift like sand, but the counsel of the Lord endures forever. No puzzle of human existence, no problem of society, no crisis of the soul lies beyond His ability to resolve. What baffles the most extraordinary minds is but a whisper to the One who knows the end from the start.

Colossians 1:16-17:

"For in him all things were created: things in heaven and on earth, visible and invisible, whether thrones or powers or rulers or authorities; all things have been created through him and for him. He is before all things, and in him all things hold together."

He is the Eternal Problem-Solver, with no mystery beyond His wisdom. For every locked door, He holds the keys for every tangled knot of life; His hand alone can loosen the strands of every soul. Humanity wrestles with questions of purpose, suffering, destiny, and truth; however, Christ embodies the eternal solution. His wisdom is not bound to time or culture, for He Himself is timeless. When the heart aches for direction and the mind cannot find peace, Jesus offers the clarity that only the eternal can give.

As the supreme Designer, He orders all things with precision. The orbit of the planets, the succession of seasons, the rise and fall of nations and governments, all are under His sovereignty. He is the only mighty King who reigns forever. His kingdom holds the secret book of every living soul, the names of all those who bow before His majesty, more than 2.9 billion souls already registered to live eternally in the new city of the heavenly kingdom.

He is the perfect Equation in which all solutions find their balance. Just as numbers obey immutable laws, the most profound realities of existence find their harmony in Him. He is the infinite Spirit who solves all the mysteries under heaven, unravelling both the visible and the invisible with an intelligence that no intellect can match.

Jesus is the One who makes the impossible possible. When human strength reaches its limit, when resources and connections fail, His power begins to prevail. **He is the Wisdom of God, in whom are hidden all the treasures of knowledge (Colossians 2:3).**

The mysteries of life, the depths of creation, the purposes of eternity, all rest securely in Him. He is the Alpha and the Omega, the beginning and the end, the place where every solution rests. Christian Families are under his protection.

The Lord God says in Apocalypse 1:8:
"I am the Alpha and the Omega, who is, and who was, and who is to come, the Almighty."

For those who are weary, He is the Light that illuminates all paths of confusion. For those who are lost, He is the Guide who leads to truth. For those who are broken, He is the Healer who restores integrity. In Him, life is restored and finds its resolution, the questions of the soul find their answers, and the desires of the heart find their right rhythms.

All creation testifies that the Master Architect of creation, Jesus, holds all eternal life and the blueprint in His hands. You are His design, inscribed in the Book of Life before the foundation of the world. Before anything under the sun came into existence, He was already there, eternally present, sovereign, the unchanging King.

Jesus said this to King Solomon in **Proverbs 8:27-30:**
I was there
When he set the heavens in place, when he traced the horizon on the face of the deep, **I was there.**
When he established the clouds above, when he secured the fountains of the great abyss, **I was there.**
When he gave the sea its boundary, that the waters should not overstep his command, **I was there.**

When he laid the foundation of the earth, at his side constantly, delighting in him day after day, rejoicing always in his presence, so now, my children, listen to me. Blessed are those who keep my ways. Receiving my instruction and being wise. Blessed are those who wait at my door, who watch daily at my threshold.
For whoever finds me finds life, and receives favor from the Lord. Those who reject me harm themselves; all who hate me love death.

The Christian family values

Once, family was synonymous with reputation, respect, and legacy. A father's honor and a grandfather's integrity defined the worth of an entire lineage. Whether someone was Christian or not, in many cultures, the first question asked when considering marriage was not:

"Do you love this person?" but **"What is their family's reputation?"**

It was understood that a person carried the weight of their heritage, and that to unite with them was to join their family's story, virtues, and even shortcomings. In many traditions, marriage was not merely about two individuals, but about the merging of households, where honor, respect, and reputation were cherished above all else.

In fact, in numerous cultures, marriage was considered not just a personal decision but a communal and even political one. To marry was not only to gain a spouse but to be grafted into a family tree with all its responsibilities and privileges.

Historically, unions often served as strategic alliances, sometimes connecting entire tribes or nations.

Love, while valued, was not always the foundation of relationships. Instead, stability, continuity, and the preservation of heritage guided the path to marriage. Contrast this with today's world, where marriage is frequently reduced to fleeting feelings or material calculations, and the difference becomes striking.

Modern culture has shifted toward new ideals. Many young women, influenced by societal narratives, are drawn to men who embody a specific image of wealth, status, and physical attractiveness. Terms like "high-value man" are increasingly tied to salaries, possessions, or social stature, rather than character, faith, or family values. In this mindset, many people seek a partner, but not necessarily a spouse.

Material desires often blind people to the qualities that truly build a lasting home: loyalty, integrity, faith, and sacrifice. The pursuit of temporary gain usually overshadows the quest for eternal values, leaving relationships unstable and families fractured.

Yet the Word of God reveals a different standard for husbands, one that transcends cultural trends and economic fashions.

In **Ephesians 5:25**, the apostle Paul commands: *"Husbands, love your wives, even as Christ also loved the church, and gave himself for it."*

A godly husband is not defined by wealth or worldly recognition but by sacrificial, unconditional love. He is called to place his wife's well-being above his own desires, to serve and honor her with humility and grace. A biblical husband is loyal and trustworthy, bound by a covenant made not only before his wife but also before the living God.

Such a husband leads with prayer, instructs his household in the Word of God, and fosters a spirit of discipleship within his home. His mission is to provide not only physical security but also emotional stability and spiritual covering. He honors his wife, forgives readily, and protects diligently.

He guides his children with wisdom and grace, modeling what it means to be a servant-leader. This is why a wife is prepared and instructed by her mother, not merely for outward appearances or social ambition, but for the sacred duty of joining her life to a man called to love as Christ loves. A valid biblical marriage is not solely about wealth or reputation; it is about building a godly legacy rooted in faith, obedience, and eternal love.

Psalm 91:1

He that dwelleth in the secret place of the Most-High shall abide under the shadow of the Almighty.

HEAVENLY CITIZEN

CHAPTER TWENTY-FOUR

Citizens of the Kingdom, the last word of grace.

You are not just a parent. **You are one of the 2.9 billion citizens of the Kingdom of Heaven.**

« *As the heavens are higher than the earth, so are My ways higher than your ways and My thoughts than your thoughts.* » (Isaiah 55:9)

This citizenship cannot be earned by your good deeds, nor inherited through your earthly lineage; it's a gift of grace, received through faith in Jesus Christ. From the moment you said, "Yes, Lord Jesus, I accept you as my Lord and Savior. I confess with my mouth and my heart that you are my salvation, now and forever," you were adopted into a divine family. Your soul is protected; you have become a chosen vessel, set apart for God's glory, carrying the weight and wonder of His kingdom into your home.

With your passport to heavenly citizenship, God has given the family a sacred foundation to move forward. He first placed the headship of the family on the shoulders of fathers, not for power or pride, but to fulfil His purpose.

From the beginning, God created man first to work, lead, teach, and protect. In His divine order, fathers are called to take responsibility for the family before God. They are to serve as God's chosen representatives in their homes, leading with humility, courage, and unfailing obedience to God. Mothers and children are to follow this leadership, not in a spirit of inferiority, but in unity, so that the home may prosper according to God's purpose.

Genesis 2:19-20 *Whatever the man called each living creature, that was its name. The man gave names to all the livestock, the birds of the sky, and all the animals of the field. This means that fathers are endowed with incredible intelligence to lead. In the father's mind, when a problem arises, he immediately focuses on finding a solution, rather than dwelling on the problem itself. Because the Lord has taught him a sense of responsibility and discipline, even in his voice, one can hear the roar of a lion, masculinity, and discipline.*

A daughter of God understands her purpose. She would never reject the blessing of having children, nor would she ignore God's call to marriage. As she pursues her education and personal growth to become a wise and capable helper, she remains faithful to the Lord's voice.

She respects God's timing, values her parents' advice, and prepares herself, through her mother's guidance, to become a godly wife and, ultimately, a loving mother.

This is not regression; it is wisdom. It is a life rooted in eternal values, not in fleeting social media trends or the crazy movement of independent women. This is real life, and the Lord designed it this way for the good and benefit of families.

Moses said in Exodus 34:23-24:

"Three times a year, all your men shall appear before the Lord, the God of Israel. I will drive out nations before you and enlarge your territory, and no one will cover your land when you go up three times a year to appear before the Lord your God."

God expects men to rise and appear before Him. God entrusts men with a sacred responsibility, and in response to their obedience, He protects their homes, their territory, and their inheritance. The man who walks in the fear of the Lord becomes the protector of his family, and the Lord, in turn, becomes his divine protector.

This divine position has nothing to do with domination, but rather with responsibility. The father is the bearer of identity, vision, and spiritual protection. He must love as Christ loves the Church, lead as a servant, and sacrifice as a shepherd. In homes where this order is respected, children are safe. Sons walk in respect and confidence, and daughters behave with grace and discernment. The atmosphere in these homes reflects honor, discipline, and joy, for God's order brings peace.

When you meet a child raised in a home where both parents are devoted to God, you often notice a notable difference. This child shows stability, discipline, and genuine respect, qualities rooted in consistent love and biblical teaching.

The father's influence is evident in how the child speaks, obeys, and treats others. The father's reputation becomes a legacy that the children carry within them.

And girls raised in such homes walk with dignity; they do not seek refuge in unhealthy relationships but wait patiently and purely for a righteous man who honors their parents.

In God's kingdom, being a parent is more than a role; it is a calling. Fathers, you have been chosen to wear this cloak. Mothers, you have been trained to raise your children alongside this leadership. And you, children, are arrows in the hand of a warrior, destined to fly with determination and power.

Let us never forget that we are not raising our children for the world, but for the Kingdom of God. And in that Kingdom, God's order is good, His grace is sufficient, and His plan is eternal.

When God answers your prayers about your calling as a parent, it is an unfailing grace. His "yes" does not depend on your past mistakes or limitations. It comes from His goodness and sovereignty. You might feel unprepared, broken, or tired, but His ways are higher, and your strength does not restrict His blessings. They are made especially for you.

He knows what he is asking of you because raising children and caring for a family are the most important tasks for parents. I understand that some parents have given up and even given away their children.

Consider what Paul said in **1 Corinthians 10:13**:

"*No temptation has overtaken you that is not common to man. And God is faithful; he will not let you be tempted beyond what you can bear. But when you are tempted, he will also provide a way out so that you can endure it.*"

If God has entrusted you with a child, whether biological, adopted, fostered, or spiritual, it is because he has also appointed you as a vehicle for his love, healing, and truth in that child's life. That "yes" from heaven bears your name. It is not just a permission, but a mission.

God's "**yes**" means that he equips you to raise citizens of the Kingdom who reflect His character.

We live in a generation adrift, detached from eternal truths, drowning in identity confusion, absent fatherhood, and cultural chaos. But you, as a Christian, and your family will be covered by grace. Your worship is not a weakness, but the power of God to establish, protect, and sustain what He has ordained in you through the Holy Spirit.

Many families without God will still find salvation. In homes marked by failure, abuse, absence, or suffering, God has repeatedly revealed Himself as Jehovah Rapha, the God who heals. He restores broken homes and recovers lost children. Your story may have started in pain, but by grace, it will end in redemption. The Redeemer will save you and your family.

Do not believe the lie that your past disqualifies you from your family's future. When God enters a home, He rewrites everyone's story. Your prayer as a father will be heard; Jesus is listening.

True freedom for your children and grandchildren will not come from academic success, wealth, or popularity. It will come from following Jesus. When a father walks in the Spirit, he leads his children out of the desert of this world and into the light of truth. That is true freedom.

Jesus said, "***If the Son sets you free, you will be free indeed.***" (John 8:36)

This freedom is generational. When a father repents, the chains of addiction, pride, and shame begin to break. When a mother intercedes, God begins to open her children's eyes. God's grace flows through family lines when parents are willing to surrender to His lordship.

Being a father isn't about being perfect; it's about being present. It's about standing firm when others flee, speaking the truth when lies abound, and pointing to God when the world is in confusion. A godly father protects, trains, and raises the next generation in partnership with God. He understands that the battle is not his, but the Lord's.

God will be with you in the fire. That's what He did with Shadrach, Meshach, and Abednego. The battle belongs to the Lord. You are not raising your family alone. You are bound to the Savior who conquered death, strengthened by the Holy Spirit, and under the authority of the Father.

So, stand still. Watch God fight for your family. When you lift your hands in worship, you are engaging in spiritual warfare. When you kneel to pray for your children, angels move in your direction. You are not powerless.

The Shepherd of the Home

The Lord is our shepherd, and the father is called to reflect that same heart. A true shepherd lays down his life for his sheep. If a father had only one parachute, a godly man would, without hesitation, attach it to his wife or child. Why would he do that? Because he knows that love protects, that love sacrifices, and that love covers. All parents know what I am talking about.

This is not a weakness; it is divine strength. Jesus was not forced to die on the cross; he chose to do so for us. And every father who gives up his pride, his ambitions, and his comfort to raise his family in faith expresses that same love in the image of Christ.

But God never intended for fathers to act alone. His divine wisdom includes both parents, each with a unique role and equal value. Together, mother and father create a balance of greatness. In homes where one of them is absent, God fills the void with His grace and appoints others, such as grandparents, mentors, or spiritual fathers, to take up the mantle.

I Am a Citizen of Heaven

Your earthly citizenship may determine where you vote, but your eternal citizenship determines how you live. You are a citizen of heaven, charged with raising the children of the Kingdom. That means your home isn't just a shelter; it's a sanctuary. Your table isn't just a place to eat, it's a place of mission. Your family isn't just biological, it's spiritual.

Live for the Kingdom. Wait for your King Jesus, and make every decision, every discipline, and every conversation point a reflection of the greater reality: the Kingdom is here and the Kingdom is coming. Teach your children to aspire to Heaven, not out of fear, but out of deep love for the King.

This world will pass, but your investment in their souls will resonate with God's plan, which is clear:

Families built on love, led by faithful fathers and mothers, healed by His mercy, and anchored in His truth. In this sacred design, love is not a feeling; it's a force. It heals hearts, redeems destinies, and plants seeds of justice.

As you close this book, remember: you're not just a reader. You are part of God's divine legacy. He has placed in your hands the most important mission on earth: to raise the next generation in His name.

Whether you're a father, mother, or grandparent, your love can heal souls. Your faith can awaken futures. Your obedience can open the gates of heaven over your home.

So, arise, citizen of the Kingdom. Peel down your heart. Trust in the King. And build a family that will withstand not only time, but eternity.

Heavenly Father,

We present ourselves to you as citizens of heaven, called by your name, redeemed by your mercy, and appointed to walk in the beauty of your divine order.

You are the Creator of families, the Author of the plan, and the Giver of every perfect gift. You have made our home a sacred place, a dwelling where love reflects your heavenly glory. Your Word declares, "Children are a heritage from the Lord, the fruit of the womb is a reward" (Psalm 127:3).

We thank you for this precious inheritance, and we recognize that each child is a testimony to your faithfulness. May your name be blessed, along with all fathers, mothers, and children, in Jesus' name. ***Amen.***

Heavenly Father,

We pray for all fathers

On this Father's Day, we lift to You the men You have chosen, those whom You have given the job of guiding, protecting, and providing for me.

We think especially of those fathers who quietly fulfil their responsibilities, without applause, without celebration, but with unfailing faithfulness.

Men who stay, who say "yes" to their calling.

Who fight for their families and serve without seeking recognition?

Lord, today I ask You to bless my father with Your grace. Strengthen him with the courage, humility, and wisdom that come from above.

As you command in Ephesians 6:4:

"Fathers, do not provoke your children to anger, but bring them up in the discipline and instruction of the Lord." "

May every father take this to heart, remembering that his mission begins at home. May their obedience attract Your favor,

And may their faithfulness become a refuge for their home. For every father who carries the cross of fatherhood, may the Lord go before them, beside them, and within them. In Jesus' mighty name, we pray. **Amen.**

Heavenly Father,

We pray for every mother. We lift them before You, the wise builders of the home, the nurturers to whom You have granted compassion, care, and quiet strength.

May they walk each day clothed in dignity, grounded in unfailing faith, and overflowing with a love that echoes Yours. Grant them the patience to meet the demands of each moment, and clothe them with strength that endures and does not fade. Inspire their hands to bring beauty and purpose, even in the midst of life's turmoil.

As Your Word declares in Proverbs 14:1: *"The wise woman builds her house…"* Remind every mother that her labor of love is sacred, seen by You, cherished by heaven, and eternally meaningful.

Bless them with good health, renewed joy, and perfect peace. We pray in the mighty name of Jesus. **Amen.**

A Prayer for Children

Lord, we pray for every Christian child, the heritage of Your hands, the fruit of the womb, arrows in the quiver of a faithful generation.

As Psalm 127:3 reminds us: *"Children are a heritage from the Lord, the fruit of the womb is a reward."* May they grow in wisdom and stature, in grace before God and men. Teach them to honor their parents with respect and love. As Ephesians 6:1-3 promises: *"Honor your father and mother… so that you may be happy and live long on the earth."*

May Your sons and daughters become peacemakers, pure in heart, faithful in their words, and bold in their righteousness, ready to pass on the heritage of faith to each generation. May they be the children of promise, as You declared in Revelation 21:7: *"Those who overcome will inherit all this, and I will be their God, and they will be my children."* In the name of Jesus. **Amen.**

NUMBER *12*

The number 12 is present throughout the biblical narrative, symbolizing divine order, completeness, and the founding of God's people. In designing a book that addresses the sacred responsibility of Christian parenting, the number 12 grounded the learner in God's blueprint for spiritual leadership, generational inheritance, and covenant identity.

For the world's 2.9 billion Christians, the number 12 holds not only historical significance but also a present-day significance. It invites every believer to see themselves as part of something greater than their individual family history. When we read the story of the 12 tribes of Israel, we are reminded that God's plan of covenant and blessing has always included ordinary people; a commonwealth called to be holy, obedient, and faithful.

The twelve sons of Jacob (Genesis 35:22-26) became the original representatives of the 12 tribes of Israel, which later formed the nation God chose to reveal His laws and love to the world. The structure of this book is not accidental; it's a demonstration of God's intentionality.

In Joshua 4:1-9, after Israel had finished crossing the Jordan, the Lord instructed Joshua to select twelve men, one from each of the twelve tribes of Israel, to gather twelve stones from the river where the priests stood. These stones were carried to their camp as a memorial to their fallen comrades. Joshua said, *"When your children ask what these stones mean, tell them the waters of the Jordan stopped before the ark of the covenant. These stones will be a sign for Israel forever."*

And the twelve stones remain as a witness to this day.

This act symbolized God's commitment to leading His people into the Promised Land. It was not just a miraculous crossing, but a generational memorial of God's provision. Similarly, 12 loaves of bread were placed in the Tabernacle (Leviticus 24:5), representing the tribes and their ongoing presence before God.

In Numbers 1:44, He nominated 12 leaders, one for each tribe, again to prove that God's governance of

His people required order, direction, and accountability. These patterns were no accident: **they were divine instructions for building a holy society.**

When Jesus inaugurated the New Covenant, He did so in accordance with a divine pattern that echoed the wisdom of eternity. **His choice of twelve disciples was no accident of culture or tradition; it was a prophetic declaration.** By calling twelve men, Jesus was proclaiming the birth of a *new Israel*, not defined by **lineage** or **ethnicity**, but by faith in Him as the promised Messiah.

These men were more than students; they were the chosen foundations of a reborn spiritual family, destined to become the patriarchs of a holy nation born of the Holy Spirit.

In Matthew 19:28, Jesus reveals the weight of this calling: **the twelve will sit upon thrones, judging the twelve tribes of Israel.** This imagery unveils the unbroken thread between the Old Covenant and the New, the continuity of God's plan, fulfilled in Christ.

The vision reaches its climax in Revelation 21:14:

"**The wall of the city had twelve foundations, and on them were the names of the twelve apostles of the Lamb.**"

Where New Jerusalem is again represented by

the number twelve, each bearing the name of one of the apostles of the Lamb. The eternal dwelling place of God's people is founded on their testimony, obedience, and sacrifice, so that we may have this gospel today.

Through them, the Church received its spiritual DNA. Their hands healed the sick, their voices proclaimed the gospel, and their authority in Christ cast out demons (Matthew 10:7-8; Mark 3:14-15).

These first apostles were entrusted as stewards of the Kingdom, bearing the good news beyond Jerusalem to the very ends of the earth. Their faithfulness marked the beginning of a spiritual nation that continues to grow, a people redeemed by the blood of Christ, called to be His holy dwelling, and destined for the eternal city whose builder and architect is God.

Thus, when **The Citizenship of Christian Parenthood** is written to serve as a **symbolic extension** of this sacred framework, each chapter can be seen as a "**tribe**" or "**foundation for families**", a distinct yet unified contribution to the call of godly parenting. It speaks to the **divine government** of the Christian home, where the father leads in righteousness, the mother nurtures in wisdom, and children are raised in the "*discipline and instruction of the Lord*" (Ephesians 6:4).

The structure invites Christian parents to see their household as a miniature reflection of God's spiritual nation.

To the Christian reader, every chapter of this book reminds us that parenting is more than a personal responsibility; it is a **kingdom assignment**. Each lesson, discipline, and prayer offered to a child is like placing another stone in God's eternal memorial. Christian parents are not simply raising children; they are forming **citizens of heaven**, future leaders in the spiritual Israel Jesus came to build. By aligning the book's structure with this sacred number, the message becomes more than educational; it becomes **prophetic**.

In conclusion, the chapters of *The Citizenship of Christian Parenthood* are not merely thematic; they are a **theological architecture**. Just as God built His people upon 12 sons, 12 stones, 12 leaders, and 12 apostles, this work seeks to help families make their homes on the same divine pattern. In doing so, every reader is invited to participate in restoring divine order within their household and contribute to the unfolding story of God's eternal Kingdom.

Heavenly Father,

Your greatness stretches beyond the void. Before time began, you were unshaken, eternal. When darkness was upon the face of the deep, Your Spirit moved upon the waters. Breathing order into chaos, Light into shadow, Hope into nothingness.

You are the **Light of our family**,
The Flame that never flickers, the Anchor of every soul that calls Your name. We don't ever want to be separate from You, not for a breath, not for a moment.

As you spoke and said,
"Let the earth bring forth the living creature after his kind," So we, your children, arise. Created in Your image,
Held in Your hand, thriving under Your divine design.
We are thankful, Lord, to rest beneath your **protection**
To stand within the fortress of Your love.
Though unseen, **your angel armies surround** us:
Each one stationed, each one sent, guarding the faithful,
Empowering the weak, allowing us to walk in holy liberty. Our battle is real, but we fight not with our strength.
The blood of Jesus is our salvation.
We don't need to earn what has already been won.
The price is paid. The tomb is empty. The veil is torn. It is finished.
Our mighty Christ Jesus, you bore the weight so we could rise. You drank the cup so we could be free.
We praise You not only for what You've done, but for who You are.
King of Glory, Lamb of God, Redeemer of our souls.
Let Your light shine in our homes. Let Your Spirit dwell within our hearts. Let Your Word guide our steps.
Let Your peace reign in our midst. Forever and always, we are yours. Amen.

A Psalm of Healing, Freedom, and the Victory of Christian Men.

My scars shall glorify God and never shame me. My testimony shall inspire faith in every heart. The story of my healing and redemption Shall echo through generations yet unborn. Through Christ, I am more than a conqueror. My life stands as a living witness to the power of the cross. For He has set me free, and I will never go back.

Fear no longer controls me, for the Lord is my peace. Every chain is broken in the name of Jesus. I walk in the liberty of the Spirit, and my family shall dwell in the freedom of the Kingdom. The blood of the Lamb redeems me. No sin from my past has any power over me.

Paul reaffirms in 2 Corinthians 5:17 that in Christ, we are made new. I am a new creation in Christ. The chains of guilt are shattered;

the voice of condemnation is silenced. My life is marked not by shame, but by the righteousness of Christ.

By His stripes, I am healed in my spirit, soul, and body. The Lord heals my wounds and restores my joy. Sickness has no final authority over me because Christ has triumphed forever. Every broken part within me is converted by the hand of my God.

I shall walk in the fullness purchased at Calvary. The cross stands as proof of His sovereign plan and the assurance of my victory. No suffering is wasted; the Lord's blood was shed for me.

I am saved and redeemed.
Jesus is Lord over my life, my family, my future, my destiny. Every battle I face lies beneath the authority. Of the risen Christ. I live not in fear but in victory. For my King reigns forevermore.

The Lord is my strength and my defense.

He has become my salvation. (Psalm 118:14) My confidence is not in human strength, but in God's power. Although I grow tired, He renews my strength like that of an eagle. He delights in me because my hope is in His mercy. My weakness is the stage for His power.

My surrender is the key to His victory. His grace is sufficient, His power endless, His will is perfect and true. The Lord, who enumerates the stars, knows me by name. His administration presides over the universe and safeguards my existence. No adversary's scheme can succeed against His counsel. His vision for me is clear. His sovereignty provides my stability, his wisdom directs my path, and my moments are entrusted to His care. He has borne my griefs and carried my sorrows; By His wounds, I am healed. No condemnation remains, for Christ has paid my debt in full. My identity is not shame, but redemption; not fear, but love, not defeat, but victory.

The cross is my confidence, the resurrection my eternal song. The Lord is great, His greatness beyond measure. No obstacle is higher than His throne, no enemy stronger than His angel armies. No darkness is deeper than His light. My life, my family, and my future are secure in the hands of the Almighty. His greatness brings me peace; all of my worship is not in vain. His wisdom gives me confidence, and His presence is my joy.

Isaiah 53
Who hath believed our report?

And to whom is the arm of the LORD revealed? For he shall grow up before him as a tender plant, and as a root out of a dry ground: he hath no form nor comeliness; and when we shall see him, there is no beauty that we should desire him. He is despised and rejected of men; a man of sorrows, and acquainted with grief: and we hid as it were our faces from him; he was despised, and we esteemed him not.

Surely, he has borne our griefs and carried our sorrows: yet we did esteem him stricken, smitten by God, and afflicted. But he was wounded for our transgressions, he was bruised for our iniquities: the chastisement of our peace was upon him; and with his stripes we are healed.

All we are like sheep have gone astray; we have turned everyone to his own way; and the LORD hath laid on him the iniquity of us all.

He was oppressed, and he was afflicted, yet he opened not his mouth: he is brought as a lamb to the slaughter, and as a sheep before her shearers is dumb, so he opened not his mouth. He was taken from prison and from judgment: and who shall declare his generation? for he was cut off out of the land of the living: for the transgression of my people was he stricken.

And he made his grave with the wicked, and with the rich in his death; because he had done no violence, neither was any deceit in his mouth. Yet it pleased the LORD to bruise him; he has put him to grief: when you make his soul an offering for sin, he shall see his seed, he shall prolong his days, and the pleasure of the LORD shall prosper in his hand.

He shall see of the travail of his soul, and shall be satisfied: by his knowledge shall my righteous servant justify many; for he shall bear their iniquities. Therefore, I will divide him a portion with the great, and he shall divide the spoil with the strong; because he has poured out his soul unto death, and he was numbered with the transgressors; and he bore the sin of many, and made intercession for the transgressors.

PSALM 147

Praise the LORD!
For *it is* good to sing praises to our God; For *it is* pleasant, *and* praise is beautiful.
The LORD builds up Jerusalem;
He gathers together the outcasts of Israel.
He heals the broken-hearted. And binds up their wounds.
He counts the number of the stars;
He calls them all by name.

Great *is* our Lord, and mighty in power; His understanding *is* infinite.
The LORD lifts the humble;
He casts the wicked down to the ground.
Sing to the LORD with thanksgiving;
Sing praises on the harp to our God,
Who covers the heavens with clouds, who prepares rain for the earth, who makes grass grow on the mountains?
He gives the beast its food, *and* to young ravens that cry.
He does not delight in the strength of the horse; He takes no pleasure in the legs of a man. The LORD takes pleasure in those who fear Him, in those who hope in His mercy.

Praise the LORD, O Jerusalem!

Praise your God, O Zion! For He has strengthened the bars of your gates; He has blessed your children within you.

He makes peace *in* your borders *and* fills you with the finest wheat.

He sends out His command *to the* earth; His word runs
very swiftly.

He gives snow like wool.
He scatters the frost like ashes;
He casts out His hail like morsels;
Who can stand before His cold?
He sends out His word and melts them;
He causes His wind to blow, *and* the waters flow.

He declares His word to Jacob,
His statutes and His judgments to Israel.
He has not dealt thus with any nation;
And *as for His* judgments, they have not known them.

The Greatness of God and His Promises

"Great is our Lord, and of great power: His understanding is infinite."

There are seasons when healing seems to take longer, when results last longer than expected, and when the heart bears the weight of unanswered prayers. Still, even in such a wilderness, the soul can continue to sing of God's glory. One word from heaven is enough to remind us how close our Lord is.

Psalm 147 anchors us in this truth:

"Great is our Lord, and of great power: His understanding is infinite." This single verse is a fortress for the weary soul. It declares that God's power is not reckless force, but strength guided by perfect wisdom. He sees what we cannot know, He understands what we cannot explain, and He weaves every fragment of our lives into the tapestry of His eternal design.

To meditate on the greatness of God is to lift our eyes from fear into his power, full of grace. His Kingdom is not only a future hope but a present reality. His reign is active, His counsel unshakable, His hand at work in every breath we take. The One who measures the stars and calls them each by name also knows the secret wounds and deepest needs of your heart.

This greatness is not abstract. It is personal. It is living. It is for you and for your family. When doubts whisper and trials roar, you may answer with the psalmist: *"Great is our Lord!"* You are not abandoned in the storm; you are carried by the One whose voice commands the waves. His greatness is your shield, His wisdom your compass, His presence your abiding comfort.

Beloved child of God, never forget: your trials are not wasted. The One who bore the cross walks with you now. The same Jesus who was despised and rejected has become your eternal High Priest, your Advocate, your Healer. By His wounds, you are healed; by His sacrifice, you are forgiven; and by His resurrection, you are secured in an everlasting hope.

At the heart of the Gospel lies a promise that cannot be shaken: God heals His people. The psalmist proclaims that He draws near to the broken-hearted, binding up their wounds with the tenderness of a Father. This finds its ultimate fulfilment in the vision of Isaiah: The Suffering Servant who bore in His body the sickness, sin, and sorrow of all humanity.

The healing Christ offers is complete; it touches every part of us. It reaches into every corner of the heart, every broken part of the soul, and every weakness of the body. His stripes are not signs of defeat but the very tools of our renewal. By His wounds, we are healed from guilt, despair, and the power of sin, and we are healed unto eternal life.

God's healing goes beyond the physical. It repairs relationships damaged by bitterness, restores minds troubled by anxiety, and renews hearts exhausted by life's burdens. Isaiah 53 reminds us that Christ bore not only our sins but also our sorrows. No wound of the spirit is too great for Him. Where there is brokenness, He provides wholeness. Where there is division, He promotes reconciliation. Where there is despair, He instils eternal hope.

Ezekiel 36:26:

"**I will give you a new heart and put a new spirit within you; I will take the heart of stone out of your flesh and give you a heart of flesh.**"

The beauty of His Kingdom is this: God does not simply mend the broken; He makes them strong. He lifts the meek and humbles the proud through life experiences. In Christ, weakness becomes a vessel for divine power; with a renewed heart, a new river of grace will flow in your wilderness. What the enemy intended for harm will turn into a testimony, proclaiming the triumph of God. The Christian family belongs to the kingdom of the Almighty, seated on His throne in paradise.

Therefore, do not despise your broken places. They won't last long; what you are now will pass. Just keep your faith and trust the Lord with everything. These are the very grounds where His glory will shine brightest. Do not fear your wounds; they are sacred spaces where His healing flows. You are not abandoned; you are being rebuilt. You are not forgotten; you are being restored.

Psalm 46:7:

"**The Lord Almighty is with us; The God of Jacob is our fortress**."

The psalmist invites us to see this amazing truth of God's grace: the same God who rules the galaxies cares enough to heal the brokenhearted. His sovereignty is not distant or cold; it is the loving reign of a Father-King who holds all things together by the power of His word.

"*God's promises are **Yes** and **Amen** in Christ.*"

(2 Corinthians 1:20)

When the Christian family proclaims the greatness of God:

We declare that no force of darkness, no scheme of man, and no power of hell can overturn His will. His reign is absolute, His counsel unchanging, and His decrees are eternal. Even the cross, which seemed like the triumph of evil, was in fact the unveiling of His redemptive plan.

"It was the will of the Lord to crush Him"

(Isaiah 53:10), and through that crushing, salvation came to the world through our Lord Jesus Christ. Such is the greatness of our God. Infinite in wisdom, unsearchable in power. Near to the broken, and faithful to every promise.

O Lord, rebuild the broken homes, restore the weary marriages, redeem the wounded children, and revive the sleeping hearts. Let the sons of God arise with boldness, let fathers lead with integrity and love, let every man walk in purity, strength, and surrender to Christ.

Heavenly Father, your greatness extends beyond the void. Before time started, you were unshaken and eternal. When darkness covered the deep, your Spirit moved over the waters, bringing order to chaos, light to shadow, and hope to emptiness.

You are the **Light of our family**,
The Flame that never flickers,
The Anchor of every soul that calls Your name.
We don't ever want to be separate from You.
Not for a breath, not for a moment.

As you spoke and said:

"Let the earth bring forth the living creature after his kind,"

So, we, your children, arise.
Created in Your image,
Held in Your hand,
Thriving under Your divine design.
We are thankful, Lord,
To rest beneath Your **protection**
To stand within the fortress of Your love.
Though unseen, **your angel armies surround** us:
Each one stationed, each one sent,
Guarding the faithful,
Empowering the weak,
Allowing us to walk in holy liberty.
And though the battle is real, we fight not in our strength.
The blood of Jesus is our salvation. We don't need to earn what has already been won.
The price is paid. The tomb is empty.
The veil is torn. Our Lord has risen again.
It is finished.
Our mighty Christ Jesus, you bore the weight so we could rise. You drank the cup so we could be free. We praise You not just for what You've done, but for who You are: ***King of Glory***, Lamb of God, Redeemer of our souls.
So, Father,
Let Your light shine in our homes,
Let Your Spirit dwell in our hearts, let Your Word guide our steps, let Your peace reign among us.
Forever and always, we are yours.
In Jesus' name. Amen

Final Acknowledgment

The Citizenship of Christian Parenthood was never a difficult book to write, because as a Christian parent myself, it was a calling. Every page was born out of prayer, meditation, and the profound joy of knowing the Lord and serving Him for 27 years. Christian parents do not simply raise their children; they watch over their souls for eternity.

This book serves as a reminder that we, the 2.9 billion believers worldwide, are not a scattered people. We are citizens of an eternal kingdom, "the kingdom of God.

Our shared **citizenship** *transcends geography, language, culture, and religious affiliation. And within this Kingdom, the sacred mission of being a parent is one of the greatest honors.*

My mindset in writing this book was grounded in obedience. I wanted to speak to the **mother who prays silently**, the **father who leads faithfully**, the **grandparent who showers generations with blessings**, and the weary parent who feels invisible.

You are all part of God's sacred government on earth, raising ambassadors for Christ in your homes and embodying His love through your daily sacrifices. I also recognize that I am just one voice among many. I stand on the shoulders of the faithful, those who taught me, prayed for me, corrected me, and showed me what it means to walk in the light. This book is the fruit of that legacy.

To all parents, foster parents, adoptive parents, guardians, and mentors: thank you for answering the call. May God strengthen your hands and deepen your joy as you continue to build homes that mirror the heavenly realm.

I conclude this work with respect, humility, and hope, knowing that as you raise your children, heaven rejoices and the Kingdom advances.

The Lord will teach all your children, and great will be their peace. (Isaiah 54:13)

"But our citizenship is in heaven. And we eagerly await a Savior from there, the Lord Jesus Christ." (*Philippians 3:20*)

Psalm 121:7–8

The LORD shall preserve thee from all evil: he shall preserve thy soul. The LORD shall preserve thy going out and thy coming in from this time forth, and even for evermore.

HEAVENLY CITIZEN

CHAPTER TWENTY-FIVE

God's Unchanging Love and Our Return home

Since the beginning of creation, long before humanity spoke its first words or took its first breath, God's love was already devising a way to stay connected with humanity. It was within the peaceful setting of Eden. The tranquillity of each sunrise when God longed to speak with man, and the harmonious melodies carried by the wind, reflected the presence of the Almighty. That steadfast love endured through many years as the Lord guided and disciplined humanity, even after individuals chose to forge their own paths rather than follow their Creator.

Though we may turn away, God's heart remains unchanged, His mercy as steady as the stars shining in the sky. His original plan remains unchanged: to live with us in a way that allows Him to visit and speak to us without the need for prayer, fasting, or lamenting to receive His grace for eternity. As the Lord says to Paul: My grace is sufficient for thee: for my strength is made perfect in weakness. Most gladly, therefore, will I instead boast in my infirmities, that the power of Christ may rest upon me.

Are you a believer in our Lord Jesus?

He was not a religious man, nor part of any denomination, but his heart was aching with sadness to see how lazy we are about seeking the kingdom of God first. So, when the disciples asked him what the greatest commandment was, he responded with a secret that every Christian family should already know. Remember how long we've been in church, believed, and been baptized; we've done everything right and followed all the rules to the letter.

Somehow, Christians are suffering because we have ignored the teachings of the only most excellent Teacher who ever lived. He was teaching His disciples to trust God for their daily needs, including food, clothing, and shelter, and reminding His followers that if they prioritized God's kingdom and righteousness, everything else they needed would be provided.

Matthew 6:33:

"But seek first the kingdom of God and His righteousness, and all these things shall be added to you."

He then continued teaching and said, "I have loved you with an everlasting love; therefore, with lovingkindness I have drawn you" (Jeremiah 31:3). He also quoted, "The steadfast love of the Lord never ceases; His mercies never come to an end; they are new every morning; great is Your faithfulness" (Lamentations 3:22-23). These words gently remind us that no mistake, failure, or sin can diminish the eternal love that God has for His children.

When Adam and Eve ate from the tree of the knowledge of good and evil, they did not simply break a rule; they broke fellowship, exchanging divine intimacy for human reasoning, and stepped out of the light into confusion. Yet even in that moment of rebellion, the father's plan of redemption was already at work; for Scripture declares that "the Lamb was slain from the foundation of the world" (Revelation 13:8). God's foreknowledge of our weakness did not cancel His purpose to save us; instead, it revealed the depth of His commitment to restore us.

Humanity hid behind leaves and fear; we love pretending to have a lot or to show up without discerning real wisdom, but God came walking in the cool of the day, calling, "Where are you?" (Genesis 3:9).

Many Christians bear a quiet burden of past sins and mistakes, haunted by feelings of guilt and shame, or moments of weak faith and doubt, crying out like the man in Mark 9:24, 'Lord, I believe; help my unbelief!" They have faith, but not enough to get them out of certain situations. They face ongoing struggles with sin, experience seasons of spiritual dryness, and mourn their lack of adequate knowledge or prayer. Some are influenced by condemning voices that tell them they'll never be good enough, forgetting their true identity in Christ.

However, Jesus never demanded perfection, only repentance and relationship. His love remains constant and unconditional, for "while we were still sinners, Christ died for us." (Romans 5:8)

Now, as your brother in Christ, I ask you: Where are you with your faith?

Because you'll need to seek the kingdom of God first today and every day, before asking for abundance, please get your condition in order with Jesus.

Hebrews 11:6

"But without faith it is impossible to please him: for he that cometh to God must believe that he is, and that he is a rewarder of them that diligently seek him. ***Faith comes first; reward (abundance) follows. Jesus referred to this as the law of receiving.***

Not because He did not know the location of your heart, but because He longed for reconciliation. Since that first moment of separation, all history has been the story of God calling His people back; every covenant, every prophet, every word of Scripture is a thread woven into the same design of restoration. **"Return to Me, and I will return to you," says the Lord of Hosts (Malachi 3:7).**

Imagine, right now, at this very moment, as you read this book, that He is searching for you, your soul, to return to Him in faith, with small prayers and thanksgiving. Do you truly understand what it means for the Lord of Hosts to be looking for you? Yes, you! He is searching for you by name. Can you say, 'Yes, Lord, here I am,' starting right now with a humble heart?

Put your name here ....!

Lord of Hosts, we humbly bow before Your presence, seeking forgiveness for all. We thank You for never giving up on us. I surrender myself to You now, Lord, guide and teach me each day to learn how to prioritize Your kingdom. I entrust my life and family to You; please bless and protect us in the name of Jesus. Amen.

Even when humanity filled the earth with violence and Israel turned to idols, God kept sending His messengers, offered grace, and prepared the way for His ultimate revelation in Jesus Christ. The divine patience of the Lord is not weakness; it is salvation extended across generations, as Peter wrote: "The Lord is not slow in keeping His promise, as some understand slowness; instead, He is patient with you, not wanting anyone to perish, but everyone to come to repentance"

(2 Peter 3:9).

I extend that same invitation to you today, brethren: every sunrise is a renewal of mercy, and every heartbeat is a reminder that Heaven still waits for your response. God's unchanging love is not just a passive emotion; it is an active force drawing us back to Himself. I have seen church members crying out daily with tears, praying without fully understanding the secret Jesus shared with us in His teachings. The secret to reaching heaven is right in front of us, on the pages of the Bible.

Lord of Hosts, thank you for giving every Christian this knowledge.

Philippians 4:6-7:
"Do not be anxious about anything, but in every situation, by prayer and petition, with thanksgiving, present your requests to God. And the peace of God, which transcends all understanding, will guard your hearts and your minds in Christ Jesus.

With everlasting kindness, I will have mercy on you, says the Lord your Redeemer (Isaiah 54:8); His love is the reason the world still spins, the reason grace still speaks louder than judgment. The waters don't flood the earth, and the master said, "Never again will there be a flood to destroy the earth." Genesis 9:11

Many observe the brokenness of the world and assume that God has turned away; however, the truth is the opposite: it is humanity that has turned its back further away from the Lord, while God remains with open arms for every soul. Jesus demonstrated this in His parable of the prodigal son: the father did not chase his son into the other country, but he waited daily at the gate, ready to run and embrace him the moment he appeared on the road (Luke 15:20). This exemplifies the posture of our Heavenly Father, always patient, always welcoming, and never changing no matter what we've done, he is waiting on you to come back to Daddy.

I advise my friends not to play games with a man's daughter because, as a father myself, I understand the deep responsibility, care, and time invested in raising her. If you're not prepared to ask for her hand in marriage, it's better to stay away. A father's love is immense; many fathers cry when giving their daughter away in marriage. I see this as a transfer of responsibility: to care for, hold, and cherish her until death.

Faith begins when we recognize that every longing in the human soul is a call back to its origin; every hunger for meaning, every thirst for justice, every ache for love is a whisper from eternity saying, *Come home.* Augustine of Hippo once said, "**Our hearts are restless until they rest in You, O God,**" and Scripture echoes that truth: "He has made everything beautiful in its time; He has also set eternity in the human heart" (Ecclesiastes 3:11). God placed eternity within us so that even in a fallen world we would never feel fully at home until we returned to Him.

Have you ever attended a funeral or been in a hospital room while feeling unwell?

What goes through your mind in those moments? What if... right? Yeah, we all feel the same emotions, but not quite yet. Yes, you are reading this book before it's time to head home, and making sure he knows who you are. "Nothing unclean and no one who practices abomination and lying, shall ever come into it, but only those whose names are written in the Lamb's book of life." Revelation 21:27.

This, then, is the story of every believer, the long journey from distance to closeness, from ignorance to understanding, from rebellion to redemption; and throughout that journey, the constant element is not our faithfulness, but God's. The Psalmist declares, "If we are faithless, He remains faithful, for He cannot deny Himself" (2 Timothy 2:13). His character is covenantal; He keeps His word not because we deserve it but because He is love, and love does not fail.

So, when we speak of our journey back to Him, I find this to be a response to what has already been extended; we are not climbing toward Heaven by our own Christian strength, but we are being drawn by divine mercy. "**No one can come to Me unless the Father who sent Me draws him**," said Jesus (John 6:44). Our repentance is therefore not a punishment but an invitation; our obedience is not slavery but a participation in divine restoration. The more we understand this, the more our hearts overflow with gratitude, for salvation is not the story of man reaching God but of God reaching man, of the Shepherd leaving the ninety-nine to find the one who was lost (Luke 15:4-7).

Once you study and understand the Lord's devotions for you, you come to realize that God will bring back what was lost to you, broken, or stolen, and make it even better than before. **"I will restore to you the years that the locust hath eaten."** *(Joel 2:25)*

Thus, from Genesis to Revelation, ***from the garden to the cross to the empty tomb, and to the last 40 days of teaching of our Lord Jesus, the theme remains unbroken: God's love never changes***; His mercy never ceases; His purpose never fails. And as we accept that truth, faith awakens, hope arises, and the journey to home begins again within every willing heart. He told Isaiah to tell his people this in Isaiah 44:22:

"I have swept away your offenses like a cloud, your sins like the morning mist. Return to me, for I have redeemed you."

God's Provision for Life on Earth: Critical Thinking for Christians.

God has never left His creation without provision; that brings a couple of questions:

God's Provisions:

- If God has already provided everything we need, what exactly does "daily bread" mean in the Lord's Prayer?
- How does free will fit into a world where everything is already provided for?
- Why do some people still live in lack if God's provision is universal?
- Is provision only physical (food, shelter, air) or also spiritual with peace, wisdom, love?
- **Prayer and Asking**
- If we already have what we need, what is the true purpose of prayer?
- Is prayer meant to *ask* or to *align* ourselves with what God has already given?
- Why did Jesus still teach us to "ask, seek, and knock"?
- How can believers learn to recognize the difference between asking for what we already have versus what we truly need?

Look in the bible to see if it's not a complete manual for the survival of Christians. All of these laws, teachings, and lessons, God has forethought of everything we'll need to sustain us before we go home permanently.

Human Responsibility

- If God gave everything, does that mean humans are failing to use His gifts properly?

- How can humanity restore balance to creation if provision is being misused or wasted?
- Are poverty and inequality signs of human disobedience rather than divine withholding?
- What role does stewardship play in manifesting God's provision?

Paul said in 2 Peter 1:3

"His divine power has given us everything we need for life and godliness"

He established the earth as a complete system of provision long before humanity understood agriculture or science. The rivers carried water before we learned irrigation, the trees bore fruit before we learned trade, and the seasons turned before calendars were invented. "The earth is the Lord's, and the fullness thereof, the world and they that dwell therein" (Psalm 24:1).

Nothing in creation is accidental; every mountain, seed, and drop of rain testifies that the Maker prepared the world not only as a dwelling place, but as a testimony of His goodness.

When Scripture says, "His divine power has given us everything we need for life and godliness through our knowledge of Him who called us to believe, this reveals that the believer's problem is not lack of resources, but lack of revelation. Many pray for what they already have, asking for open doors while the keys rest in their own hands. God's design is that man would steward, cultivate, and multiply what was given, not live-in fear of shortage. From Eden to today, the mandate has remained the same: "Be fruitful and multiply; fill the earth and subdue it; have dominion" (Genesis 1:28). Dominion is responsible authority guided by righteousness.

Over time, deception took hold of people's hearts, and even among believers, truth was exchanged for manipulation. Crossing borders comes at a high cost. To visit a different continent, whose land all belongs to our God, specific qualifications are required. Reflect on this and find meaning in it! Our disobedience goes so far that one can't grasp how many laws exist within their own country and territory. We keep each other in slavery without any feeling or thought, but under certain conditions.

The Apostle Paul warned the Corinthian church and our modern church today: *"Unlike so many, we do not peddle the word of God for profit, but in Christ we speak before God with sincerity"* (2 Corinthians 2:17). Sadly, the same spirit of commerce that Jesus drove out of the temple still hides behind the pulpits; the same tables of exchange now take the form of manipulated offerings and false promises. Christians often do so much to receive blessings from God. These teachings are only valid if they enrich oneself. Christ overturned the tables not because giving was wrong, but because the motive was corrupted. He said, "My house shall be called a house of prayer, but you have made it a den of thieves" (Matthew 21:13).

Giving was designed as worship, not as transaction; generosity was meant to express gratitude, not to buy miracles. **Do you know anyone who is selling miracles like they are the only one who knows where the Lord's heart is?** The early church understood this balance: they shared all things in common so that none among them lacked (Acts 4:34-35); it was unity, not manipulation.

However, in modern times, some leaders have transformed stewardship into a system of control, replacing faith with fear, and turning worshipers into customers. And the business is money every week. They teach that God's favor can be purchased through the next "seed," "prophetic offering," or "breakthrough fund," when the Word clearly says, "Freely you have received; freely give" (Matthew 10:8). Now, they will instruct you to give a specific amount to receive a double portion. From now on, I want you to keep it in your Bible until God comes personally to take it from you. If He does not, begin investing it, so the Lord can grant you a better portion.

It is not wrong for believers to give; indeed, Paul wrote, "God loves a cheerful giver" (2 Corinthians 9:7). The danger lies in giving through compulsion, fear, or manipulation. A pure heart knows that the tithe and offering are acts of worship, not payment for favor. The widow who placed two small coins in the temple treasury gave more than all the rich because she gave from love, not leverage (Mark 12:42-44). The Kingdom measures obedience by sincerity, not by amount.

God's provision is already at work all around us; He designed the soil to yield food, the mind to create solutions, the body to labor, and the Spirit to inspire creativity. The more we recognize this divine structure, the less we fall prey to manipulation. "The blessing of the Lord makes rich, and He adds no sorrow with it" (Proverbs 10:22). True blessing carries peace, not pressure. Not to give non-stop every month. The believer who learns this truth becomes unshakable; he no longer chases prophetic promises for sale, for he already walks in the inheritance of sonship of the Almighty. "All things are yours, and you are Christ's, and Christ is God's" (1 Corinthians 3:21-23).

Still, the Lord calls His people to discernment, for not every voice that says "Lord, Lord" speaks from His Spirit.

"**Beware of false prophets**, who come to you in sheep's clothing but inwardly are ravenous wolves" (Matthew 7:15). Their words are sweet, but their fruit reveals greed. They prophesy gain yet ignore holiness; they build crowds yet neglect character. But the Spirit teaches the humble: "You have an anointing from the Holy One, and you know all things" (1 John 2:20). Every believer who walks in the Word and prays sincerely will recognize truth from deception.

Therefore, believers should return to the simplicity of the gospel, where Christ alone is enough. We need to rediscover the value of gathering not for show with cameras in church to make money online, but for authentic presence, not for performance, but for prayer. The Book of Acts never portrayed believers as consumers; instead, it depicted them as disciples committed to "the apostles' teaching, to fellowship, to breaking of bread, and to prayer." When these four pillars are upheld, the Church becomes resilient once again.

The call of this generation is to move from religion to relationship, from performance to purity of authentic worship. The prophet Amos cried, "I hate, I despise your religious festivals; your assemblies are a stench to Me. But let justice roll on like a river, righteousness like a never-failing stream" (Amos 5:21-24). God desires better from us, worship from a clean heart, giving that flows from compassion, to care for our widows in prayer that flows from communion. When believers return to this posture, revival becomes inevitable, for where sincerity reigns, the Spirit moves freely.

So, when you look around and see corruption in the name of Christ, do not lose faith in Christ Himself; for He warned us, "**Many** will come in My name, saying, 'I am He,' and will deceive many" (Mark 13:6). The presence of **counterfeits prophets** today does not diminish the value of the original; instead, it proves how precious the truth is. Therefore, to what is pure, measure every teaching by Jesus; pray for discernment; and remember that God Himself is the Provider, not men, not systems, not movements.

"For every good and perfect gift is from above, coming down from the father of lights, who does not change like shifting shadows"

When Jesus died, the veil in the temple tore from top to bottom (Matthew 27:51); this was no coincidence. That heavy curtain had separated the Holy of Holies, the dwelling place of God's presence, from the rest of humanity. Its tearing signified the end of separation; access was restored, not for a select group of churchgoers, but for every believer washed by His blood. "**We have confidence to enter the Most Holy Place by the blood of Jesus, by a new and living way He opened for us through the curtain**" (Hebrews 10:19-20). For this, every believer must say Amen, Hallelujah, and thank you, Lord.

To understand redemption is to understand exchange; our guilt was placed upon Him, His righteousness was put upon us. "God made Him who knew no sin to be sin for us, that we might become the righteousness of God in Him" (2 Corinthians 5:21). This divine transaction restores not only our status, but our purpose; we are no longer wanderers seeking meaning, but sons and daughters carrying a mission. This was the highest point of trade, if you understand business. We are the Lord's business; He saw us losing in the negotiation of life. We could no longer go before heaven to negotiate or seek reverence. We've lost all access to holiness. Then Jesus made a trade negotiation for us and said: "Once you were not a people, but now you are the people of God" (1 Peter 2:10).

Christ did more than forgive sin; He re-created identity. "If anyone is in Christ, he is a new creation; old things have passed away; behold, all things have become new" (2 Corinthians 5:17). The Kingdom of God is not a faraway realm reserved for death; it is righteousness, peace, and joy in the Holy Spirit, experienced now by those who walk with Him. He said to every believer, "The Kingdom of

God is within you" (Luke 17:21), meaning that access to Heaven begins in the transformed heart of those who believe.

Jesus's ministry constantly pointed people back to this relationship. **He rebuked religious leaders who laid heavy burdens on others**, but would not lift a finger to help them. He said, "Come to Me, all you who labor and are heavy laden, and I will give you rest" (Matthew 11:28). The rest He offered was not laziness but relief from striving to earn what grace freely gives. In Him we find both rest and purpose, both forgiveness and transformation.

Redemption also restores authority. When Christ rose from the dead, He declared, "All authority in Heaven and on earth has been given to Me; therefore, go and make disciples". Not to pastors, or fake prophets who will come and tell lies, ask them when they saw God and how. They don't know. Why, if they could see the Lord, are not all their children always serving Him? Stop following these fools. Begin reading the Word and grow in spirit and truth, one prayer at a time. You will see how a deeper understanding of God transforms your life.

The same power that raised Jesus from the grave now works in believers. We are ambassadors of reconciliation, carrying the message that God is no longer counting people's sins against them (2 Corinthians 5:18-19). Every act of kindness, every prayer, every word of truth is a continuation of His ministry on earth. Which means every time you apply kindness, helping someone you don't even know, you are qualified to be called a Christian.

To accept Christ is to return home. Like the prodigal, we come with weary steps and broken pride, only to find the Father running toward us with open arms. He places the robe of righteousness upon us, the ring of authority on our hands, and rejoices over us with singing (Zephaniah 3:17). Redemption is not about signing a contract to pay a fixed monthly fee for blessings, as some frantic churches portray. Instead, it is a celebration, focused on restoring a relationship rather than religion. This renewal spans from Bethlehem to Galilee, Jesus' cross to your heart, from heaven's throne to your home, and extends to our families during worship.

True Prayer, Faithful Understanding, and Direct Access to God

When a believer realizes that redemption restores both relationship and authority, prayer shifts in meaning; it stops being a desperate cry from a distant sinner to God for help and becomes a confident dialogue between a child and their Father. Prayer then is the language of restored fellowship, a breath of a soul walking again with its Maker. It is not about performing to impress others but about a posture to connect with Heaven. "When you pray, go into your room, close the door and pray to your Father, who is unseen; and your Father who sees what is done in secret will reward you openly" (Matthew 6:6). Whether you desire wealth, a baby, marriage, graduation, a promotion, a blessed home, or a peaceful life, pray privately. Your prayer should not be just a ritual but a genuine conversation between a child and their daddy.

Take a moment and think: everything required for survival and for growth has already been placed within creation, food in the ground, water in the rivers, wisdom in the mind, strength in the body, community in the heart. Eternity in the reflection of the family. To pray for what is already given is to miss the purpose of prayer; for prayer was meant not only to ask but to align. "Seek first the Kingdom of God and His righteousness, and all these things shall be added to you" (Matthew 6:33). Faith is the posture of alignment; it listens as much as it speaks.

Recently, my wife's friends came over for dinner. Among them were a couple of single women and single men, what better place to find a spouse! One girl mentioned she needs to feel something just by looking at a man without speaking to him. I said, "You don't know him, and I don't either. Let me describe what I see, and you can tell me if I'm wrong." I observed a handsome young man in his late 20s, from the same country and speaking the same language as you. He might be everything we expect, but since we haven't talked to him or learned about his family background, he's like a potential husband waiting to be chosen.

Imagine this woman meeting the Lord and asking, 'Why didn't you send my husband my way earlier, before I turned 35?' When she sees the video where I tell her this man could be a potential husband for her, do you realize how many people overlook what the Lord has provided for them?

Samuel looked around and asked Jesse, "Are these all your sons?" Jesse replied, "There is still the youngest, but he is out tending the sheep." Then Samuel said, "Send for him; we will not sit down until he arrives." So, Jesse sent for his youngest son, David, and when he came in, he was healthy, with a good appearance and handsome features. The Lord then told Samuel, "Get up and anoint him; this is the one." 1 Samuel 16:11-12. The king was not in a fancy office, from an Ivy League college, tall, with a good job, a high salary, a big house, and nice cars. Don't overlook your king. **God has over 4 billion daughters and sons** on earth; don't tell the Lord you are unable to move and travel to find one of them.

There is a season for fasting, a season for petition, and a season for thanksgiving; wisdom discerns them. When the need concerns what human hands can provide, God expects diligence, stewardship, and faith in action; for "faith without works is dead" (James 2:17). But as Christian, you will know when the matter exceeds human reach of each other here on earth: the healing no doctor can achieve, then prayer and fasting become the believer's spiritual weapon. "This kind can come forth by nothing but by prayer and fasting" (Mark 9:29). In that sacred place of surrender, strength is exchanged; "they that wait upon the Lord shall renew their strength; they shall mount up with wings as eagles" (Isaiah 40:31).

Many believers continue to live as if they need a prophet, pastor, or mediator to reach the throne of heaven, but the gospel states otherwise. Through Christ, the veil was torn, and Heaven was opened. Often, the same person will ask for prayer. "Let us then approach God's throne of grace with confidence, so that we may receive mercy and find grace to help in times of need" (Hebrews 4:16). The Holy Spirit living inside every believer is the real proof of that access. "The Spirit Himself testifies with our spirit that we are children of God" (Romans 8:16). Ignoring that presence is like living as an heir who never claims his inheritance.

You can pray for yourself and for others, and Heaven will hear. "**Whatever you ask in My name, that I will do, that the Father may be glorified in the Son**" (John 14:13). The promise is not limited to apostles; it belongs to every child of God walking in faith. "The prayer of a righteous person is powerful and effective" (James 5:16). When a mother prays for her children, when a husband prays for his home, when a believer prays for the sick or the lost, the same Spirit that raised Jesus from the dead works through that prayer. No distance or hierarchy separates your voice from God's ear; for Scripture says, "Before they call, I will answer; while they are yet speaking, I will hear" (Isaiah 65:24).

In a world full of noise and counterfeit spirituality, silence before God becomes a weapon of discernment. Elijah did not find the Lord in the wind, the earthquake, or the fire, but in the gentle whisper (1 Kings 19:11-12). So, it is with us; revelation often comes not through what you see online, the spectacles of shows and experts, but through stillness. The more you quiet the outer world, the louder His peace becomes within you.

When believers grasp this truth, they live no longer as spiritual beggars but as beloved sons and daughters who carry Heaven's authority into earthly spaces. Jesus said, "Behold, I give you power to tread on serpents and scorpions, and over all the power of the enemy" (Luke 10:19). That authority is not arrogance; it is delegated grace. It operates through humility and obedience; for "God resists the proud but gives grace to the humble" (James 4:6).

Therefore, build confidence while remaining humble. Walk in faith, but stay rooted in love, because love is the most significant revelation; it is the law and a demonstration of spiritual maturity. "If I have the gift of prophecy and understand all mysteries but have not love, I am nothing" (1 Corinthians 13:2). Knowing God means loving as He loves, with steadfastness, sacrifice, and sincerity.

God's unchanging love brought humanity out of darkness and into light; His provision sustains us; His Spirit empowers us; His Son restores us.

I will end this chapter with, in the heart of a God whose love never changes and never fails. From Eden's loss to Calvary's cross to the glory still to come, His story toward us remains one of mercy, truth, and restoration. He is the same yesterday, today, and forever. His invitation still stands: "Return to Me, and I will return to you." And to those who answer, Heaven replies, "Well done, good and faithful servant; enter into the joy of your Lord" (Matthew 25:21).

The throne of heaven is our Lord Jesus Christ, waiting for every family to come home as heavenly citizens.

"For our citizenship is in heaven, from which we also eagerly wait for the Savior, the Lord Jesus Christ." (*Philippians 3:20*)

The Lord Jesus declared that although the physical world will one day fade away, His teachings, the truth of God's Word will remain **eternal and unchanging**. This powerful truth reminds us of the everlasting authority and unfailing reliability of Christ's words. The **King** of kings said **three times** that: **"Heaven and earth shall pass away, but my words shall not pass away."** (Luke 21:33; Mark 13:31; Matthew 24:35)

This journey of faith is often hard and challenging for all of us who are citizens of the Kingdom. Yet in the end, we will rejoice to stand before the Lord Jesus: *"I have fought the good fight, I have finished my course, I have kept the faith."* (2 Timothy 4:7) **Amen.**

We belong to the same kingdom.
Author & Fellow Citizen of God's Kingdom

Gabriel Marcelin

www.ingramcontent.com/pod-product-compliance
Lightning Source LLC
Chambersburg PA
CBHW052016070526
44584CB00016B/1780